A JOURNAL

OF THE

DISASTERS IN AFFGHANISTAN,

1841-2

BY

LADY SALE.

SANG-E-MEEL PUBLICATIONS
25-SHAHRAH-E-PAKISTAN (LOWER MALL) LAHORE

Reprinted by Permission of the Government
of Punjab Under terms of the Publication
of Book Ordinance (1969)

958.1 Sale, Lady
Journal of the disasters in Afghanistan, 1841-2/Lady Sale. — Lahore: Sang-e-Meel Publications, 1999
xvi, 451p.
Appendix p. 449-51
1. Afghanistan — History.
I. Title.

1999

Published by :
NIAZ AHMAD
Sang-e-Meel Publications
Lahore

ISBN - 969 - 35 - 0895 - 5

Sang-e-Meel Publications
Chowk Urdu Bazar Lahore. Pakistan.   Phone : 7667970
Showroom : 25-Shahrah-e-Pakistan (Lower Mall),
Lahore.PAKISTAN.   Phones: 7220100-7228143 Fax:7245101
email: smp@sang-e-meel.com   http://www.sang-e-meel.com

Printed at : Combine Printers, Lahore.

A

JOURNAL

OF THE

DISASTERS IN AFFGHANISTAN,

1841–2.

BY

LADY SALE.

SEVENTH THOUSAND.

LONDON:
JOHN MURRAY, ALBEMARLE STREET.
1843.

CONTENTS.

	Page
Vocabulary	ix
Introduction	1

CABUL.

The Zoormut Expedition	6
Revolt of Tézeen and Bhoodkhak	8
Departure of Gen. Sale's Brigade from Cabul	10
Losses at the Khood Cabul pass	11
Terms made with the Chiefs	21
Outbreak in Cabul	31
Captain Johnson's Treasury plundered	35
Supineness of the British Chiefs	38
Capt. Campbell's regiment repulsed	39
State of the cantonments	42
Return of the 37th N. I.	43
Attack on the Commissariat fort	50
Loss of Mackenzie's fort	54
Outbreak in the Kohistan	56
Want of provisions	58
Loss of the Commissariat fort	59
Disastrous attempt to recapture the small fort	62
Shah Zeman declared King	66
Recall of Gen. Sale	69
Position of the cantonments	70
Arrival of Brig. Shelton in cantonments	83
Losses at the Rikabashees' fort	87
Death of Col. Mackrel	89
Losses at Kandahar	95

	Page
Action on the Western Heights	97
Affairs in the Kohistan	103
Accounts from Jellalabad	108
Dissensions in the British councils	120
Action on the hills above Behmaru	121
Terms proposed by the enemy	135
Reply of the Envoy	142
Difficulty of obtaining supplies	149
Attack on the captured fort	152
Disgraceful loss of the fort	157
The General urges the necessity of negotiating	168
Terms made with the enemy	173
Hostages demanded by them	176
The forts given up to them	181
The seizure of the Envoy by Mahommed Akbar Khan	194
News received of the Envoy's death	197
Negotiations resumed	201
Preparations for evacuating cantonments	208
Departure postponed	215

RETREAT FROM CABUL.

Cantonments evacuated	221
Difficulties encountered by the rear guard	227
Loss of the guns and ammunition	231
Terms made with Mahommed Akbar	235
Losses in the Khoord Cabul pass	236
Akbar demands possession of the ladies and children	244
Destruction of the rear column	264
Attempt of the remnant of the army to reach Jugdaluk	259
Gen. Elphinstone and Brig. Shelton go to Mahommed Akbar	264
Deliberations of the Chiefs	267
Attack at Jugdaluk	273
The final struggle at Gundamuk	278

THE CAPTIVITY.

	Page
March of the prisoners towards the Lughman valley	279
Accommodation at Buddeabad	284
Accounts from Jellalabad	288
Severe earthquake	297
Adventures of Capt. Bygrave	300
Accounts from the garrison at Ghuznee	305
Ferocity and cruelty of Mahommed Akbar	307
Change of jailors	309
Offers for ransoming the Prisoners	311
Report of the murder of Shah Shoojah	317
March for Tézeen	321
Major Pottinger expostulates with the Sirdar	328
Death of Gen. Elphinstone	332
Insults offered to his corpse on its way to Jellalabad	334
Akbar acknowledges that he slew the Envoy	337
Treachery of Shumshudeen at Ghuznee	340
Visit to the ladies of Mahommed Shah's family	345
Accounts from Jellalabad	351
Proceedings at Cabul	351
March to Khoord Cabul	352
Offers for exchange of Prisoners	357
Reports from Cabul	365
The Bala Hissar is surrendered to Akbar	367
Sufferings of Col. Stoddart and Capt. A. Conolly in Bokhara	376
Friendly conduct of the Nawaub, Zeman Shah Khan	381
Gen. Pollock offers to treat with the Sirdar	384
Gloomy prospects	386
Policy of Mahommed Akbar Khan	386
Death of Capt. John Conolly	392
Accounts of the Kandahar force	397
Newspaper controversy	399
Review of Akbar's conduct	400

A 4

CONTENTS.

	Page
His treatment of the Prisoners	403
Futteh Jung challenges Akbar to battle	409
Removal of the Prisoners to the Loghur country	410
Proposed plan for their release	415
March to Bamean	421
Terms made by the Prisoners with their jailor	425
He hoists the flag of defiance on the fort	426
The Prisoners are joined by several native Chiefs	427
They commence their MARCH	430
Arrival of Sir Richmond Shakespear	432
Rescue by Gen. Sale	436
ADDENDA	439
APPENDIX	445

VOCABULARY

OF

PERSIAN, HINDOSTANI, AND OTHER ORIENTAL WORDS

EMPLOYED IN THIS VOLUME.

Akukzye. The name of one of the great Affghan tribes.
Aloo-baloo. The wild sour cherry.
Aman. The cry for mercy — quarter.
Ameer. Commander or chief.
Ana. A small coin; sixteen of which make a rupee. Its value is about three halfpence.
Ashurpee. A mohur — a gold coin. Its value is about thirty shillings English.
Ayah. A female attendant — a nurse.
Bahadur. A bravo — a boaster or braggadocio; also a brave man — a hero.
Bahadur (verb). To boast or brag.
Bala Hissar. Upper citadel — royal palace.
Barats. Legal documents — assignments — promissory notes.
Barukzye. The name of one of the five great Dooranee tribes.
Bash or *bosh.* Nothing — humbug.
Bashee. A head-man.
Bédanas. A sort of mulberry.
Behmaru. The name of a village near Cabul. The word signifies "the husbandless."
Bhanghys. Baggage. — Boxes. They are boxes hung at each end of a pole and carried on a man's shoulder.
Bheestees. Water-carriers.
Bhoosa or *Boussa.* Chopped straw — chaff. *Hindostani.*

VOCABULARY.

Bhoodkhees. Presents.
Bildars. Excavators — sappers.
Bourj or *Burj.* A fortified hill or tower.
Bukshees. Gifts — presents — *douceurs.*
Bukhraeed. A Mahommedan feast. The festival of the goat; held to commemorate the history of Abraham and Ishmael (Isaac).
Bunneah. A trader — a corn-merchant or dealer in grain, flour, &c.
Cafila. A caravan — a convoy.
Cass. A kind of furze.
Caupoochees. Porters.
Chaoney. An encampment — cantonments.
Charpoys. A bed on four poles, with ropes crossed over them.
Chattak. A measure for grain, &c. The 16th part of a seer, or about 2 ounces English.
Chebootras. Small thick mats, on which slaves usually sit or *squat.*
Chillum. The part of the hookah, or pipe, containing the lighted tobacco — hence used for the pipe itself.
Chillumchee. A washand-basin.
Chiragh. A lamp.
Chogah. A sort of cloak.
Chokey. A police station.
Chouk. A bazaar — a street. Also the portion of the taxes *excused* to the native Chiefs for keeping the passes open, and for keeping the tribes in check.
Chowdry. The chief man or head of a bazaar.
Chuddah. A sheet or veil.
Chupao. A night attack — a surprise — a foray.
Chupao (verb). To attack by night — to surprise by stealth.
Chupatties. Unleavened cakes, made of ottah.
Chuprassy. A messenger — a servant bearing a badge or brass plate.
Chuttah or *chatta.* An umbrella or parasol.

VOCABULARY.

Compound. An enclosed space — the ground round a house.
Cossid. A courier — an express — a foot messenger.
Crore. Ten lakhs of rupees, or one million pounds sterling.
Dāk. Letter post.
Dallies. Baskets for fruits, &c. — panniers.
Dewan. A steward.
Dhal. A kind of split pea — pulse.
Dhooley. A palanquin for the sick.
Dhye. Sour curds.
Dooranee. The general name of the five great tribes; the Populzye — Barukzye — Nurzye — Barmizye and Abkhuzye.
Durbar. Levee.
Duffodar. A non-commissioned officer of cavalry.
Elchee. An ambassador — an agent.
Eusofzyes. An Affghan tribe north of Peshawer.
Fakirs. Devotees — mendicants.
Fatcha. The prayer for the reigning monarch — a part of the Mahommedan service; the reading of which is equivalent to doing homage.
Feringhees. Europeans — Franks — foreigners.
Fernez. Sweet curds.
Fouj. An army.
Ghee. Clarified butter.
Ghuzee or *Ghazeea.* A champion of religion — a fanatic.
Gilzye. The name of a great Affghan tribe.
Gobrowed. Dumbfounded — at a *non-plus*.
Godowns. Storehouses — granaries.
Golees. Balls — bullets.
Golundaz. Artillerymen — literally, throwers of balls.
Goor. Coarse brown sugar or molasses.
Goorkha. A native of Nepaul; literally " Cowherd."
Gulas. Cherries.
Hamaum. A hot bath — baths; commonly written *Hummums*.

VOCABULARY.

Haut. A measure equal to half a yard — a cubit.
Havildar. A serjeant in the native troops.
Hazir-Bashes. The king's body guard. The words imply " Ever ready."
Hookm. An order — permission — the word of command.
Hoosseinee-Angoor. A peculiarly fine sort of grape, of immense size, called " the bull's eye."
Huft Kohtul. The seven passes.
Hurharu. A messenger.
Janbaz. The Affghan cavalry.
Jee. Life — spirit — " with right goodwill."
Jeerga. An assembly or council — a diet.
Jemadar. A native officer holding the rank of lieutenant.
Jhala. A raft.
Jingals. Wall pieces, carrying a ball of about a quarter of a pound.
Jorabs. Boots.
Jung. The fight or battle.
Juwans. Young men.
Juzail. The long rifle of the Affghans.
Juzailchees. Riflemen.
Kaffirs. Infidels.
Kaloss. Safe — free. Finished.
Kazanchez. A treasurer — a treasury.
Keshmish. Raisins — grapes.
Khan. A nobleman. In Cabul the title is assumed by every one.
Khelluts. Dresses of honour.
Khootba. The prayer for the king.
Kirkee. A wicket or window.
Kos. A measure of distance, equal to about two English miles.
Kote. A fort.
Kotilla Taj-i. The name of a pass — literally, the crown of the mountains.
Kotilla Murdee. The dead men's pass.

VOCABULARY.

Kujavas. Camel-panniers.
Kulassy. A tent pitcher — a baggage servant.
Kulma. The Mahommedan creed.
Kuneh. A private dwelling.
Kurtoot. The name of a village — literally, the donkey's mulberry.
Kurwar, or *Khurwah.* A measure; equal to 700 lbs. English.
Kuzzilbashes. Persians; or persons of Persian descent, residing in Cabul.
Kyde. Prison. The root of the vulgar English "quod" — to put in quod.
Kysee. The white apricot.
Lakh. One hundred thousand.
Lakh of Rupees. Ten thousand pounds sterling.
Larye. A battle — an engagement.
Lascar. An attendant on guns, magazines, &c.
Loonghee. The cloth of a turban.
Loot. Plunder.
Loot (verb). To sack — to plunder.
Mast. Curds.
Maund. A measure of grain; about 80 lbs. English.
Maush. A sort of grain.
Meerza. A secretary — a Mahommedan writer.
Meer Wyse. A teacher — the high priest.
Mehmandar. A cicerone — a man of all work — a *factotum.*
Mehter. A class of camp-followers — a sweeper.
Mohur. A coin, generally gold; its value is about thirty shillings English.
Moollah. A priest.
Moong. Pulse.
Moonshee. A secretary or interpreter.
Muezzin. The call of the *Faithful* to prayers.
Mushk. A leathern bag for holding water — a goat's skin.
Musjid. A temple or place of worship.

Nagura. A set of drums which the natives beat to announce the presence of the king or any great chief.
Naib. A deputy or lieutenant.
Naich. A corporal in the native troops.
Nal. A horse-shoe.
Nalbunds. Farriers.
Nalkee. A palanquin.
Nans. Cakes of bread. (? Latin, Annona.)
Nawaub. A prince. Nabob.
Nazir. A master of the household.
Neemchees. A kind of spencer made of sheep-skins.
Neencha. A coat.
No-roz. The Vernal Equinox. The Mohammedan New Year's Day.
Nullah. The bed of a river; also used for a river.
Numdas. Coarse felt carpets.
Ooloos. The tribes or clans. To summon the Ooloos, answers to our " calling out the militia."
Oorsees. Open-work lattices.
Ottah or *Attah.* Ground wheat — flour, or rather what is called pollard.
Palkee. A palanquin.
Pall. A kind of tent.
Pesh Khedmuts. Attendants.
Pillau. A dish of meat and rice.
Posha Khana. An armoury.
Poshteen. A sheep-skin; also a fur-pelisse.
Pushtoo. The language of the natives of Affghanistan.
Pyjania. Loose trowsers.
Raj. A government — a province.
Rajah. A prince.
Ressalah. A troop of horse.
Rezai or *Resaiz.* A counterpane — a quilt.
Rui-band. A veil.
Rupee. A silver coin; its value is about two shillings English.

VOCABULARY.

Saces. A groom.
Sahib. Sir — master.
Salaam. Salutation. To make salaam — to pay one's respects.
Seer. A measure; about equal to two lbs. English.
Shah Bagh. The king's garden.
Shah Guzees or *Shahghasses.* The household troops — the "yeomen of the guard." Officers of the court.
Shah-zada. A king's son — a prince.
Shalu. Red cotton cloth from Turkey.
Shikar. Field sports.
Shikargurs. Hunting grounds — preserves.
Shoke. A hobby — a mania.
Shroffs. Native bankers — money changers.
Shubkoon. A surprise at night.
Shytan. The devil.
Siah Sung. The black rock.
Siahs. A large sect of the Mahommedans; opposed to the Soonees.
Sipahees. The native Hindostanee troops. Sepoys.
Sir-i-chusm. The name of a village — the words signify "the head of the spring."
Sirdar. A general. The title assumed by Mahomed Akbar Khan.
Sirdar-i-Sirdan. The chief of the generals. Generalissimo.
Soonees. A large sect of the Mahommedans.
Subadar. A native officer, holding the rank of captain.
Sugs. Dogs. *A term of contempt.*
Sungah. Breast work. Fortifications.
Surda. A species of melon. The *cold* melon.
Surwans or *Surwons.* Camel drivers — grooms.
Setringees. A kind of small carpet.
Suwars. Horsemen — troopers.
Syud. The title of a chief of the Ooloos.
Syud. A holy man — a saint.

Syuds. A sect of the Mahommedans; claiming to be the descendants of the prophet; and who therefore wear the green turban.
Tattoes. Ponies.
Topes. Tombs — mounds — barrows. There are several in Affghanistan, built in the time of Alexander.
Topshee Bashee. The commander of the artillery. " The master-general of the ordnance."
Turnasook. The red plum.
Tykhana. A cellar.
Usufzyes. An Affghan tribe north of Peshawer.
Vakeel. A deputy — a commissioner — one who acts or negotiates for another.
Wuzeer. Vizier.
Wuzeerat. The office of vizier.
Xummuls. Coarse blankets.
Yaboos. Affghan ponies.
Yaghi. Rebellious — in a state of rebellion — or of independence.
Zenana. A harem.
Zerdaloos. Apricots.
Zilzilla. An earthquake.
Zubberdust. Overbearing — " with the strong arm."
Zuna. A dwelling.

JOURNAL

OF

LADY SALE.

INTRODUCTION.

* * * * I have not only daily noted down events as they occurred, but often have done so hourly. I have also given the reports of the day, the only information we possessed; also such news as was telegraphed from the Bala Hissar, or sent in by the King or by Capt. Conolly to the Envoy; and many other reports brought by Affghan gentlemen of Capt. Sturt's* acquaintance, and by others of lower degree, who having had dealings with him in the engineer department and public works, and having received kindness from him, gave him such intelligence and warning as was in their power: all of which he communicated [to his superior officers] at different times; but the warnings were not attended to; and as when he gave his advice it was seldom

---

* Lady Sale's son-in-law.

adhered to, he became disgusted, and contented himself with zealously performing his duties and making himself generally useful, acting the part of an artillery officer as well as that of an engineer. Had poor Sturt's life been spared, it was his intention to have worked up my Rough Notes, and to have added much valuable information: he was too much overworked to afford leisure to give me assistance at the time. His plans, drawings, &c., with his public and private papers, were lost, except a note or two that were, just a few days before we left Cabul, put with my Journal. I believe several people kept an account of these proceedings, but all except myself lost all they had written; and had recourse to memory afterwards. I lost every thing except the clothes I wore; and therefore it may appear strange that I should have saved these papers. The mystery is, however, easily solved. After every thing was packed on the night before we left Cabul, I sat up to add a few lines to the events of the day, and the next morning I put them in a small bag and tied them round my waist. I am indebted to Capt. Souter, of H. M. 44th Regiment, for a plan, from recollection, of the cantonment and forts. The inaccuracies, if any, are but trifling; and it is sufficiently clear to indicate the positions of the principal places alluded to.

INTRODUCTION. 3

A much better narrative of past events might have been written, even by myself; but I have preferred keeping my Journal as originally written, when events were fresh, and men's minds were biassed by the reports of the day, and even hour.

It is easy to argue on the wisdom or folly of conduct after the catastrophe has taken place. With regard therefore to our chiefs, I shall only say that the Envoy has deeply paid for his attempt to out diplomatize the Affghans. Gen. Elphinstone, conscious that his powers of mind had become enfeebled with those of his body, finding there was no hope of Gen. Nott's arrival to assume the command, called in another officer to his aid, who had but one object in view (to get back, at all hazards, to Hindostan). He averred that a retreat to the Bala Hissar was impossible, as we should have to fight our way (for one mile and a half)! If we could not accomplish that, how were we to get through a week's march to Jellalabad? Once in the Bala Hissar, which would have been easily defended by one thousand men, we should have had plenty of troops for foraging purposes; and the village of Ben-i-shehr, just under the Bala Hissar, would have given us a twelvemonth's provisions if we had only made the demonstration of a night march, to have the appearance of taking them by force. Sallies from thence might also have been made into the town, where there was always a party, particularly the Kuzzilbashes, who would have covertly assisted us, until our returning fortunes permitted them to do so openly.

Independent of ———'s determination to return to India, he often refused to give any opinion when asked for it by the General, a cautious measure whereby he probably hoped to escape the obloquy that he expected would attach to the council of war, composed of Gen. Elphinstone, Brig. Shelton, Brig. Anquetil, and Col. Chambers. I might say nominally composed; numerically it was much more extended. Capt. Grant, with cold caution, obstructed every enterprise, and threw all possible difficulties in the way; Capt. Bellew was full of doubts and suggestions, all tending to hamper and retard operations; and numbers of young men gave much gratuitous advice; in fact, the greater part of the night was spent in confusing the General's ideas, instead of allowing a sick man time by rest to invigorate his powers. Brig. Shelton was in the habit of taking his rezai with him, and lying on the floor during these discussions, when sleep, whether real or feigned, was a resource against replying to disagreeable questions. Major Thain, a sincere friend and good adviser of the General's, withdrew in disgust from the council: and Sturt, who was ever ready to do any thing or give his opinion when asked, from the same feeling no longer proffered it.

As a proof that Sir William Macnaghten's confidence in Shah Shoojah was latterly much shaken, he wrote to the Governor of India, proposing that, if it really should be proved that His Majesty was acting treacherously against us, the Dost should be restored to his country. But it is very doubtful whether this despatch ever reached the Governor-General.

I shall not refer back to many small insurrections that took place, but only allude to the events that immediately preceded the grand insurrection at Cabul.

I believe I have indifferently written the name of a village as Dehmaru and Behmaru; it is called both, but Behmaru is the correct name, signifying the husbandless: Dehmaru would be the Husband's Village. It takes its name from a romantic legend of a girl of rank betrothed to a chief who was said to have been slain in combat, and she consequently pined away and died also; but the lover recovered from his wounds, and placed a stone, said to be one of those white ones that look like women in Bourkhor, over her grave on the Behmaru hill; and when he died he was buried beside her, with a similar stone to mark the spot.

JOURNAL.

CABUL.

September, 1841.—Sir William Macnaghten obtained a force to be sent out to the Zoormut country. A chief, contemptuously designated as a robber, was said to have gone into the town of Zaho beyond Gurdez. The information given to Capt. Hay, commanding one of the Shah's corps, represented the place as contemptible. He went there with some few troops supported by guns, found that the place was much stronger than he had supposed, and that he could not do anything against it, and that he was fired at from six forts. On this intelligence reaching Cabul, a large force was sent out on the 28th of September, under Col. Oliver of the 5th, consisting of half of Capt. Abbott's battery, two iron nine-pounder guns, a wing of the 44th Queen's, the 5th N. I., Capt. Warburton's guns, Capt. Backhouse's mountain train, Anderson's horse, the Kohistan corps, and two others of the Shah's, with the King's sappers and miners and the Hindostanee sappers and miners under Capt. Sturt, as sole engineer.

The first day's march was through the city, with narrow streets and sharp turnings, very unfavorable for guns, as was also a bad road afterwards, a nullah, and a steep ascent; all which circumstances kept them from getting into camp until late in the evening; after that the road was good, with the exception of the Al-Timor pass, which was very steep. It rises 9600 feet above the level of the sea. The crest was represented as being as much as a man on horseback could surmount, and the artillery would never have been got over it had not the natives given their assistance: 800 of them dragged the guns up. The great difficulty (as far as I could learn) lay, not so much in the acclivity, as in the roughness of the road, which was perfectly filled with huge blocks of stone. Here it was dreadfully cold, and snow fell. Beyond this pass the people of the country fled, abandoning their property, and consequently their suffering must be very great in the approaching winter.

The chiefs declared that they were ready to submit, but the orders were peremptory to destroy the forts that had fired on the Shah's troops. Lieut. John Conolly and Lieut. Burnet (54th) chupao'd* Akram Khan, riding sixty miles at night with 300 horsemen. They surprised the chief, his wives, and families; it was however done through the treachery of the chief's son-in-law, who dis-

* See Vocabulary for this and other Oriental terms.

closed his retreat. The Shah has ordered Akram Khan's execution. Whilst these events were going on, disturbances had broken out near Cabul, where much had occurred to incite the chiefs to rise. In former times, under the feudal system, when the sovereign of Cabul required troops, each bold chieftain came forward with his retainers; but these vassals had been taken from them, and were embodied in corps commanded by British officers, to whom they owed no affection, and only paid a forced obedience, whilst their hearts were with their national religion; their chief's power was now greatly limited, and the chouk guaranteed to them was withheld on the plea that the Company had commanded retrenchments. But the saving required by Government was a curtailment of those expences which were defrayed by its own rupees, whereas the 40,000 rupees now the subject of dispute were, in fact, no saving at all to us, as that money was never paid by the Company, but was the chouk or money excused to the chiefs out of the revenue or dues owing to the King, on condition of their enforcing the submission of the petty chiefs and the payment of their rents. This sum whether paid to Shah Shoojah or not, would never have replenished the Hon. Company's coffers; and by upholding the Shah in such an act of aggression we compromised our faith, and caused a pretty general insurrection, said to be headed by Meer Musjude.

The Kohistanee chiefs are urged on by the Dooranee Chiefs in Cabul, and all the country about Tézeen and Bhoodkhak is in a state of revolt. It is only wonderful this did not take place sooner.

The Indian government have for some time been constantly writing regarding the enormous expenditure in Affghanistan, every dāk has reiterated retrench; but instead of lessening the political expences and making deductions in that department, they commenced by cutting off these 40,000 rupees from the chiefs.

Affairs having assumed this gloomy appearance, the Envoy sent in all haste for the force under Col. Oliver to return as quickly as possible, leaving it to Capt. Macgregor's diplomatic ability to patch up the Zaho business as best he might, and come to the rescue with his advice regarding the Tézeenites, with whose customs, &c. he had much familiarity. Macgregor strongly advised the not stirring up a hornet's nest, and wished to try what he could do by diplomacy. Valour, however, was the order of the day; and various were the suggestions of the politicals. One plan was, that Gen. Sale's brigade, on its way down to the provinces, should make a detour viâ Nigerow. The troops were not to fight but only by their presence to overawe the Nigerowians, whilst some neighbouring tribes, who had a blood feud with them, should make the attack. Plans of the country were sent in, with imaginary roads drawn on them from various points, whilst supervening obstacles to the march of an army, such as hills and passes, were omitted. The scheme was not considered feasible, in consequence of the advanced state of the season, it being now October, and from the apprehension that the cold would destroy the camels requisite to carry the tents and provisions.

9th October. — The 35th N. I., commanded by Col. Monteath, C. B., with two six-pounder guns under Lieut. Dawes, were suddenly sent at a day's notice to Bhoodkhak, partly as being the first march towards the provinces (they forming a part of Sale's, or the 1st brigade), and partly in consequence of the disturbances.

11*th.* — The 13th light infantry, commanded by Lieut.-Col. Dennie, C. B., were also sent at a few hours' notice to Bhoodkhak; but as they were not to proceed on their march until the arrival of Capt. Abbott with his guns, I remained at Cabul with my daughter, Mrs. Sturt, who had been staying with us during her husband's absence with Col. Oliver's force; and Sale took his departure from Cabul, fully expecting me to follow him in three days at the latest.

12*th.* — The 13th and 35th, with the two guns

under Dawes, moved forward, the whole under Sale, their object being to go through the Khoord Cabul pass, and place the 35th N. I. in an advanced position at Khoord Cabul, after which the 13th were to fall back again on Bhoodkhak. This movement was effected, but with considerable loss. The Khoord Cabul is a narrow defile, enclosed by high and rugged rocks; it is said that the number of the enemy did not exceed 60 men, but they possessed considerable advantage over our troops in their knowledge of the country and in the positions they took up; for until they commenced firing, not a man was known to be there. They were concealed behind rocks and stones, and by a stone breastwork that they had hastily thrown up, behind which, on our troops entering the pass, they laid in wait, and appeared to pick off the officers in particular. The number of the enemy were, however, underrated, as I am assured there were fully 200 of them. The 35th lost, in killed and wounded, about 40 men; and Capt. Younghusband, of the same corps, was badly wounded in the foot. The 13th had 8 men killed and 19 wounded. Gen. Sale was wounded in the left leg; the ball entered near the ankle, shivered the small bone, and was taken out from the skin on the other side where it had lodged. Lieut. Mein of the

13th, while leading his company up to the breastwork, was severely and dangerously wounded in the head; the skull was fractured by the ball, which entered it. Lieut. Oakes, of the same regiment, had also a very narrow escape, being wounded in the head also. It rained very heavily that night, and the 13th had the full benefit of it, for they were out all night, having two alertes; one of the sentries was mortally wounded, being shot on his post. Exertions were made to discover the persons who fired on our sentries: three men were seized who had in their possession the soldier's belt, which was a tolerable evidence of criminality; but the Envoy wrote to say, that the people about the King said that those men were good men and true, and they were to be released without any punishment!

13th. — Two companies of the 37th N. I. and two guns under Mr. Waller, were sent to reinforce the 13th at Bhoodkhak, leaving only the remainder of the 37th in cantonments, and no guns. Should there be a rising in Cabul, we should be entirely without the means of defence. The Shah's troops have moved from their camp behind, to Siah Sung, for protection, as, from the force which has gone with Col. Oliver, they have not guards enough to protect their camp, or the stores left there: their sentries are fired on constantly. Lieut. Mayne, of the Shah's service was reported to have been shot when going his rounds last night, but it was a mistake; the suwar who accompanied him was the sufferer.

A poor woman, a Mrs. Smith, the wife of a conductor, was travelling up the Bolan pass to Kandahar, with a few suwars as a guard. She was attacked by the Belooches; the suwars fled, Mrs. Smith got out of her palkee and ran a short distance, but was soon overtaken and killed; the body was not plundered, and her rings were found on her fingers, and her earrings in her ears; not that they committed the act from hatred to the Feringhees and disdain of plunder, but that, according to the superstition of these tribes, it is a most unlucky circumstance to kill a woman; and finding their victim of the gentle sex, they fled, and left her as she fell.

17*th*. — Col. Oliver's force returned; Capt. Abbott's guns have had their carriages much damaged; the spokes of sundry wheels are absent, thanks to the acclivities and declivities of the Al-Timor pass, so that he requires a few days to put all to rights before he can go to join Sale with the 37th: when they do so, the brigade will move on on Tézeen.

18*th*. — The enemy came down (a chupao or night attack), 400 strong, on Khoord Cabul, where an action was fought with great loss on both sides; Lieut. Jenkins of the 35th was mortally wounded, and lingered in great agony, having been shot through the spine. Col. Monteath sent to Sale for reinforcements, who despatched to him the two companies of the 37th that had lately arrived at Bhoodkhak.

19*th.*—The remainder of the 37th marched from Cabul to Bhoodkhak; also Capt. Abbott and his guns, and the Shah's sappers and miners under Capt. Broadfoot. Sale and Sturt have agreed that I am to remain with him and my daughter at Cabul, and to come on with the Envoy, who is anxious to go to his government at Bombay, and Gen. Elphinstone, who returns to the provinces in consequence of ill health.

Sale's brigade is to move on to Khoord Cabul to-morrow. Seventy-seven of the wounded men from thence and Bhoodkhak have come in to cantonments, as also Lieut. Mein, of the 13th. It appears that the Hazir Bash, the escort sent by the King with Capt. Trevor to Capt. Macgregor (political agent), were the people who let the Ghilzyes into the 35th's camp; they were partly of the same tribe, and whilst the rest were fighting, these ever-ready gentlemen did a little work of their own, cutting down surwans and hamstringing camels. Whilst they were thus employed Capt. Wyndham came up with a company

of the 35th, and fired into the midst, putting them to rout. Col. Monteath turned these people out of his camp as unsafe to be trusted; the Envoy has ordered them to be sent back to Cabul, and to be kindly treated, and will not believe them to be in fault. The Hazir Bash, as their name imports, are " aye ready for the field," but I fear that just now —
> "At a word it may be understood,
> They are ready for evil and not for good,"

like Walter Scott's goblin page.

20*th*. — Lieut. Jenkins's body was brought to Capt. Sturt's house; he died just after he was placed in the dhooley, and was thus saved the additional pain of the journey.

21*st*.—Lieut. Jenkins's funeral took place. As the 35th lost ninety camels, and fifty more were sent in with the sick and wounded, the force is detained until more camels can reach them from Cabul.

23*d*. — Much firing has been heard, and great anxiety prevails. All the forts about Cabul are empty, and the Juwans have gone (it is said) to aid in the fight against us at Tézeen: Sale writes that the report is, that the people at Tézeen say they are unable to cope with us in battle, but that they intend to plunder and annoy the force on its way down.

24*th.*—Sturt sent me a note before I was dressed this morning to inform me, that at Tézeen one small fort had been evacuated, and that Lieut. E. King, of the 13th light infantry, was killed. In the course of the morning I heard that the 13th, having expended their ammunition, were obliged to retreat; that poor King, being the last man to do so, was shot dead on the spot. The men could not stop to take up his body then, but they returned shortly after, and obtained it before the enemy had time to do more than take off his jacket. He was a gallant high-spirited young man, universally beloved, and consequently is much lamented. He was interred under a tent at night, lest the Affghans should recognise the grave and disinter the body. We afterwards were informed that the attack was made on the rear guard before they quitted their ground; that the enemy cut in, in rear of the baggage, took ninety camels with all the treasure of the 13th, a large quantity of ammunition, and other stores.

Gen. Elphinstone told me, that Sale had been very imprudent in using his leg, and had consequently been suffering a great deal of pain, but that the remedies applied had given him relief; he expressed great regret that he had not communicated any information to me, taking it for granted that the Envoy had done so, if I had not a letter from Sale himself; but he was wounded, and with plenty of military occupation, could not always find time to write me many particulars, as he had to send his despatches off as quickly as possible to the General.

A letter from a friend with the force that was sent from Kandahar mentions, that the force had arrived at the extreme point of their tour (Dehwarah) on the 15th of October, and that they were to set out on their return the following day. Capt. Leeson, of the 42d, in temporary command of the Shah's 1st cavalry regiment, was to march twenty-five miles and over a pass (the Kotilla Meercha), to be out of the way of the others, on account of the scarcity of water. The troops had not had any thing to do, nor was there even a chance of their having a foe to contend with, for the people of that part of the country got such a lesson in the fight of Secunderabad, that the chiefs could not have collected 200 men; the forts were mere shells, their walls of no thickness.

The fort against which the eighteen-pounder guns were sent out, has been an utter ruin for years, not only indefensible but uninhabitable. The troops have been terribly distressed bringing the guns over and through the passes, which are more difficult than can be imagined by those that have not seen them; the last, the Dana Thunghee, is described as resembling what the Khyber would be about Ali Musjid, if it had a deep and very rapid river flowing through it, the said river having to be crossed thirteen times.

The Kotilla Taj-i (crown of the mountains), is very steep, and as nearly impracticable as it can be, without being actually so. To avoid these passes, the troops are to go through the Kotilla Murdee (dead men's pass), which Capt. Leeson reports, from what he has seen of it, as practicable but difficult. He writes to me that it will take a great deal of labour to get the guns over it. From thence they steer for Kurtoot (the donkey's mulberry), but it was not known whether the route by that place was practicable; if not, they must face the Kotilla Taj-i, bad as it is. Major Rawlinson, the political agent, had obtained the blessings of the force for leading them such a wild-goose chase; he seems to have received information that Akram Khan had a fort there, but not to have known what that fort was like. It is a pity the army were harassed unnecessarily; but in Major R.'s defence it is but justice to say, that information is difficult to procure, and that it all comes from our enemies.

25th.—I received a letter from Sale, in which he informs me, that the conduct of the troops employed in the affair at Tézeen was good beyond all praise; but, concluding that I had heard all the particulars, he did not enter into detail. He wrote me that he was to halt that day (the 24th), as Macgregor was in treaty with the chiefs, who he says are willing to refrain from all further opposition, and say they are convinced they have no chance against us. Sturt has seen a letter from Lieut. Cunningham, of the Shah's sappers and miners, by which it appears that no enemy showing themselves, Capt. Paton, Qr.-Mr.-Genl., was on the point of pitching the camp, when some of the advance guard were fired on, upon which two companies were sent from each corps, with the sappers, who all behaved gallantly; they went up the hills, and down again, chased the enemy into their fort, and the sappers, commanded by Capt. Broadfoot, drove them through it, and followed them through the wicket they escaped by. The 13th having expended their ammunition were obliged to retreat, and it was then that Lieut. E. King fell.

Lady Macnaghten called on me, and told me that Capt. Macgregor, Political Agent, wrote that the chiefs received him with great politeness, and were pleased at the confidence reposed in them by his going to meet them attended only by one suwar. They appeared to be unanimous, and many in number, mustering 700 followers, who were daily increasing. They agreed to all the conditions but one; whatever that is, it appears to be the main point to be conceded, and we suppose that it relates to the 40,000 rupees. One day has been allowed to the chiefs to deliberate. The Envoy was some time since warned by three Affghans not to ride so early in the morning or so late in the evening as was his wont; but, whether from policy or natural fearlessness, he has not attended to their advice. The Akhoonzadah has also told him that three men have sworn on the Koran to take his life. The people of Tagow and Lughman are leagued with those of Tézeen. Capt. Macgregor writes that a great quantity of ammunition was left on the road for want of camels to carry it on, which must have proved a great prize to the enemy, who were much in want of it.

26th. — There being a report that all was peaceably settled at Tézeen, I became very anxious for intelligence. Two letters were brought to me, but alas! neither of them were to my address, one being from Capt. Havelock to Gen. Elphinstone, the other from Capt. Paton to Major Thain. After giving them a reasonable time to ruminate over their news, I wrote to Major Thain, requesting him to give me any information in his power; and informing him that I had no letter, I got the provoking reply that the Sahib was gone out. Some time afterwards Major Thain called: he owned he was puzzled as to what was going on, but hoped that affairs would remain quiet until we got out of the country. He said it was the present intention, that the sick should move out on Saturday next, and the Envoy and the General should leave Cabul on Monday the 1st. Shortly after he left me, he sent me the two letters to read; he had expressed his surprise that they had not arrived sooner, both being dated the 24th; and my letter of the same date from Sale had arrived the day before! Capt. Havelock mentions that all is settled and hostages given, but remarks that, since the pacification, the camels have been fired on, as also our outposts, but says, the one may be attributable to the arrival of a chief who was in ignorance of the treaty, and the other, to their people not being well in hand, a pretty sounding phrase; but are we to understand that our men are so well in hand as not to resent it? Capt. Paton writes mysteriously, that he has much to communicate, "better spoken than written," and says the enemy have consented regarding the obnoxious chief, (some person who they did not wish should participate in the benefits of the treaty). He adds that a force to be of any use in that country must not be hampered with camels, tents or baggage, and that the ammunition should be carried only on mules or yaboos. If all remained quiet, Paton and Havelock were to return, and the force to go on to Kutta Lung. Paton hints that something had gone wrong which would not have done so, had Gen. Sale not been confined to his dhooley. Thain tells me that there is no mention in Sale's despatch of the gallant conduct of the sappers and miners as related by Cunningham; he being wounded probably did not observe all that passed, and did not have the circumstances brought to his notice in time to write them; but had he done so, it would have been very immaterial, for, excepting from private letters, no intelligence transpires.

Last year, when Sir Willoughby Cotton commanded, and during the disturbances in the Kohistan, every despatch from Sale, who commanded the troops there, was promulgated in orders, and the present system of keeping information close is disgusting; there can be no secrets regarding what passes in action in the field. The general impression is that the Envoy is trying to deceive himself into an assurance that the country is in a quiescent state. He has a difficult part to play, without sufficient moral courage to stem the current singly. About two months since Sir William wrote to Lord Auckland, explaining to him the present state of Affghanistan, and requesting that five additional regiments should be sent to this country, two of them to be European. To these statements a written war succeeded between the Envoy and the Supreme Government of Bengal. Letter after letter came calling for retrenchment. Sir William had been appointed from home Governor of Bombay, and was particularly chosen for the office from his being a moderator and a man unlikely to push any violent measures; he hoped affairs might take a turn for the better, and was evidently anxious to leave Cabul and assume his new appointment. In an evil hour he acceded to the entreaties of Sir Alexander Burnes (who appears to have been blinded on the subject) and wrote to Lord Auckland to nullify his former request for additional troops, and to say that part of those now in the country might be withdrawn. The 1st brigade under Sale was accordingly ordered to be in readiness to move down; and it was generally understood, that all would be withdrawn as soon as the Shah had raised five more regiments of his own. The letter of recal, as we may term Sir William's, was sent off only two days before the breaking out of the Zoormut affair.

Great stress has been laid upon the chiefs having given us hostages, but this is no certain proof of their sincerity; we have been long enough amongst them for them to know the

British character; they also know that the Dost's family were safely and honourably treated under our protection, whilst he and his son were in arms against us, and they naturally consider their safety as a proof of that of any hostages they leave with us.

The dāks, which have not arrived since the 2d (nor have been despatched since the 4th), are confidently asserted to be now on their way, and are expected in to-morrow at the farthest. No one appears to have been made acquainted with the terms of the treaty, which have been kept close by the Envoy, who, however, observed that Macgregor had given them better terms than he himself would have done. They are to get the 40,000 rupees the quarrel began about, and they promise to return us any property they can find of ours: so that we leave off where we set out, barring our killed and wounded, expence, loss of ammunition and baggage, and annoyance of the detention, if not loss, of our dâks, bhanghys, &c.

27*th*.—I hear that Macgregor writes to the Envoy that the country about Tézeen never was in so tranquil a state as it is at present! Now, with a little variation in the wording, he might have cautiously written to the Envoy, so as to be understood by him alone, and have intimated that the country was now as quiet as it ever was; which, to those who know the wild tribes thereabouts located, indicates any thing but a state of pacification.

The sick are again ordered to be off to-morrow, with a wing of the 54th, to Tézeen, where the 37th awaits their arrival; and at present it is supposed that the Envoy and General will follow on the 1st.

28*th.* — Sale has written me that he arrived at Seh Baba on the 26th at 1 P. M.; that the rear guard was fired on a mile from camp, and three men wounded. They were in a snug post for the night. His leg was doing well, and all inflammation had subsided. They had grain and bhoosa in plenty. Capt. Grant tells me that a chief goes on daily in advance, to keep the country quiet, and bring in grain.

29*th.* — We hear that since the force left Khoord Cabul, they have never pitched a tent. The rear guard has been attacked daily, and the bivouack fired on every night. The camels are dying forty of a night from cold and starvation. Lieut. Jennings (13th) has been wounded severely in the arm, the bone broken, and the ball went through into his side. Lieut. Rattray (13th) wounded, and a sergeant killed and 3 men wounded; 4 or 5 Sipahees* of the 35th wounded.

* Commonly written Sepoys.

30th.—A small dâk has come in for the Envoy and General only, and that only newspapers; the Envoy sent orders to have the dâk sent by a private path, which succeeded.

It seems that the terms made with the chiefs of Tézeen were, the remission of the money which gave rise to the dispute. They were required to call out the *Ooloos*, which they represented would be attended with considerable expense, so they received 10,000 rupees to enable them to do so, when they pocketed the money, but omitted calling out the militia! Macgregor writes that he suspects the chiefs are at the bottom of all the plundering and attacks on our force, though they profess to have nothing to do with it, and that the depredators are the robber-tribes.

Last night as the cavalry videttes went their rounds at Siah Sung, a party of men rushed out of a cave and fired at them; some were taken prisoners; part of them were Affghans, but four were Hindostanees, and one of them was a Chuprassy of Capt. Bygrave, who endeavoured to excuse himself by saying, he fired at the party supposing them to be Affghans, but could give no reason for being there himself.

Mr. Melville was attacked last evening, but set spurs to his horse and galloped off, on which the Affghans set up a shout; this is the fourth attempt on the part of the Affghans to assassinate British officers within a short time. I before mentioned Mr. Mayne's escape; Dr. Metcalfe was also nearly cut down; and Lieut. Waller, of the Artillery, was wounded on the head whilst riding close to the Siah Sung camp.

31*st.* — The invalids, whose march had been countermanded, are again under Orders to go out to Siah Sung on Tuesday, to be in readiness to march on Wednesday the 3d of next month. When the barracks for the men and the officers' quarters were erected in the Cabul cantonment, a committee assembled to value them and fix the house rent, both for them and for the two houses to be occupied by the Commander of the forces and the second in command. It was fixed at ten per cent. on the actual outlay as specified by the engineers' department. We paid ours monthly, as did the 13th, through the regimental paymaster. The 35th also paid their rent monthly. There was some dispute regarding it with some others, in consequence of the rooms not being all quite finished; but as Capt. Sturt was not ordered to collect the money, but only to pay over whatever he received, the business remained in abeyance. An inquiry is now making about the house rent that has not been paid by the officers who have gone away, so I feel quite delighted that Sale and

I are out of the scrape. Brig. Shelton has written officially to the General, to say that it is very hard that he is kept at Siah Sung, when there is a good house in cantonments to which he has a right, and applies officially to the General to give him up either his own house or ours. Now, as long as Brig. Shelton's duty keeps him at Siah Sung, he has no business in cantonments. This is Sunday: both the General and I expect to march on Wednesday, so, *par complaisance,* we neither of us expected to be turned out; however, if we do not go, we both intend vacating our habitations, when our house will be made over to Capt. Sturt, to undergo repairs, so as to be ready for the reception of the next Commander of the forces. Gen. Nott has been written to, to come up immediately, and Gen. Elphinstone is to give up the command to him from the 1st of Nov. The reason that our house is in future to be appropriated by the chief arises from its being the best and most commodious. Sir Willoughby Cotton gave his plan, and Sale his, when the houses were built; and Sir Willoughby living *en garçon* had omitted many little comforts that we had considered indispensable. Added to which, Sale had a *shoke* for gardening, and had an excellent kitchen-garden; whilst I cultivated flowers that were the admiration of the Affghan gentlemen who came to see us. My sweet peas and geraniums were much admired, but they were all eager to obtain the seed of the edible pea, which flourished well; and by being sown as soon as the frost was over we had plenty of succession crops, and we still have peas growing which we hope, if not cut off by frost, will give a crop next month.

The potatoes thrive well, and will be a very valuable addition to the *cuisine*. The cauliflowers, artichokes, and turnip radishes are very fine, and peculiarly mild in their flavour; they are all from seed we brought with us from our garden at Kurnaul. The Cabul lettuces are hairy and inferior to those cultivated by us; but the Cabul cabbages are superior, being milder, and the red cabbage from English seed grows well.

Regarding the fruits of Affghanistan, I should not be believed were I to state the truth. Selected grapes off a bunch of those in the Kohistan have been known to weigh 200 grains; the largest I ever weighed myself was 127 grains. It was the kind denominated the Bull's Eye by the English; I believe the natives call it the Hoosseinee-Angoor; its form is nearly round, and the taste very luscious; it is of a kind not generally purchaseable. At Kardunah they grow in great perfection. Those I ate were sent as a present from a native gentleman to

Captain Sturt, as were also some very delicious pears from Turkistan. The largest peaches I have myself weighed turned the scale at fifteen rupees, and were fully equal in juiciness and flavour to those of the English hothouse. The finest sort are in the Kohistan, but are so delicate they will not bear carriage to Cabul. I have been assured by my friends who have been there in the peach season that the best fruit of the kind at my table was quite inferior to those above mentioned. The Orleans blue plum is excellent. There is a green one resembling in appearance a greengage, but very tasteless. There are also many other kinds, with a great variety of melons, Water, Musk, and Surda, which is accounted the best.

It is reported that Sale's brigade are very badly off for carriage and provisions, and we have here no camels to send to them. The 37th N. I. and the Shah's sappers and miners are ordered back to the Huft Kotul, to await the arrival of the invalids at that place. It is now said that, from the difficulty experienced in procuring carriage, the sick and wounded must be left here.

In the evening we heard that the Envoy had received a hurried note from Capt. Macgregor, by which it appears that between Jugdaluk and Soorkhab the troops were attacked by about 400 men; that ours were unable to force the hills. The enemy left the pass open, by which the brigade proceeded; but they came down in force on the rear-guard, who are stated to have been panic-struck. Our loss is stated at ninety killed and wounded. Capt. Wyndham of the 35th killed, and Lieut. Coombes severely wounded; Lieuts. Rattray and Halcombe of the 13th Light Infantry wounded. There has been great loss of baggage and camels; seventy of the latter carried off, which were returned to us on paying ten rupees each for the Hindostanees, and twenty each for the Affghan animals. This is instituting a premium for plunder, but it was caused by dire necessity.

There were no despatches for the General, nor letters for me, but we hope to receive further accounts to-morrow.

1*st November.*—No letters from camp, which has caused both surprise and anxiety.

2*d.*—Last night a party of Kohistanees entered the city; a large body of horsemen were also seen proceeding towards the city from the road that leads by the Shah's camp behind Siah Sung.

This morning, early, all was in commotion in Cabul; the shops were plundered, and the people were all fighting.

Our Affghan servant, Mahomed Ali, who used to sleep in the city, when he passed out to come to my house in the morning was threatened, and reviled as the chuprassy of the Feringhee General, who, they asserted, had been beaten at Tézeen, and that all his troops had run away, and he with them!

The Shah resides in the Bala Hissar, and his guns from that fortress were constantly firing; the Affghans in the city were doing the same from six in the morning. Capt. Sturt hearing that Capt. Johnson's (paymaster to the Shah's force) house and treasury in the city were attacked, as also Sir Alexander Burnes's, went to Gen. Elphinstone, who sent him with an important message, first to Brig. Shelton at Siah Sung, and afterwards to the King to concert with him measures for the defence of that fortress. Just as he entered the precincts of the palace, he was stabbed in three places by a young man well dressed, who escaped into a building close by, where he was protected by the gates being shut. Fortunately for my son-in-law, Capt. Lawrence had been sent to the King by the Envoy, and he kindly procured a palkee, and sent Sturt home with a strong guard of fifty lancers, but they were obliged to make a long detour by Siah Sung. In the mean time, Lawrence came to tell me all that had passed, and to break the bad news to my daughter, Mrs. Sturt.

Lawrence (military secretary to the Envoy) had had a very narrow escape himself. An Affghan, grinding his teeth, and grinning with rage and hatred of the Feringhees, aimed a blow at him with a sword, which Lawrence parried, and putting spurs to his horse he escaped: one of his suwars received a cut in the leg, which was revenged by another horseman shooting the fellow.

It was Lawrence who came to tell me of Sale's wound; he is always kind and friendly, though he has now been twice the herald of ill news. It struck me as probable that the suwars would take Sturt to his own house; and as he and my daughter were staying with me, there would not even be a bed to place him on there. I therefore determined not to lose time by waiting till the bearers could get my palkee ready, but took my chuttah and walked off as fast as I could towards Sturt's house. I fortunately met Major Thain (aide-de-camp to Gen. Elphinstone), for I soon saw a crowd of about fifty suwars in his compound. Thain ran on, and told the bearers to bring him on to my house. I cannot describe how shocked I felt when I saw poor Sturt; for Lawrence, fearing to alarm us, had said he was only slightly wounded. He had been stabbed deeply in the shoulder and side, and on the face (the latter wound striking on the bone just missed the temple):

he was covered with blood issuing from his mouth, and was unable to articulate. From the wounds in the face and shoulder, the nerves were affected; the mouth would not open, the tongue was swollen and paralysed, and he was ghastly and faint from loss of blood. He could not lie down, from the blood choking him; and had to sit up in the palkee as best he might, without a pillow to lean against. With some difficulty and great pain he was supported up stairs, and laid on his bed, when Dr. Harcourt dressed his wounds, which having been inflicted about ten o'clock, now at one were cold and stiff with clotted blood. The tongue was paralysed, and the nerves of the throat affected, so that he could neither swallow nor articulate; and the choking sensation of the blood in his throat was most painful to witness. He was better towards evening; and by his wife's unremitting attention in assisting him to get rid of the clotted blood from his mouth by incessant applications of warm wet cloths, he was by eleven at night able to utter a tolerably articulate sound. With what joy did we hear him faintly utter *bet-ter;* and he really seemed to enjoy a tea-spoonful of water, which we got into his mouth by a drop or two at a time, painful as it was to him to swallow it.

It was most gratifying to see the attention and

kind feeling manifested on the occasion by the sergeants of the engineer department, and their anxiety (particularly Sergeant Deane's) to make themselves useful to Sturt.

Capt. Warburton, Capt. Johnson, and Capt. Troup were all fortunately in cantonments; for their houses in the city were plundered and burnt. At Johnson's (the King's treasury) the guard of forty men was massacred, as also all his servants but one, who luckily was not at home. The insurgents looted a lakh and 70,000 rupees of public property, and Johnson lost above 10,000 rupees of his own property.

There were of course various reports. We first heard that, on the affair breaking out, Sir A. Burnes went over to the Wuzeer's to ascertain what could be done; and that he was safe there, excepting having been shot in the leg. The King, from the Bala Hissar, sent intelligence to the Envoy "that Burnes was all right;" but a few hours afterwards the King acknowledged that he did not know any thing of him, neither did the Envoy at seven in the evening, when Capt. Lawrence and Capt. John Conolly came to inquire after Sturt's health. Our only hopes of Burnes' safety rest on the possibility of his having obtained refuge in some harem. His brother's fate is as yet unknown. Capt. Broadfoot was shot in the breast, and killed. He was breakfasting with the two Burnes's: before he fell he had killed six men with his own hand. Capt. Drummond is protected by Osmar Khan, Kariez-i-Umeer, chief of a domain, the first stage from Cabul towards the Kohistan. Capt. Mackenzie, political assistant to Capt. Mackeson at Peshawur, came up to Cabul some time since; and when Lieut. Milne (in the Commissariat) was sent to Khelat-i-Gilzie, Mackenzie took his place in the Shah's commissariat. He was located in a fort divided into two by the range of Commissariat Godowns, — one side inhabited by Brig. Anquetil, commanding the Shah's forces, the other by Mackenzie, who (the Brigadier being in cantonments) held out in both, with some sappers and miners, a few of the Shah's 6th Regt., and 130 Juzailchees: the latter are good men, and mostly Usufzyes. In this fort were stored 8000 maunds of ottah and wheat. Capt. Trevor hopes to defend his tower as long as it is not fired. Another report states that Trevor, his wife, and one child, have escaped, whilst his six other children have been murdered. Another, that he has escaped, but that his wife and seven children are all murdered.

The Kuzzilbash quarter of the city is said to be all quiet. Naïb Shureef's son has been killed in some of the scuffles in the city. Abdoollah Khan, Amenoollah Khan, and a few other Dooranee chiefs, are said to be the instigators of the insurrection.

The King (who resides in the Bala Hissar) says if the rebellion is not all over to-morrow morning, he will burn the city,—by no means an easy task: the houses are all flat-roofed and mud-roofed. It is true Cabul has been burnt three times before, and therefore what has been may occur again. By throwing shells into the houses you may fire them; and the individual house fired, being ceiled with wood, blazes fiercely until the roof falls in, and the mud and dust smother the fire without danger to the adjacent buildings. The King has also declared that if the Meer Akor (who protected the man that stabbed Sturt) does not give the assassin up, he will hang the Meer Akor himself. It appears a very strange circumstance that troops were not immediately sent into the city to quell the affair in the commencement; but we seem to sit quietly with our hands folded, and look on. On the breaking out of the insurrection the King sent Campbell's Hindostanee regiment into the city, with some guns, who maintained an arduous conflict for some time against the rebels; but being wholly unsupported, were obliged eventually to give way, when the greater part of them were cut to pieces, and several of their guns were captured.

The state of supineness and fancied security of those in power in cantonments is the result of deference to the opinions of Lord Auckland, whose sovereign will and pleasure it is that tranquillity do reign in Affghanistan; in fact, it is reported at Government House, Calcutta, that the lawless Affghans are as peaceable as London citizens; and this being decided by the powers that be, why should we be on the alert?

Most dutifully do we appear to shut our eyes on our probable fate. The Shah is, however, to be protected, whatever may be the fate of the English in the city; and Brig. Shelton is sent with the Shah's 6th, some of the 44th Queen's, and three horse artillery guns under Capt. Nicholl, to the Bala Hissar. The King, as he well may be, is in great consternation. At about 9 A.M. Capt. Sturt arrived at Siah Sung from the cantonments, bearing orders from Major-Gen. Elphinstone for the 54th N. I., Capt. Nicholl's three horse artillery guns, and a company of the 44th, accompanied by the Shah's 6th regiment, to hold themselves in readiness to march at a moment's notice to the Bala Hissar. As they had all been on the *qui vive* since daybreak, they were ready in an instant, and eagerly expecting orders to march, when a note came from Capt. Lawrence (the Envoy's military and private secretary), dated Bala Hissar, 10 A. M., telling them, "Stay where you are,—all is quiet; you need not come." This caused great surprise, as the firing was brisk in the city. After waiting another hour under arms, the Brigadier ordered Sturt to go in and see what was going on: this he gladly did, and, accompanied by eight suwars of the Shah's 2d cavalry, went to the Bala Hissar. In half an hour a suwar returned, saying he had been badly wounded entering the palace gates, and bearing an order for an immediate advance of the troops. "Forward" was the word; and, anticipating an attack on the city, the troops gladly set out, and arrived unopposed in presence of the King, when, to their sorrow, instead of receiving *hookm* to enter the city, the Shah almost rudely inquired why they had come! After standing under arms another hour, firing being heard towards the Shôr Bazaar, the Brigadier sent Lieut. Melville of the 54th to inquire what was going on. On going down to the gate towards the city, he found the fugitives from Campbell's regiment flying in, and reporting that their regiment was entirely cut up: this he reported to the Brigadier, who ordered him to take the light company down to the city gate, and whilst taking charge of that position to protect as best he could the retreating regiment. On arriving there, Lieut. Melville placed a section as a guard, and took the remaining three to the entrance of the Shôr Bazaar, and formed them up facing the street: he had not been there more than five minutes, when he observed a disorderly rabble retreating at a quick pace towards him, pursued by a large body of Affghans, whilst others from the tops and windows of the houses kept up a brisk fire upon them.

Immediately after the colours had gained the rear of his detachment, Lieut. Melville retreated slowly, facing the enemy, towards the gate, pouring in volley on volley; but, owing to the protection afforded the rebels by the walls, it is to be feared with but little effect. On reaching the fosse he formed his men up again, to allow the two guns to pass to his rear; but the Affghans made a rush, and the golundaz of the Shah took to a disorderly flight. As the idea of rescuing them with three sections was entirely out of the question, and the fire was becoming very hot, Melville sent Lieut. Macartney (of the Shah's service), who in the meantime had come to his assistance with one company of the Shah's 6th to man the walls over where the guns were left, and prevent the enemy carrying them off; this being done, Melville got a few of the golundaz to go back and spike one of the guns, after which he retired inside, having lost one subadar and three men wounded, and one man killed. On arriving inside he placed the men on the ramparts; and being accidentally bayoneted in the thigh, he was released from duty, making over charge of the men to Macartney.

It being found impracticable to bring in the guns, from the carriages being broken, the European horse artillery, who had been sent out for that purpose, came back; and some guns having in the meantime been mounted on the wall and brought to bear on them, they were so broken by the shot as to be perfectly useless: and it may here be remarked, that to the day the troops left the Bala Hissar, notwithstanding frequent attempts were made by the enemy, they never succeeded in gaining possession of them.

The King, who had been in a great state of excitement during the day, on hearing of the loss of his guns, and that 200 of Campbell's regiment had been killed or wounded, was excessively agitated; the more so that, immediately on the rebellion breaking out, almost all the Pesh Khedmuts and Shah Guzees had deserted him. He ordered a dinner for the officers in the evening; as, to their extreme disgust, they were obliged to stay the night in the fort, neither men or officers having an article of any sort or kind besides what they wore. The 5th cavalry, who had accompanied the detachment to the Bala Hissar, had, after taking all the baggage from Siah Sung to cantonments, remained in the latter place.

The King, sitting with the British officers around him, was anxious to obtain their advice in the present crisis, and particularly asked that of ———; whose conduct was represented on the emergency as pitiful and childish in the extreme, not having a word to say, nor an opinion to offer.

In cantonments all was confusion and indecision. The Envoy mounted his horse and rode to the gateway, and then rode back again,—the best thing he could do; for had the Affghans either killed him or taken him prisoner, it would have given them a decided advantage on their part. Sir William and Lady Macnaghten had vacated the residency before 11 o'clock A. M., and came into cantonments; a circumstance which no doubt was soon known to the insurgents, and must have given them an idea that we greatly dreaded an attack from them, which was threatened at night. The guns were placed in battery, and the walls manned with double sentries. The Kohistanees are reported to have 500 men assembled at Deh Hadji in the Kohistan. The villages about the Lake are all in a state of insurrection. The whole force from the Siah Sung cantonments are come in: the Shah's 6th, the 5th cavalry, Anderson's horse, and Skinner's are in the Mission Compounds; the escort in cantonment. Lawrence has kindly promised in case of an attack to come over to us; but we are so anxious about Sturt that we do not think much of danger.

Two Sipahees were cut down near the gate of the Commissariat Fort to-day; another was killed who only attempted to cross the road. We have good news to-day from Sale at Gundamuk, dated the 1st. They were all quite well, and supplied with all that they required. Bukhtar Khan, the new governor there, had sent 500 of his tribe to Jugdaluk; 250 of Ferris's corps and 300 of Burns's Khyberries were to follow quickly, to secure the passes, and open the road to Seh Baba. The Tagow chief who attacked Sale's force on the road is said to have withdrawn his men; and now that all seems clear for our march down, this insurrection has risen up here. It was only two days ago Lady Macnaghten told Mrs. Sturt that the country was all quiet, except the little outbreak near Tézeen!

3*d.*—At three in the morning the drums in cantonments beat to arms, in consequence of a large body of men coming over the Siah Sung hill; they proved to be the 37th from Khoord Cabul, who, about half-past 2 P.M. yesterday, received an order to march on its receipt to Cabul. Poshteens arrived about an hour afterwards in safety, with no other guard than a couple of suwars; however, before the regiment was ready to move off its ground, the Ghilzyes had taken possession of the mouth of the pass, and were with some difficulty dislodged by two companies of the 37th, and two guns of the Shah's mountain train; the latter under Lieut. Green. The order received by Major Griffiths to march the detachment under his command on receipt of the order was accompanied by a note from Capt. Paton, Assistant Quartermaster-General, telling Major G. that all Cabul was in insurrection, &c. The Laird of Pughman (who had held the pass from the time Sale left Bhoodkhak), with all his followers, joined our force as soon as they reached his post, and marched into Cabul with them. The rear-guard of three companies and one Mountain T. gun were hard pushed, as they had to fight all the time the regiment was getting ready, and also kept up a skirmishing fight all the way in, in which all the corps joined; they had four men killed and thirty wounded. The Mountain T. gun they had in the rear eventually broke down, but was brought into cantonments. One officer, Lieut. Gordon, was wounded. Notwithstanding this, they came in with all their baggage in as perfect order as if it had been a mere parade movement; and great praise is due to Major Griffiths on this occasion. I observe I have mentioned the Laird of Pughman, — a sobriquet applied to a good man, and a true one to the Shah and us. His proper name was the Syud Mahommed Khan; and for the good service he did in the Kohistan with Sale's force he obtained the honorary title of Jan Fishan Khan, or the nobleman who is the exterminator of his sovereign's enemies. It is a difficult sentence to render into English.

Jan means life; *Fishan*, heedless of the life of your enemies; *Khan*, a lord or nobleman. I am no linguist myself, but friends who understand Persian well give the above as the best translation. The common one is, "The khan or noble who throws away his life upon his enemies."

This day there was a great talk of the Kohistanees being expected to arrive to attack us. The double sentries are loaded to-day, as also the sentries placed round the ammunition and stores.

In the evening the rebels appeared in considerable numbers near Mahommed Khan's Fort, and between that and the Commissariat Fort, situated 300 yards from cantonments. We have only three days' provisions in cantonments: should the Commissariat Fort be captured, we shall not only lose all our provisions, but our communication with the city will be cut off.

This fort (an old crazy one, undermined by rats) contains the whole of the Bengal commissariat stores, valued at four lakhs of rupees, including about 12,000 maunds of ottah, wheat, and barley, and all the medical stores, &c.

No military steps have been taken to suppress the insurrection, nor even to protect our only means of subsistence (the Godowns), in the event of a siege. The King, Envoy, and General appear perfectly paralysed by this sudden outbreak: the former is deserted by all his courtiers, and by even his most confidential servants, except the Wuzeer, who is strongly suspected of having instigated the conspiracy; and suspicion attaches to his Majesty again. It is here necessary to observe, that several months ago letters calling on all true Mussulmans to rise against the Kaffirs (English unbelievers) were widely disseminated: they bore the King's signature; but Sir William Macnaghten always insisted that they were forgeries of a very peculiar description, that papers bearing the veracious signature had had their contents washed out, and these seditious writings inserted. The Shah of course said, " An enemy has done this;" and, as dead men tell no tales, much of the obloquy was allowed to rest on Moollah Shekoor, who had paid the penalty of other state crimes.

In Affghanistan the English act as they do in all other countries they visit, — keep to themselves, and even (generally) employ only servants brought with them. The Envoy kept but few Affghans in his employ: he had a news reporter, at 150 rupees a month, who had the credit of concocting splendid untruths; an old moollah picked up at Kandahar, who, I believe, receives 200, — a man greatly in Sir William's confidence; there is also an old cossid. These people adhere to the Envoy, and flatter him into the belief that the tumult is *bash* (nothing), and will shortly subside.

This day there was a grand bustle, getting guns into all the bastions. Capt. and Mrs. Trevor, and their seven children, came into cantonments. Trevor's Hazir Bashes brought them in safe; but they had to walk through the river, and to carry the children, saving only the clothes they had on. As they escaped at one gate, their tower was taken possession of by the rebels from another.

That the insurrection could have been easily crushed at its commencement, is evident from the circumstance that on the 2d of November a considerable number of chiefs went to Capt. Trevor's house to lend him assistance; amongst them were Osman Khan, Abdool Rahim Khan, Khan Shireen

Khan, Taj Mahommed, Gholam Moyenoodeen, &c. The Nawaub Zeman Khan sent one of his younger children to Trevor, and desired him to keep him as a hostage; but finding that no assistance came from cantonments Trevor declined keeping the boy, and, accompanied by some of the above-mentioned persons and their followers, he made his way into cantonments on the 3d.

It is further worthy of remark, that Taj Mahommed Khan went to Sir Alexander Burnes the very day before the insurrection broke out, and told him what was going on. Burnes, incredulous, heaped abuse on this gentleman's head; and the only reply he gave him was, "Shuma beseeah shytan ust!" on which Taj Mahommed left him. This anecdote was told us by himself.

Two of the Shah's mountain train guns, under Lieut. Green, and 400 of the 54th N. I., were sent, escorted by cavalry, to take ammunition and carcasses to the Bala Hissar, as also bedding for the men.

There is a report that the city is about to be fired.

A large party bearing the religious flag (green) came towards the rear gate: they fought with much *jee;* but one of our guns played on them, and then the cavalry dashed out and cut them up. Lieut. Le Geyt, of the Shah's service, with a small party of Anderson's horse, feigned to fly, and drew a party after them, on whom they turned and dealt destruction.

At the Bala Hissar the troops were allotted to their different stations; though, in consequence of a great portion of the 54th N. I. being in cantonments, as yet no permanent division of the troops could take place.

One of the most important posts was the tower on the summit of the hill, which was held by 100 men of the 54th, the same number of the King's Juzailchees, one gun of the mountain train, with two officers. The centre post, being a commanding position over the town, was occupied by four companies of the Shah's 6th, two of Nicholl's H. A. guns, and some large guns of the King's. The rest of the troops were scattered in different parts of the fort, two companies being at each of the gates.

During this day many projects were entered into for the purpose of putting down the rebellion, but none were put into practice. The Wuzeer went into the town, accompanied by some troops; but soon returned, having made no impression. The King wrote to Sir William Macnaghten, proposing that a free pardon should be offered to all offenders, and that all should be forgiven and forgotten if the leaders of the insurrection would come to his durbar, and, acknowledging their

D

faults, return to their allegiance. This, of course, was never carried into execution. Five companies of the 54th, commanded by Capt. Corry, accompanied by some cavalry, arrived; having lost on the way, between cantonments and the Bala Hissar, the baggage and clothing of the grenadier and light companies, who, consequently, were exposed to the rigorous nights without a single article of clothing. Although fired on the whole way, they had only three men wounded. The cavalry returned, but the 54th remained with the headquarters of their regiment.

4th. — At two in the morning firing recommenced at the city. Khan Shireen Khan and some others are conjectured to have driven the fighting party out of the city; but we do not hear of the heads of the faction (Abdoollah Khan, the proprietor of the Pisheen Valley, Amenoollah Khan of Logur, and Sekunder Khan) being seized. The insurgents in great numbers took possession of Mahmood Khan's fort, the Shah bagh, Mahommed Shureef's fort, and the garden between the Godown fort and the fort called the Bazaar of the European regiment.

Our guns from the south bastion opened early, and played almost all day on Mahmood Khan's fort, and on any body of Affghans that showed themselves. Lieut. Warren, who held the Commissariat fort with fifty men, wrote to the General to say, that, unless reinforced, he could not hold out; that he was surrounded by the enemy, who he feared were mining the walls, and they were preparing ladders for the escalade; adding also that some of his men had already left him.

In the evening a party of cavalry and infantry were sent to aid him in evacuating his position! Capt. Boyd, the Bengal Commissariat officer, on hearing the object of this force from Capt. Grant (Assist. Adjt. Gen.), proceeded in person to Gen. Elphinstone, accompanied by Capt. Johnson (the Shah's Commissariat officer). They urgently entreated him to recall them, and, instead, to send such reinforcements as were required to hold a position of such vital importance; pointing out the certain destruction of the whole force in cantonments, in the event of the capture of all our supplies. The General acquiesced in their views, and promised to issue the order for reinforcements. The above detachment was very shortly obliged to return to cantonments, having suffered most severely in men and horses, who were fired upon from behind every face and from every loophole of Mahommed Shureef's fort, without their being able even to see an enemy. Previous to this detachment going out, a party of Europeans, under Capt. Robinson, went down the Kohistan road to effect the same object. Capt. Robinson (H. M. 44th) being killed, this small party was obliged to retire, having suffered severely. Two horse artillery guns accompanied the party. Lieut. Waller, H. A., and Lieut. Fortye, 44th, were wounded. The whole of this occurred within 250 paces of the south bastion. In the evening no reinforcements had been sent to Warren, and the two heads of the Commissariats, Johnson and Boyd, again went to the General, to entreat he would not lose any more time in sending aid to that officer, and informed him there were but two days' provisions left in cantonments; pointed out the great fears entertained that we could not procure supplies from the surrounding country, with the enemy in force in the neighbouring forts, and the consequent destruction of our force from famine, unless the Godown fort were taken possession of at all hazards. The General conceded to these opinions. As Mahommed Shureef's fort commanded the only gate of the Commissariat fort, it would be requisite first to take possession of that fort. The political authorities had no persons from whom they could obtain information! For a reward of fifty rupees one of Johnson's servants proceeded to the fort, and brought back intelligence (in about half an hour) that he saw twenty or thirty men with lighted matchlocks sitting on either side of the wicket;

he judged, from the silence that prevailed, there were but few then within, and affirmed there were none on the road. Johnson subsequently sent another man, who confirmed the reports, but did not see any lights near the wicket. All this was made known to Gen. Elphinstone, who determined on taking possession of the fort, and Capt. Boyd volunteered to carry the powder to blow in the gate. The General, however, afterwards listened to other advice from other of his staff officers, who were averse to the proceeding, as involving too much risk! During this time another letter was received from Lieut. Warren by the adjutant of his regiment, stating that unless he was immediately reinforced, he must abandon his position, as many of his guard had gone over the wall to cantonments, by which his force was much weakened. Capt. Boyd and Johnson left the General about midnight under the impression that Mahomed Shureef's fort would be immediately attacked and the Commissariat one reinforced.

A letter was written by order (by Capt. Bellew) to assure Lieut. Warren that he should receive reinforcements by two o'clock in the morning. Capt. Mackenzie held his (the King's Commissariat) fort until his ammunition was entirely expended, and then cut his way through the town; but in so doing was wounded in three places. Strange to say, this officer owed his life to beating a woman! He told his people to abandon their property and save their lives. A woman put down her child to save her pots and pans; and expostulation being of little effect, and time most precious, Mackenzie drew his sword to strike her with the flat of it, by which means he had it in his hand when he was attacked immediately afterwards.

Trevor's tower has been burnt. Had reinforcements and ammunition been sent to Trevor's tower and Mackenzie's fort, they might have held out for ever against any force the rebels could have brought against them. The Hazir Bashes refused to stay to defend them, because they saw they must be sacrificed, and that no reinforcements were sent. Had they arrived, the Kuzzilbashes would have declared openly in our favour, with Khan Shireen Khan at their head but unless supported by us, they dreaded giving offence to the insurgents.

Another party has been sent out with guns; it is said they are to fire the city, but most likely it will be a mere demonstration. Such it has proved. The guns were sent to take possession of the Lahore Gate; they got not quite to Mahmood Khan's fort, and had to come back again.

The enemy have now possession of the Commissariat fort, the fort opposite the Bazaar fort, or Mahommed Shureef's, and the Shah bagh; the two latter posts appear to have been left unoccupied for the enemy's especial advantage.

The only mortar we have being a five-and-half-inch one, has little more effect than a popgun of large calibre.

A gun has been sent to attempt to blow open the gate of the Shah bagh, which Sturt says will be a work of time with a gun; and they cannot use a powder-bag, as the gate is not *get-at-able* for the crowds of people fighting all the way from the Bazaar fort to the Shah bagh, and thence to the city.

A large party of horsemen have shown themselves coming down the Siah Sung hill: the cavalry are sent to look after them. Mahmood Khan's fort is occupied by the enemy, who are to be shelled out, it is said; but we have been throwing shells into the small fort opposite the Bazaar (Mahommed Shureef's) since 12 o'clock, and now at 4 they are still at it, and seem to have done nothing.

A Kulassy of Capt. Maule's has just come in from the Kohistan half naked: he reports, that the Kohistanees are all up; that Maule and Wheeler were killed at Kar Durrah, and that they were overpowered.

This day Lieut. Gordon, of the 37th, was killed; Capt. Swayne, 44th, ditto; Lieut. Walsh, of the Shah's service, wounded in the thigh; Hallahan, 44th, in the shoulder; Warren, 54th, wounded; Capt. Robinson and four men, 44th, killed, and sixteen wounded.

The cavalry had brought in six wounded, and had thirty-one missing at 5 o'clock. The 5th cavalry went up to the gate of the Shah bagh in gallant style; but it was shut too quickly for them to get in. Hamilton's horse shot under him in the ditch under the gate.

At tea-time we had an alarm, and very smart firing like a *feu de joie;* but it was a false alarm. I believe no enemy was seen: it occurred on the rampart near to Sale's bastion.

After we had, as we thought, settled poor Sturt for the night, between 8 and 9 o'clock Capt. Lawrence came to see him and ask his advice. Sturt had wished to have communicated with the General on the defence of the cantonments, and, ill as he was, he had written a letter to him; but thinking that advice from so young an officer might not be relished, he, notwithstanding my remonstrances on the subject, tore it up. About 10 o'clock, Lieut. Eyre, Deputy Commissary of

Ordnance, and Capt. Warburton, the Shah's Topshee Bashee, came; and as they had received information that there are men posted outside the gate of the captured fort, with matchlocks all ready, the plan in agitation of blowing open the gate with a bag of powder would not answer: they, therefore, with Sturt, decided on getting the two nine-pounders into the bastion, and on setting to work forthwith to cut the embrasures to fit them; and between 2 and 3 o'clock in the morning was fixed upon as the time to commence playing on the fort to breach it, and at the same time to throw in a proportion of shells to create confusion. The place to be taken by assault. If this does not succeed, we shall probably have to retreat to Jellalabad. Sturt strongly advises the troops being all thrown into the Bala Hissar, and the cantonments being abandoned until we get up reinforcements; but the cry is, how can we abandon the cantonments that have cost us so much money?

The enemy's force are estimated at from 1500 to 2000. Brig. Shelton is expected in from the Bala Hissar, where they are said to be short of provisions. Here we got six seers of ottah for the rupee yesterday, but to-day none is procurable. The servants are to get half rations from the commissariat to-morrow.

At the Bala Hissar. two companies!!! were warned for service under Capt. Corri, 54th, for the purpose of entering the town to cause a diversion during the expected attack which it was understood there was about to be made from cantonments. However it was, as usual, only one of the theoretical plans so often talked of, and so little practised. Conolly, Troup, and Hay had gone there for the purpose of assisting with counsel; but there was "great cry and little wool," and nothing was done.

The supplies are become very limited, and it becomes a question how the troops and Horse Artillery horses are to be fed: to-day there were only three days' provisions left; but owing to the great exertions of Capt. Kirby, Acting Assistant Commissary-General, a very large quantity was laid in, Damel Khan and Timor Khan, two Armenian merchants, being very instrumental in procuring them. Immediately in the neighbourhood of the Bala Hissar were fields of wheat stretching out for many acres; the wheat being the second crops, and some half a foot high, was found to be excellent food for the cattle: the groves also, in the vicinity, were all cut down for fire-wood, which, as long as it lasted, was very liberally distributed to the troops by the King.

5th.— At 5 o'clock A. M., no reinforcement having gone to the assistance of Lieut. Warren, although promised by 2, that officer vacated the Commissariat fort. No blame can attach to him, but much to those who withheld aid. The enemy took possession, depriving us of our only means of subsistence. Nor was this all the mischief: it gave both confidence and much plunder to the enemy, and created great disgust amongst the Europeans, who lost all their rum; a worse loss was all the medical stores, sago, arrow-root, wine, &c. for the sick.

The men in cantonments were employed all day, the guns and mortars throwing shot and shell at the Mahommed Shureef's fort; Major Swayne being ordered with a very insufficient force to attack it, only two companies with two Horse Artillery guns, under Lieut. Eyre. The latter were ordered to be placed on the Kohistan road, outside the gate of cantonments, and to keep up a heavy fire on the fort; whilst Major Swayne was to advance rapidly on the fort, and blow open the gate with a bag of powder. Lieut. Eyre obeyed his orders; but his ammunition was all expended before the arrival of Major Swayne's party, who, instead of advancing, had, on a fire of matchlocks being opened from the fort, taken cover under some walls from the heavy fire of the enemy; and having expended all their ammunition ineffectually, the whole had to retire with some loss of men and horses. This was the only opportunity that offered of retrieving our loss. The enemy were busied in hundreds all day in carrying off our stores, all which we plainly saw from cantonments. The troops retired by order of Gen. Elphinstone, to my no small surprise, for the enemy had begun to run out from a broken bastion; but when they found our people retreating, they took courage, and no more left the fort, on which shot and shell kept playing all day. After stating this, it is unnecessary to add that Sturt's suggestions had not been acted on.

When the 44th retreated from Mahommed Shureef's fort, all were in amazement; the 37th asked leave to go and take it, but were not permitted to do so. The Sipahees are grumbling at short allowance, and not being allowed to do any thing. The 37th were anxious to be employed in recovering the Commissariat fort, though no actual proposition to that effect was officially made to the General.

On this day a report was carried to the King and Conolly that the rebels had mined from the Shôr Bazaar to immediately under H. M.'s palace, which said mine was to be sprung the same evening. The King instantly left the palace, and took up his abode at the Gate of the Haram Serai, where he remained during the rest of the siege; and all day, seated at a window commanding a fine view of cantonments, telescope in hand, watched anxiously the course of passing events in that place. He was at this time quite sunk into a state of despondency, and would gladly seize any opportunity of asking the opinion of any of the officers as to what was likely to be the issue of the struggle. He put off for the time all the insignia of royalty, made the officers sit by him on chairs, and seemed quite *gobrowed* (an expressive eastern term, to be rendered something between dumbfounded and at one's wits' end). The Shah's conduct in the particular of the chairs is the more worthy of remark, as he had been in the habit of keeping the officers for hours standing with folded hands silently in his presence, and then ungraciously dismissing them without even a passing remark. He now sent to each Sahib a warm silk resaiz and a pillow, which were very acceptable, as they were all starving with cold.

6th. — Major Kershaw, Lieut. Hobhouse, and eleven soldiers of the 13th Lt. In. (who had been left at Cabul in consequence of illness) this day volunteered their services.

Sturt, having fretted himself half mad at every thing going wrong, determined, weak and ill as he was, to go out and do his duty. He is the only engineer officer at Cabul. He was unable to dress, but went out in his shirt and pyjania to the works. Although he was out himself a little after 6 o'clock, he could not get things or people into their places until 10. General Elphinstone gave him permission to make any arrangements he considered as safe from chance of failure for taking the small fort; but when he had with great exertion got three nine-pounders and two twenty-four pound howitzers at work (the latter across the road), Major Thain was sent to him to desire he would be careful not to expend ammunition, as powder was scarce! there being at the time a sufficiency for a twelvemonths' siege! However, Sturt made no alteration in his proceedings, and by 12 o'clock an excellent breach was made, the bastion being thrown down and great part of the curtain, so that ladders were not required: the gate was blown in at the same time by Capt. Bellew, Assist.-Adjt.-Gen. There was a small crack in the rampart near Sale's bastion, of which I used to take advantage, as a stepping-stone to enable me to see what was going on; and from my position I saw the storming party ascend the breach, under a heavy fire, with a commendable steadiness and great alacrity: they quickly drove the enemy from their stations, who then escaped through the wicket into the Shah's garden. The storming party was commanded by Major Griffith, of the 37th N. I., consisting of the light company of the Queen's 44th, Lieut. Hobhouse and ten men of H. M. 13th Lt. Inf., one company of 5th N. I., one company 37th N. I.; in all about 150 men. Lieut. Raban, 44th, killed whilst waving his sword on the highest point of the breach; Mr. Deas, 5th, wounded. I believe we had nineteen killed, and several wounded; amongst the latter, one of the 13th. The flag taken from the enemy was waved on the crest of the breach by a Sipahee of the 37th, who captured it, and who was promoted for the act. He and a havildar of the same corps, though belonging to the rear company, were, with Lieut. Raban, the first into the fort. But few of the enemy were found killed; but it is difficult to estimate the numbers of their slain, as they are so particular regarding Moslem burial that they always, when practicable, drag the bodies away. Great numbers escaped to the hills behind, which were quickly covered with horsemen, from 2000 to 3000 men. A party of Anderson's horse charged straight up the hill (just to the left of the gorge leading to the lake) in most gallant style, and drove the enemy along the ridge to the extreme left. Meantime, the 5th cavalry rode along the foot of the hill to the left, and charged up at that end; by which manœuvre the enemy were hemmed in, in the centre of the two cavalry corps, when a very severe encounter took place. From the top of our house we saw every thing distinctly; the gleaming of their swords in the sun, and the fire of their pistols and matchlocks: fresh horsemen came pouring on to the assistance of the enemy from the back of the hill; they buried our cavalry and Anderson's horse, who, overpowered by numbers and a most galling fire, were forced along the ridge to the spot whence the first charge took place.

The Affghans have many advantages over our troops: one consists in dropping their men fresh for combat; each horseman takes a foot soldier up behind him, and drops him when he is arrived at the spot he is required to fire from. Their horsemen are either gentlemen or yeomen (as we should denominate them), all well mounted, and their baggage ponies can manage the hills much better than our cavalry horses; in fact, the Affghan horses seem to me to climb about with as much unconcern as goats do. As regards pistols, we are on a par, as most of theirs have been presents from the Posha Khana; but their juzails carry much further than our muskets, and, whilst they are out of range of our fire, theirs tells murderously on us.

A standard bearer with a white flag was killed;

he was evidently a person of some consequence, from the great anxiety evinced to obtain possession of his body. There were two red flags in another division.

Capt. Anderson distinguished himself, killing four men with his own hand; he rode up the gorge to challenge the enemy again, but they had the advantage of position, and would not come down.

The enemy continued to crown the heights: our guns were out of range, and the shot fell short. We had infantry out in skirmishing order, but the whole was little more than a very exciting and provoking spectacle; for we made little impression, although the whole of our cavalry was out: so cavalry, infantry, guns, and all, came back again, and soon after the enemy came down the hill, some evidently returning to the Shah bagh, and others dispersing more to the left, and probably returning to the city.

Lady Macnaghten told me to-day that Sir William had written to inform Sale that we had been in siege since the 2d, and to request his return with the force under his command; to leave the sick and wounded in safety at Gundamuk, under charge of the troops there. To this the General assented, and signed the letter; but afterwards he said it would be abandoning the sick and baggage, and refused to recall Sale's brigade.

I was asked if I could send a letter from Sir William to Sale, through Sturt's influence with the natives; but if, with secret service money at his command, the Envoy cannot bribe a messenger, how are poor people like us to do so?

Sir William has given one of the Kuzzilbash chiefs 50,000 rupees to raise a diversion in our favour, and has promised him two lakhs more if he succeeds.

The insurgent chiefs have set up a king, and a wuzeer; they went to the mosque, and read the fatcha, or prayer, for the reigning monarch. Several of the Moollahs refused to recognise the name of Shah Zeman: they said they would allow that of Shah Shoojah as a legitimate monarch. There was a long and wordy dispute; but Shah Mahommed Zeman seems at present to possess most power in Cabul. This is not the blind Shah Zeman, Shah Shoojah's brother, but a relation of the Ameer Dost Mahommed. He is an old man, and said to be the son of an elder brother of Dost Mahommed's, and used to be called the Nawaub. He has struck coin in his own name.

Abdoollah Khan has sent a messenger to treat with the King, who replied that he would receive no such low person, and that some person of respectability must be sent. The King is also said to have seized the man who stabbed Sturt, and to have declared his intent to put him to death; but just now I believe he dares not do so.

This day there was a report that Sir Alexander Burnes and his brother were still living, but that the people, in whose power they were, were treating for a very large ransom.

Capt. Warburton left two guns in the city at his house; the Affghans have taken possession of them (six-pounders), and use them against us either with their own balls, or ours returned to us in that manner. They hammer our nine-pound shot into an egg shape. One of them that fell in Sturt's compound attracted attention, as we all supposed that they could not be hammered to fit other guns.

Paton and Bellew meet in council with Sturt at nine most evenings at our house. To-day arrangements were made for carrying the Shah's garden and the Commissariat fort at daybreak, every thing being so clearly explained that even I understood it as well as hemming the handkerchief I was making. The captured fort, as it is called, is now held by three companies. It is proposed to be blown up: they are quietly to cut embrasures in the wall for three guns, to cover the attack on the garden. There is to be a simultaneous attack on the Commissariat fort; and the signal for escalading the breach with a company of Europeans, and one of natives, will be the explosion in blowing up the gate. Plans were sketched, and all the minutiæ written out, so that the General might have no questions to ask. It is now midnight, and no reply has been sent from him, though an answer was to have come to say whether the work should be done or not.

This day Gen. Elphinstone wrote to the Envoy to state that we were in want of ammunition, requesting him to endeavour to make arrangements with the enemy!

Capt. Bellew told me that the General has at length agreed that Sale's brigade shall be recalled. Had we more men, a brigade might be sent out on the hill, to punish the enemy who defy us there.

The men are greatly harassed; their duty is very heavy, and they have no cover night or day, all being on the ramparts. The weather is cold, particularly at night.

There was a good store of grain in the captured fort, but very little of it was brought into cantonments by the Commissariat, though a great deal found its way into the Bunneahs' shops, or was carried off by the Sipahees and camp-followers.

A great quantity of wheat has been brought in to-day and yesterday from the villages, and we are promised further supplies.

A note from Thain mentions that Sale has been sent for, but, from the very cautious wording of the order, it appears doubtful whether he can take such responsibility upon himself as it implies. He is, if he can leave his sick, wounded, and baggage in perfect safety, to return to Cabul, if he can do so without endangering the force under his command. Now, in obeying an order of this kind, if Sale succeeds, and all is right, he will doubtless be a very fine fellow; but if he meets with a reverse, he will be told, "You were not to come up unless you could do so safely!"

There has been much talk of bringing Brig. Shelton from the Bala Hissar into cantonments, to aid with counsel and prowess; the plan is, however, for the present abandoned.

The troops in the Bala Hissar are better off than we are, as there are yet some supplies in the shops there, though at an exorbitant rate.

Despatches have been sent for reinforcements from Kandahar. If Gen. Nott's brigade had not proceeded on their way to the provinces further than the Kojuk pass, they are to return.

Accounts have been received that Codrington's corps at Charikar is surrounded. Capt. Rattray, the political agent there, and Lieut. Salisbury, killed. Capt. Codrington and the other officers wounded, as also Major Pottinger, political agent.

There has been great talk of withdrawing the troops from the Bala Hissar into cantonments; but if this were done, the King, with his 800 ladies (wives, daughters, &c., and their attendants), would follow, and we should soon be starved out. If we make an inglorious retreat to Hindostan, he will still accompany us; and as we brought him to the country, we must stand by him.

When there was first an intention of building for the army at the Company's expense, Capt. Sturt gave it as his decided opinion, (which opinion is on record in the letter book of his office, in a letter to Sir A. Burnes,) that the garrison should be placed in the Upper Bala Hissar, from whence (with plenty of ammunition and food, which might always be procured from the city, either purchased from friends, or taken zubberdust from the enemy) we never could be dislodged. A large outlay (I write from memory, and therefore do not name a sum) was expended in commencing barracks, bombproofs, &c.; and last, not least, a new wing was added to a palace for the Envoy, and another, to make all square, was laid out, when the King sent to say he would neither have the Envoy nor the troops in the Bala Hissar: so all the money spent was thrown away, and the King had the new wing and the whole palace thrown down because it was originally erected by the Dost.

The camp was pitched at Siah Sung; but that site would not answer for a cantonment for many reasons detailed by Sturt in his public letter, which I propose appending to my Journal.* I shall therefore only notice two of them, — the distance from good water, and the whole spot being commanded by the heights that surround it, except on one side, which is a morass, and from that cause not particularly healthy at some seasons.

There was ground on the further side of the city, but that would not answer, as should an insurrection occur in Cabul it would cut off our communication with Jellalabad.

Eventually the King gave up a garden or orchard, the present site of cantonments, with water at hand, good and plentiful, and always procurable by digging two feet for it in any direction.

Sturt urges the absolute necessity of our now withdrawing our forces from the cantonments into the Bala Hissar, but is still met by the cry

* This letter was lost, together with all the rest of the documents of the army. (See p. 2.)

of, " How can we abandon the good buildings and property ? "

The ammunition might be buried and concealed, the guns spiked, &c.; but a great deal of the former might be sent into the Bala Hissar by the cavalry carrying each man a proportion on his horse nightly, and many of the latter might be taken to the citadel.

To Sergt. Deane, of the engineers' department, the army are very greatly indebted for his great personal exertions in getting in grain. He is a particularly intelligent man, and very superior to his present station in life; and the fluency with which he speaks Persian enables him to pick up information, and also to go about at times in disguise for the same purpose.

If we can only continue to obtain provisions as we have done for the last two days, we shall be able to hold out on half rations, and in another month, it is said, the Kohistanees cannot touch us for the snow, which fell heavily on the hills last night.

We had rain here late in the evening, and at night; and this morning I saw a great increase in the snow on the hills.

In the Bala Hissar, Lieut. Melville having recovered from his wound sufficiently to do his duty, was sent down to take charge of the

Lahore gate of the fort, which was now the only opening into the Bala Hissar, the others having been built up with almost solid masonry.

The troops there were isolated in a fort closely besieged, actually without a single case of amputating or other surgical instruments amongst them, and hardly a grain of medicine! — most culpable negligence, as they might easily have been sent from the cantonments, though a little foresight would have suggested their being taken there with the troops; and they might easily have been got ready during the time they were under arms — more than an hour — before they marched.

There has been constant firing for the last day or two on the city side of the fort, and the enemy have made several unsuccessful attempts to carry off the two guns that are lying beneath the walls. Food is already scarce in the bazaar; and although plenty is stored up in the private houses of the natives, yet in the shops the price of two seers of wheat or two and a half is a rupee.

The Sipahees complain bitterly of the severity of the weather, particularly at night, and above sixty men are in hospital at the Bala Hissar already, besides the wounded: they are attacked with pneumonia, which carries them off in the course of a couple of days. The King sent strict orders to Melville at the gate, to allow no one to pass either in or out without a pass from either the wuzeer or Conolly, except the surwans in charge of the grazing cattle which go out at 8 A. M. and return at 2, protected by a resallah of the King's Sikh regt.: in case of an alarm from without, a flag is ordered to be waved from the ramparts, on which signal all the cattle are immediately to come in. The above-mentioned resallah are, without any exception, the worst set-up and most disorderly body of troops calling themselves a regiment that can be imagined: their horses are ill-conditioned, their arms and accoutrements nominal, as each man dresses as he pleases, a stick with a bayonet on the top being the sole offensive weapon of many of them. And this is the imperial guard of the monarch of Affghanistan! Besides this regiment his majesty has with him in the fort, of his own troops (not reckoning those of the subsidiarised force), his orderly regiment (Campbell's), 400 Juzailchees, and 500 of another Hindostanee regt. The orderly regiment are certainly better men of the sort (not being the Company's soldiers) than are usually met with, although they did run away in the city on the 2nd, but it was not until they had lost 200 men and fought gallantly. Campbell himself is the King's right-hand man.

Associated with Melville at the gate was Raja Jeenial Sing, a man whose father was prince of an extensive territory lying near Cashmere, and who, when Shah Shoojah in 1818 was a fugitive and an exile flying from Runjeet Sing, received him most kindly, gave him all he asked for: refusing every offer or command of Runjeet to surrender him up, he transported him safely to the Company's territories. For this, Runjeet deprived him of his Raj, valued at four lakhs yearly, and all his property, imprisoning both him and his sons: the latter on their father's death made their escape and arrived at the court of Shah Shoojah, for whose sake they had lost every thing. His gratitude was shown in the regal donation of two rupees eight anas daily!! Verily they had their reward, and well may they exclaim, "Put not your trust in princes!"

From an idea of an insurrection being about to take place among the Arabs (who compose a large portion of the inhabitants), a proposal was set on foot for turning all the Affghans, &c. out of the Bala Hissar, and taking all provisions found for the use of the troops both there and in cantonments. This, as well as every other energetic measure proposed, was knocked on the head either by the King or the politicals, and, instead of turning out all useless hands, an order was issued to allow no woman to pass the gate unless supplied with a pass, as an idea had got afloat that they were about to turn out their wives and children ere a general massacre of the troops took place. However, in lieu of an insurrection, food becoming very scarce, all the natives became clamorous for permission to leave the fort, and go into the city with their wives and children,—"a consummation devoutly to be wished," and to insure which it had been good policy to have paid them a high price for their houses and grain, &c. This the King positively refused to allow, but ordered a Shah-Gazee to join Melville at the gate, and, having examined them one by one to see that they carried out no arms, to allow females to pass; but no man to go on any account. In this way, in three days were passed out 750 women with their children, which was at least a good riddance!

7th.—I did not go to bed till after Mr. Eyre went away this morning: he came at a little after midnight in consequence of some frivolous objections of the General's, based I believe mostly on Capt. Bellew's doubts as to whether the trees in the garden next the Commissariat fort were planted in lines parallel to the wall or not. Now Bellew always has an "observation" to throw in, or "begs to suggest" something. He had acknowledged he had never been in this garden, though Sturt had; neither could he be made to understand that it was the custom of the country to plant the trees in lines parallel with the outer walls: neither could he comprehend, that if even a tree intervened, a shot would destroy it from the heavy nine-pounders. These trees were not gigantic English oaks, the growth of a century; but fruit trees.

The heavy iron nines would now have proved their utility against the fort, but the old objection of the difficulty of transporting them over bad roads still exists; an iron nine cannot be as portable as a brass six-pounder, but the eighteen-pounders would not have given much more trouble than the nines did on the march up, and would have done us good service had we them here. Capt. Abbott wrote for 3 eighteen-pounders ; the military board made it a case of arithmetic, and sent 6 nines; and as they had to be taken up the hills by hand, a little more manual labour would have transported the others also over the Affghanee mountains.

I often hear the Affghans designated as cowards: they are a fine manly-looking set, and I can only suppose it arises from the British idea among civilised people that assassination is a cowardly act. The Affghans never scruple to use their long knives for that purpose, *ergo* they are cowards ; but they show no cowardice in standing as they do against guns without using any themselves, and in escalading and taking forts which we cannot retake.

The Affghans of the capital are a little more civilised; but the country gentlemen and their retainers are, I fancy, much the same kind of people as those Alexander encountered.

The Juzailchees were sent out to skirmish: they attacked the Shah bagh, and cleared the west end of it; they then joined Major Thain, who, with a squadron of horse and two companies of infantry, attacked a garden beyond it, drove the enemy out with great slaughter, and burnt the garden house. Lieut. Eyre at the same time, through a small opening in the wall of the Shah bagh immediately under the captured fort, played with a six-pounder upon the gate of the garden. Not being supported, however, these advantages were lost, and the enemy being reinforced in great numbers, the above troops were forced to retreat, having lost a considerable number of men; *par exemple*, fifteen of the Juzailchees out of ninety-five were left on the field. I have not the actual numbers of the Europeans and Sipahees who were slain.

The gun was saved with great difficulty, and here a great fault was committed in sending one gun only. In the Marquis of Hastings's time an order was published prohibiting a single gun being sent out, in consequence of the disastrous consequences attending its being unsupported during the Nepalese war. But all seems confusion here. Those who; at the head of affairs, ought to have been directing every thing, appear to be in consternation. General Elphinstone from his first arrival in the country was in ill health, which gradually increased on him, till his mind became nearly as much enervated as his body ; and so conscious was he of his own state, that he had written to Government to give up the command, and also to Gen. Nott at Kandahar to come up and take his place until a new commander of the forces was appointed.

We are now in circumstances which require a man of energy to cope with them. Major Thain is said to be a good adviser, but unfortunately it is not always in the multitude of counsellors that there is wisdom; and so many proffered their advice and crossed his, that Thain withdrew his, and only now answers such questions as are put to him.

8*th*.—At four in the morning a sharp firing was heard, for which at the time we could not account, but afterwards found that it proceeded from the captured fort, which the enemy had attempted to mine and re-capture. They had succeeded in making a large hole, but being repulsed they set the fort on fire. At daybreak, finding Sturt's servant still in the verandah, and knowing that his master was to have been up at half-past four, I went to the door to inquire, and found that the General, or rather his advisers, had decided that nothing was to be done.

The enemy are using our guns against us, throwing shot into cantonments from Mahmood Khan's fort.

Our men are so over-worked that it is intended to give them rest to-day.

Sturt went out early this morning, and found the garden next the Commissariat fort unoccupied; he immediately took the sappers under Lieut. Laing with fifty of the Juzailchees under Mackenzie to cover them, and sent for two companies of Sipahees as a covering party whilst they pulled down the wall, which was quickly accomplished.

There is a report that we are to be attacked in cantonments to-night. Sturt went to Gen. Elphinstone and Brig. Anquetil, who both gave him *carte blanche,* and desired that all his instructions should be obeyed. He has accordingly placed 15 guns in position. We have only two artillery officers in cantonments that are available, now Waller is wounded; they are Eyre and Warburton. We have no laboratory men,—no other engineer officer than Sturt, who, weak as he is, has to do every thing.

When we came into cantonments last November, Sir Willoughby Cotton commanded the forces in Affghanistan; and Sale, as the second here, and commandant in cantonments, had the troops paraded and their posts assigned, in case of any sudden attack. These troops (the 1st brigade), who knew their posts, are now far from us, and no arrangement of a similar kind has been made since their departure; so Sturt has had the officers told off to their several stations, has paraded them at them, and goes his rounds before he goes to bed to see that they are all at their posts.

It is said that Mohun Lull has named the man who killed poor Sir Alexander Burnes; he also writes that there are only 500 Kohistanees in the city, and that otherwise all is going on well in the Kuzzilbash quarter of the city, where he resides.

It was reported to-day that the city was on fire, but it proved to be a village fired by the Kohistanees.

Conolly writes from the Bala Hissar, accounting for the firing we heard this morning. An attack was made on the Bala Hissar, which was repulsed: the enemy were seized with a panic, fancied they were attacked from the rear, and began to fight amongst themselves; cries of *Aman* were heard in cantonments by several persons besides myself. Conolly also writes that he has not only heard that we are to be attacked to-night, but that the enemy are making up bhoosa bags with which to fill up the ditch.

Sturt is gone to lie down to recruit his strength, knowing that I never dose now till daylight, but sit up to watch passing events, and give the alarm if need be, and have kept my nightly watch ever since the insurrection commenced. Our troops as yet are staunch; and if we are attacked, and succeed in repelling the enemy, we shall be able to keep our own until Sale's brigade arrives.

The enemy showed to-day on the heights, in force about 3000; but we cannot cope with them, so content ourselves by throwing shrapnell at them. Eyre threw some with great precision; the distance was, however, very great, and we consequently did little execution. We also greatly feel the want of laboratory men to cut fuzees, &c.

Sturt asked for a party to occupy the village of Behmaru, but it was not given. The Envoy was anxious to secure this place, but all was in vain; and as we neglected our advantages, the enemy availed themselves of them, and Meer Musjudee threw himself and 1000 followers into it. We have thereby lost 900 maunds of ottah, which was paid for.

Two forts near the village are in our possession.

An attack expected at about 3 o'clock this afternoon.

Brig. Shelton came in from the Bala Hissar with six companies of the Shah's 6th, one horse artillery gun, and one of the mountain train.

The people in cantonments expect wonders from his prowess and military judgment. I am of a different opinion, knowing that he is not a favourite with either his officers or men, and is most anxious to get back to Hindostan. I must, however, do him the justice to say that I believe he possesses much personal bravery; but, notwithstanding, I consider his arrival as a dark cloud overshadowing us. Most glad shall I be to find that, by his energy, the General is roused up to active measures. It is, perhaps, a part of his complaint (but, nevertheless, equally unfortunate for us), that Gen. Elphinstone vacillates on every point. His own judgment appears to be good, but he is swayed by the last speaker; and Capt. Grant's cold cautiousness, and Capt. Bellew's doubts on every subject, induce our chief to alter his opinions and plans every moment.

At the Bala Hissar they began to be much cramped in their correspondence with cantonments, which became very limited; a hurkaru stealing out at night, and returning with an answer early in the morning, being now the only means of communication; and the same man never went for more than five days without being either killed or confined.

The Affghans, having persons who can read English, French, and Latin, were aware of all our secrets.

Mohun Lull and the Naïb Shureef were our newsgivers from the city, and always gave intelligence of the arrival of any new chief or body of troops; also doing, or saying they were doing, all in their power to enter into some sort of terms. The King is gradually getting worse and worse, and has quite lost all his self-possession. He has warned the females of his zenana (amounting in number to 860) that in the event of the cantonments falling into the hands of the rebels he should administer poison to them all! At least these are the reports gathered from his few immediate attendants; how far they may be relied on as true, or whether they are merely set afloat to blind us to his own share in the insurrection, it is difficult to say.

Brig. Shelton made over the command to Major Ewart, 54th N. I., and left the Bala Hissar at 4 A. M., and arrived in cantonments before daybreak, without meeting with any opposition on the road.

The troops were left in position as follows:—

At the city gate of the fort were 2 companies of the 54th, 1 gun horse artillery, 1 of the mountain train. At the centre square above the palace 2 companies 54th, 2 guns horse artillery, 1 eighteen-pounder, and just under it a nine-pounder. The Sikh horse encamped in the square.

At the Lahore gate, 100 men of the 54th under Lieut. Melville, with 50 of the Shah's Juzailchees. On a bastion to the left of the Haram Khana, 1 company of the 54th. On the upper tower of the fort, commanding the whole, 100 of the 54th, 100 Juzailchees, and 1 gun of the mountain train. The remainder were in reserve at the palace square, with their different parts allotted to them in case of an alarm.

On this day the men at the Bala Hissar were put on half rations in consequence of the large supplies of ottah required to be sent to cantonments, and which Capt. Kirby is getting stored as fast as he can.

Ammunition, by the directions of the Major-Gen., is now beginning to be thrown into the Bala Hissar, under charge of Capt. Walker, commanding detachment of 4th local horse, who has orders to bring back all the ottah he can collect in time to return before daylight; but, owing to the men (who are half starved in cantonments) always, immediately on depositing their loads, leaving their ranks to forage for themselves, not more than half the loads usually arrived.

We now began to bombard the city in earnest from Nicholl's battery, beginning at eight o'clock every evening and continuing until eleven, firing at intervals of about ten minutes from the 5½-inch mortar, and the nine-pounder. The effect was beautiful to us in the cantonments; but it is to be feared that was almost the only effect it had, as, from all we could learn, four or five were the usual average of victims, being a very small number for so great an expenditure of ammunition. Amenoollah Khan's house was the principal object of attack, and one or two shells went completely through it; but as, immediately on the shelling commencing, he and all his family left it for some other residence, the loss of a few of his horses was the utmost injury he suffered.

Regarding Brig. Shelton's view of affairs, it may be remarked that, from the first of his arrival in the country, he appears to have greatly disliked it, and his disgust has now considerably increased. His mind is set on getting back to Hindostan; and it is worthy of remark that from the first, on going into the Bala Hissar, he desired Capt. Nicholl to fill all the ammunition boxes, as fast as it was expended, with flour (ottah), to be ready for provision in case of retreat.

9*th.* — The enemy showed themselves again on the hills, and were permitted to remain unmolested.

The Envoy wished troops to be sent out; but deference was paid to Shelton's opinion, who would not attack them, being all for a retreat to Hindostan.

10*th.*—Having bullied us with impunity yesterday, the enemy again showed themselves on the hills, and rushed with a shout into the village of Behmaru, which they occupy and vacate as the whim takes them. They also lined the Siah Sung hills, came down to the river, and kept up such a heavy fire, that we could not keep our gun outside the rear gate, and we had to bring it in.

The enemy are in possession of several forts near us. The 44th and part of every corps were out under Shelton, but considerable delay took place, and it was only on the Envoy assuring the General that he would take the responsibility of the act on himself that the troops were sent out.

They attacked the Rikabashees' fort. By some blunder, Bellew did not go at the gate, but blew in the wicket. Lieut. Bird, of the Shah's 6th, and a few others, got in, when the enemy's cavalry charged, and the 44th turned — " sauve qui peut." Here Shelton proved a trump. Cool and brave, he with much difficulty succeeded in rallying the men, to save those inside, and when they did return they fought like lions. It was a very fearful affair as witnessed by nearly all in cantonments; and the men, both Europeans and natives, in the second attack behaved with undaunted courage. Capt. Westmacott, 37th, had been skirmishing in front, and commanded the advance No. 2. and 3. companies of the 37th. On the retreat of the troops, Lieut. Hawtrey (37th), Capt. MacCrea (44th), Lieut. Cadett (44th), Lieut. Bird (6th), Lieut.-Col. Mackrell (44th), and two or three soldiers (44th), and a havildar and four or five of the 37th, were left in the fort, having rushed in at the kirkee (wicket). Lieuts. Hawtrey and Cadett returned to endeavour to get more of the men up. Bird's account of the affair is, that when they got in they experienced a most decided opposition, but the enemy rushing out at the opposite gate, they took advantage of it, when abandoned by their comrades, to close the entrance, securing the chain with a bayonet. The enemy, seeing the success of their own charge outside, rallied, and, cutting a hole in the door with their long knives, they got out the bayonet, and opened the gate again. Bird and one Sipahee, 37th, and one or two others, retreated to a room in which there were two horses, and through a small opening kept up a sharp fire, luckily killing the few who saw them enter, and afterwards picking off all who passed in their way. Above thirty were thus killed, fifteen of whom fell to Bird's share, and six to that of the Sipahee of the 37th, for which the Sipahee was afterwards promoted, by Bird's especial request to Major Griffith. Col. Mackrell went to the door, to look if relief was coming, disregarding Bird's advice to remain with him coolly and steadily till they got reinforcements. The Colonel was wounded and fell, and the cavalry cut him up dreadfully. He was wounded in both legs, one below the knee, the other on the thigh; he had three cuts in the back, two toes cut off, and three or four cuts on the arm, which was taken off immediately after he was brought in. Poor man! He said, "This is not battle, it is murder!" He still lives, but is not likely to survive; better had he been shot at once. To persons accustomed to civilised warfare, these details must be revolting. Even a dead enemy is never passed without a cut at the body. They cry "Aman" themselves, but never show mercy to Kaffirs.

Capt. MacCrea was in the fort all but one

arm, by which they seized him and dragged him out: his was a very similar fate, but his sufferings were less protracted, for he was dead when found, with, I believe, his skull cloven.

Poor Westmacott of the 37th was cut to pieces near the kirkee. We must have killed a great number of the enemy. Mr. Bird says he himself saw above 100 killed, but that as fast as a man fell, others came and dragged him away. Major Scott in vain tried to rally the 44th: excited to tears, he called for volunteers to follow him, when a private, named Stuart, was the only man who offered to go, and for which, on its reaching the Envoy's notice, he was, by Sir William's earnest entreaty to Shelton, promoted sergeant.

When the storming party came up the second time under Shelton, a cruel scene took place. The enemy could not have had less than 150 killed and wounded. We had ourselves fully that number. There were 26 killed and 28 wounded of the 44th; above 50 killed and wounded of the 37th. I did not hear the number of the Shah's 6th, and have not access to records; not that they are kept very correctly, for Sturt was never returned as a wounded officer.

The conduct of the 37th is highly spoken of: they drove the enemy (who had got on the top of a bastion) with their bayonets clean over the side, where they were received on the bayonets of the 44th.

The dreadful slaughter of our men is attributable to a desperate rush of Affghan cavalry. It is supposed that some very influential person was in the fort, and has been killed. A body richly dressed was found, but the head was carried away. This they do when they cannot take the body, as the head then receives Mussulman burial, which the Affghans are very particular in observing. A horse was taken, and a sword that was much bent; both are said to have been recognised as having lately been in possession of Moollah Mobend of Zoormut. Four other forts were taken, from which the enemy ran on the capture of the Rikabashees'.

Shelton led the troops out towards the Siah Sung hill, where the enemy was in force, and where Eyre did great execution with two horse artillery guns. The troops remained out till dark, when, having completely overawed the enemy, they returned. Three times the sappers were ordered (and as often countermanded) for the purpose of blowing up these forts and firing them. At length it was decided to keep the Rikabashees' fort, and to occupy it. There is known to be a large store of boussa and lucern there; and we hope also to find grain. Zulfar Khan's fort was also occupied by us. These forts were not above 400 yards from cantonments. The furthest fort is memorable as the spot where a murder was committed not long ago, and was perhaps 1000 yards distant; of this the four bastions were blown up, and the place itself fired. As Brig. Shelton has always been supposed to be greatly disliked by his men, it has excited much astonishment that the men of the 44th were all inquiring after the "little Brig.," as they call him. They say they are ready to be led to any work there may be for them to do.

This event has already produced its effect. Khojeh Meer of Behmaru has sent his salaam to know our pleasure. The Envoy's reply was, "If you wish to keep your two forts, sell us grain."

The events of to-day must have astonished the enemy after our supineness, and shown them that, when we have a mind to do so, we can punish them.

Our spirits are raised and depressed by the barometer of public events. Could any thing have roused us at first to action, the insurrection had been crushed in the bud. When the 44th turned and fled to-day, the Gen. asked the Envoy if he was prepared to retreat to Jellalabad as to-night; but Sir William replied that he would do his duty, and never desert the King; and, if the army left him, would die at his post!

Now we are uppermost we hold up our heads, and hope not to have to sculk into the Bala Hissar without baggage. Were Sturt's advice taken, we should nightly send ammunition there, and, when a sufficiency is conveyed, all make one bold night march in very light marching order, just what we can carry on our horses. In there, we can be lodged (not comfortably, I grant) in the houses of the inhabitants, who would be well paid for vacating them. They have laid in their stores for the winter, which would be bought at any price — and then we might defy all Affghanistan for any time. However it seems hopeless to think on such subjects, for those who with a great end in view might be brought to abandon public works and property for a time, will not consent to part with their own! A horse, with handsome silver-mounted saddle, &c., has been brought in by Lieut. Vanrenen, who sold it for 120 rupees to some one who fancied it because it was supposed to have belonged to a chief.

Sturt's recovery and energy appear little short of miraculous; he nearly possesses the power of ubiquity. He cannot yet mount his own tall horses, and must astonish my little Cape horse, for he gallops him the whole day from bastion to gate, and gate to bastion, laying guns, and off like a shot ; his aim being to show the enemy that all our batteries and gates had guns in position, which we could fire nearly simultaneously, — for they know how weak we are in artillery officers.

The enemy kept up a smart fire for some hours; the bullets flew about briskly, and fell plentifully in the verandahs of Capt. Boyd's house.

An artilleryman was killed whilst sponging his gun; also two bheestees in the Mission Compound.

Sir William told Sturt this morning that if we beat the enemy to-day, he felt convinced that in five days they would all be off; and the circumstance of Khojeh Meer's salaam is a favourable sign.

To-morrow early we are to endeavour to get grain from Khojeh Meer at Behmaru.

The grain in the Commissariat fort is still burning, and the fort itself still in possession of the enemy, who annoy us from thence and from the Shah bagh and Mahmood Khan's fort. The latter place we are not strong enough to take unless Sale's brigade or Nott's arrives: this is much to be regretted, for in all disturbances in Cabul, whichever party kept possession of that fort was always the conqueror in the end.

Gen. Nott may be here with his brigade in three weeks: we have plenty of ammunition, and if we can get grain we may hold out till they arrive.

11*th.* — Yesterday's lesson has made the enemy shy, and very few showed themselves on the hill, and those were all horsemen: none were seen on the Siah Sung hills.

Two regiments were sent to cover the foraging party collecting grain from the captured forts. 600 maunds of wheat have been brought in, boussa, &c.; this gives us three and a half days' provisions.

Ottah is ready for us at the Bala Hissar, and the chief of Behmaru has tendered his civilities again, now that Meer Musjudee's people have retired from the village; but our 900 maunds of grain that were paid for are gone.

A large grave, or rather pit, full of bodies has been found outside the Rikabashees' fort, which the enemy had not time to cover over before they retreated.

Bad news from Candahar. A party of the Shah's troops under Lieut. Crawford, who were escorting state prisoners, are said to have been attacked and cut to pieces, and it is feared that Capt. Sanders (Engineers) was with them. Capt. Skinner is reported to have been killed in endeavouring to escape out of the city in women's clothes. A dog of Col. Dennie's, and another of Major Kershaw's, having come into cantonments, has caused much excitement: as we have not heard from Sale's camp for some time, we think it may be a proof that they are on their way back.

To-day we have been throwing shells into Mahmood Khan's fort, both from the cantonments and also from the Bala Hissar. We hear that to-morrow night the enemy intend to take the cantonments, and that they have fifteen ladders to escalade with, and bags filled with boussa to cross by filling up the ditch. Our men are all in high spirits.

Meer Musjudee has sent to Sir William to say he will come in to treat; his vakeel was in cantonments yesterday. The Ghilzyes have been (it is said) brought off by the Envoy. It was a reinforcement of 1000 Ghazees that joined the enemy yesterday at the Rikabashees' fort; it is supposed that they suffered very severely in the action.

12th. — Arrangements have been made by Sir William with Meer Musjudee, who is to receive 60,000 rupees if he brings in Codrington's regiment: he, poor man, has died of his wounds. The expected attack on the cantonments has not taken place, but there was a good deal of firing all night, and shells were thrown from one o'clock at Mahmood Khan's fort.

13th. — The Ghilzye chiefs expressed a wish to treat: however that may be, the enemy showed themselves on their favourite heights (Behmaru); they are supposed to be reinforcements from Zoormut. They took two guns up with them, which they played upon cantonments. On this Brig. Shelton was sent with a force against them. It was with great difficulty the Envoy persuaded the General and Brigadier to consent to a force going out; and it was late before the troops were ready, consisting of—

A squadron of Anderson's horse, 120 men, under himself;

The Envoy's cavalry escort, about 60 men, under Le Geyt:

The 5th cavalry, all but their usual guards, about 250, under Col. Chambers, being two squadrons, the rest being with Sale:

A troop of the 1st and another of the 4th locals, or Skinner's and Alexander's horse, under Capt. Walker:

6 companies of the 44th, under Major Scott; 4 weak companies of 40, or 160 men, of the 37th; the Shah's 6th, the 5th, I believe six companies each.

There were three columns; two companies of the 37th led the left column under Thain, with the 44th in the centre and Shah's 6th in rear. The right column was under Scott, the reserve under Major Swayne.

Civilians and women are fond of honour and glory, and perhaps do not sufficiently temper valour with discretion.

It appears that the Affghans attribute our forbearance, whatever may be its motive, to fear, which gives them courage to beard us lions in our den.

The General again (as in the late attack on the Rikabashee fort) asked the Envoy if he would take the responsibility of sending out the troops on himself; and, on his conceding, the force was sent. The Envoy had also much angry discussion on this point with Brig. Shelton.

But all these delays of conference lost much time, and it was between four and five P. M. before operations commenced.

The Affghan cavalry charged furiously down the hill upon our troops in close column. The 37th N. I. were leading, the 44th in the centre, and the Shah's 6th in the rear. No square or balls were formed to receive them. All was a regular confusion; my very heart felt as if it leapt to my teeth when I saw the Affghans ride clean through them. The onset was fearful.

They looked like a great cluster of bees, but we beat them and drove them up again.

The 5th cavalry and Anderson's horse charged them up the hill again and drove them along the ridge.

Lieut. Eyre quickly got the horse artillery gun into the gorge between the Behmaru hills and that to the left (the gorge leading to the plain towards the lake): from this position he soon cleared that plain, which was covered with horsemen. There was another stand made at the extreme left; but we were successful on all points, captured both guns, brought one of them in, for which we had spare horses in the field; and having no means of bringing the other away, it was spiked, upset, and tumbled down the hill.

The enemy had taken these guns up the hill with the King's elephants; but unfortunately they had sent the animals back, or they would have been fine prizes for us.

Brig. Shelton, perhaps not considering the lateness of the hour, deferred his return to cantonments until the shades of evening had closed over the troops; and it being impossible to distinguish friend from foe, we could not assist with our guns from cantonments, which in daylight would have swept the plain, and have prevented the enemy from following up our return to cantonments.

The enemy cut in between cantonments and our men, and their horsemen came up close to Sale's bastion. Our anxiety was very great, for all this time our front was attacked (it is said by 400 men); the firing was sharp and long-continued. The Brigadier did not get back till 8 o'clock; and it was some time after that before all was quiet. When the men of the 37th were upbraided for turning, they replied, "We only retreated when we saw the Europeans run, and knew we should not be supported."

We moved into Sturt's house this evening, as Brig. Shelton was grumbling about the cold in a tent.

The enemy saluted our house with six-pound shot, which rattled about and passed us, and several struck the house; one was imbedded in the wall under Mrs. Sturt's window. At night we threw shell as usual into Mahmood Khan's fort, and could plainly distinguish the sound of " Ullah ul Alla" as they burst.

Major Thain and Capt. Paton were wounded; the latter had to suffer amputation of the arm; the former had a deep flesh wound in the shoulder, twelve inches long, and one deep.

Sturt, going his rounds at night, narrowly escaped being shot in the back.

14th. — We had a quiet night; which was a

great blessing, as Sturt was suffering very much from the wound in his face.

The chiefs complained that we broke faith with them yesterday in attacking them when they had expressed a wish to treat : however, we were not the aggressors, for we did not do so till they had fired at us. To-day they have requested we will not fire on the hill, which has been agreed to : they are (they say) busy searching for their dead. They had lights on the hill all night, burying their slain, and they are now searching for swords and any thing they can find, also picking up balls of all kinds.

A number of swords have been taken.

The two sons of Abdoollah Khan are said to be wounded. We could hear Abdoollah Khan's nagura beating on the hill quite distinctly.

Had Sale's brigade been here, it is probable we should not be so peaceable ; but our men are so hard worked that they require a day's rest.

The Affghan cavalry yesterday were not inclined to try a second charge : Col. Chambers invited an attack, which they declined. Their infantry seem to be contemptible in the plain, but they fight hard when cooped up in forts. They fire from rests ; and then take excellent aim ; and are capital riflemen, hiding behind any stone sufficiently large to cover their head, and quietly watching their opportunities to snipe off our people: There is also a peculiarity in the Affghan mode of fighting, — that of every horseman carrying a foot soldier behind him to the scene of action, where he is dropped without the fatigue of walking to his post. The horsemen have two and three matchlocks or juzails each, slung at their backs, and are very expert in firing at the gallop. These juzails carry much further than our muskets.

The Envoy went out to meet some chiefs in Zulficar Khan's fort: they kept him waiting a long time, and then said they could not come. Meer Jaffier Khan, the son of Naib Shureef, has returned from collecting the revenue, with 300 Hazir Bashes: being all Kuzzilbashes, we presume he will not be against us. The old Naib has been fined 1000 rupees for having associated with, and eaten with, us infidels.

Meer Musjudee is said to be sick even unto death in the city. A cossid has arrived from Macgregor, and a letter from Sale of the 9th from Gundamuk. The enemy are evidently spreading false information, through persons professing to be travellers. No travellers are on the roads now. Cossids are scarcely procurable; the few that have been sent to recall the brigade have not succeeded in their attempt. The man who went on the 6th was stopped and his letter read by a man who was educated at Loodianah. The enemy have another sçavant, who imbibed literature at the college of Delhi. There is also a prisoner, a Mr. Tierney, in the city; whether he assists them or not we do not know.

The day has passed off quietly, and we look forward to a good night's rest, which is most desirable for Sturt.

15th. — After a quiet night, we have had a quiet day.

Our camels are dying fast: we see several dragged away daily; and as they are only just thrown without the gate, the air is tainted by their carcasses.

Major Pottinger and Mr. Haughton have made their escape from the Kohistan; the former has a ball in his leg; the latter has lost his hand, and is severely wounded in the back and neck. During the time they were beleaguered in Charikar, they were, in common with the Sipahees of the Shah's 4th regiment (Ghoorkas), subjected to great misery from the want of water; the allowance for the last four days being one wine glass full per diem for each man: the horses they rode on had not had a drop to drink for ten days, nor food for five.

The site of the cantonments was badly chosen.

In addition to there being no water, which of itself rendered the site unfit for a military post, their position was completely commanded on two sides by the enemy; who, having cut off their supply of water from above, gave the few defenders no rest by night or day. Added to these trying circumstances, the garrison were encumbered with their wives and children, who had been encouraged to come up from Hindostan in great numbers. It is affirmed that they did so by permission of Lord Auckland; it being supposed that they would have no wish to quit the country with their families settled along with them.

The not being allowed to bring up their families, even at their own expence, was always considered as a heavy grievance by the Europeans; but, in their instance, the wisdom of the refusal has been proved. But to return to the Ghoorkas; harassed by the enemy, and encumbered by their families, they sank into a state of perfect apathy; not so the Punjabee artillerymen who served the guns. Part of these deserted to the enemy; and, on the following day, had the insolence to return for the purpose of seducing away their comrades. It was in trying to arrest some of these that poor Haughton was so dreadfully wounded: perceiving his intentions, the Jemadar of artillery (a Punjabee) snatched Lt. Rose's sword from him, and with it cut off Haughton's hand. It was with great difficulty that Pottinger and Haughton effected their escape. Somewhere between Akterae and Istalif during the night they strayed from the other officers. Finding themselves separated from the rest, they determined to make the best of their way, secreting themselves in a hollow during the day, and travelling all night; but Haughton's wounds, particularly those in the neck and back, prevented his urging his horse beyond a walk. On arriving at Cabul, they decided on going straight through the city in the night; they were challenged, and Pottinger gave a Persian reply; which the guard evidently judged a doubtful one, as it was followed by a volley being fired at them, but fortunately without effect, and they pursued their way to cantonments, arriving at the gate in such a state of exhaustion that had they had a mile further to go they never could have sat on their horses. From them I heard the particulars of Maule's, Rattray's, and Wheeler's deaths. They were sitting together, I believe at breakfast, when some of their own men attacked them: they are said to have set their backs against the wall and defended themselves until they were deliberately shot.

The report to-day is that Abdoollah Khan's sons are killed; that Amenoolah's two sons are killed, and Shumsoodeen's two brothers wounded; the latter are nephews of the Ameer, Dost Mahommed.

It is also reported that the enemy say they cannot meet us in the field, but they will starve us out of the country.

The Envoy has information that we are to be attacked to-night on three faces of the cantonments; this is the first night of the moon: Sturt's Affghan servants say that, if an attack is made, it will not be for three nights to come, as at present they are all feasting.

There is a native report that a Fouj has been seen at Seh Baba, which has been magnified into Sale's brigade on the way up; but from letters of the 9th, received yesterday, it is evident that at the time they were written none of our letters had reached them; and they were misled by false reports industriously spread by the enemy, in the guise of travellers.

16*th*.—There was some quick firing heard about one in the morning. The news we gather from people who have come in from the city is, that Nawaub Zeman Khan has paid his troops three lakhs of rupees, at the rate of ten rupees for each suwar and six for each foot soldier; that they are in high glee, and say they will attack the Chaoney.

The 25,000 men that were to do so last night did not make their promise good.

Some Goorkhas that came in to-day say that they have no information regarding Dr. Grant, but that they saw Lt. Rose at Karabagh.

A report has come in from the Bala Hissar that Sale has gone on to Jellalabad, which Brig. Shelton told me he believed, on the principle of "Being out of a scrape, keep so." Most people believe the report to be a ruse of the enemy, to shut out hope of relief coming to us. We, however, doubt Sale's having ever received the order to return.

The city seems to be much quieter, and some ottah and grapes were brought very early this morning to the gate to sell. The King has written to say he wishes to offer terms to the rebels; but Sir William says that they must first be sent for his approbation, lest his Majesty should offer too much.

A quiet night, as far as regarded hostilities, — with plenty of rain.

17*th*. — We had a gloomy day, with rain at intervals.

Another report that the 1st brigade is gone on to Jellalabad; coupled, however, with its being only to deposit their sick in safety, and that a force of 10,000 men have arrived there to our assistance from Peshawer.

Jubbar Khan (a brother of the Dost's) has been appointed Wuzeer to Zeman Shah Khan, who has coined rupees in his own name.

This has been a good grain day: at 12 o'clock we had got in 400 maunds, at two Cabul seers the rupee, and otta at one. The Cabul seer is equal to six Hindostanee seers. The Affghans continued bringing in grain and ottah all the day.

18*th*. — This morning, at 2 o'clock, an attempt was made to throw in ammunition into the Bala Hissar, but it failed; and Capt. Walker and Lieut. Webb reported that the bridge, which was to have been repaired by the Wuzeer, had not been touched.

Accounts received from Jellalabad by a cossid, who brought a letter to Sir William which he had torn in three pieces for the better concealment of its contents; on seeing the enemy he swallowed another small one; he was searched, but brought in the torn letter without discovery. He reports, that, after Macgregor gave him the letter, he delayed his departure a little; that there was a grand *Larye* at Jellalabad; that Sale had thrown his force into the fort there; that the enemy had come down with 40,000 men, and

Sale had sallied out and beat them, pursuing the enemy eight or ten miles to Futteabad.

Another report stated that Sale had been obliged to spike three of his guns. A few hours afterwards another courier arrived with a letter from Sale, by which it appears that the enemy surrounded the fort, in number about 5,000, and that he ordered a sally under Col. Monteath, of 600 infantry, all his cavalry, and three guns. The cavalry maintained their character, and behaved nobly, and the enemy got severely handled.

My letter, containing a précis of goings-on here from the 2d to the 8th inclusive, had reached Sale, and was the only detail of events that had been received; it was sent on to the Commander-in-chief, and a copy of it to Lord Auckland. Sale had written to Capt. Mackeson at Peshawer for provisions, ammunition, and troops.

It had been wished that this blow below should be followed up by another here; but the council at the General's was as usual both divided and wild. One plan was to sally out, sword in hand, and attack the town,—a measure that must have been attended with great loss on our side, even if victorious; with the pleasing certainty of all who were left in cantonments having their throats cut during the absence of the troops.

The next proposition was the taking of Killa Mahmood Khan. But nearly the same objection existed there. With a large force, and much probable loss, we might take it; but we could not destroy it quickly, and could not afford troops to garrison it. It is rather fortunate that the last-mentioned attack was not made: for a few hours afterwards we had certain information that, instead of 200 men, the enemy have nearly all their infantry there.

A report was this day brought to the King that the Jemadar of Juzailchees, who commanded at the Upper Town, above the Bala Hissar, had deserted his post during the night, accompanied by two non-commissioned officers of his guard. His Majesty was extremely wroth; and ordered all the men to be relieved, and another party, consisting of Rohillas from the Peshawer territory, to be sent in their place. Most fortunate was the discovery, and the prompt measures taken on the occasion; as it was discovered, from secret information sent in by Mohun Lull during the day, that the traitor had sold the tower to the rebel Sirdars for a hundred gold mohurs. This man had the effrontery to return in the evening; and declare, with the greatest *sang froid*, that he had only been away on his own business into the city; and angrily demanded why he was deprived of his command. He was, however, put in irons, and confined in the fort prison.

Mohun Lull's account stated that arrangements had been made to give up the tower that same night to a party who were to come round by the back of the hill. Had this plot succeeded, the Bala Hissar might have been taken, as the tower commands it.

19*th*. — At two in the morning an alarm; which soon died away. Shortly after this the ammunition was sent off to the Bala Hissar, under charge of Col. Oliver; who sent back to report that in consequence of the bridge being out of repair, and there being water in the Nullah, he could not proceed, and desired instructions how to act. The reply from the General was, if he could not proceed, he was to return: when this arrived, Oliver had got over with the ammunition; but I suppose he misunderstood the order, for he recrossed and came back again. With very few exceptions the 5th N. I. may be said to be inefficient from the commanding officers to the lowest rank.

In the course of the day we got in a good deal of grain; but the General appears to be kept in a deplorable state of ignorance. Although reports are sent in daily, he scarcely knows what supplies are in store, or what is our real daily consumption. Affairs are curiously carried on: for instance, the Shah's 6th indent for six maunds daily; the 37th, a much weaker corps, for about twenty! These indents are all signed by authority! The quantity required is easily calculated, as each fighting man gets a half seer of wheat, and each camp follower six chattaks per diem. There is much roguery going on in the regimental bazaars, where the Chowdrys make money in connexion with the Bunneahs.

They say the 6th have a full bazaar from loot at the forts taken lately, and do not require to draw for their followers: the 37th have 5,000 registered camp followers, and other corps much in the same proportions.

The Affghans are highly indignant at Pottinger and Haughton having ridden through the town. It certainly appears to us very wonderful that they did so in safety.

There was some firing in the city about sunset, — both guns and volleys of musketry. The rebel chiefs are supposed to have attacked the Kuzzilbashes in the vicinity of Morad Khana.

The enemy have sent to the Kohistan for the guns that are at Charikar, and on their arrival propose giving us battle. A plan was laid to sally out from the Bala Hissar towards the city, and destroy an Hamaum exactly in front of the

Ghuznee gate. In this place reside a barber and a blacksmith, two of the best shots in Cabul, who have picked off many of our men. They completely commanded the loopholes with their long rifles; and although the distance is probably 300 yards, yet they seldom fail to put a ball through the clothes or into the body of any one passing them. It was sufficient for the loophole to be darkened, for it to be fired at; and it became an amusement to place a cap on the end of a pole above the walls, which was sure to be quickly perforated by many balls.

I believe this plan was never put in execution, and only, like many others, proved a source of speculation and conversation.

20*th*. — The firing in the city yesterday was consequent upon some persons having taken refuge with the Kuzzilbashes, who refused to give them up, as being contrary to the Affghan rules of hospitality. There has been more fighting amongst themselves to-day.

The latest report is that the Ghilzyes, and Kohistanees, and all the people who come from a distance, are anxious to return to their own homes, finding that there is no more plunder to be had, and sundry hard knocks being all that they are likely to obtain. However, they have been requested to stay for a few days, just to see how the Chaoney is taken when the guns arrive from the Kohistan. These same guns cannot be very formidable, for they are said to have been spiked at Charikar; and, moreover, the carriages are broken down—all split at the elevating screw.

The enemy are now talking of pitching camps on the other side of the hills towards the Lake, and also on the Siah Sung encamping ground.

There was a report to-day that a large force was coming in with the guns, for which the rebels have sent the King's elephants. In consequence of this report, and another that the enemy had taken possession of a fort in our rear, six companies of infantry and two troops of horse were sent out, but only a few stragglers were to be seen; and the forts were all peaceably occupied by women and children as usual.

Camels and tattoos are dying fast, and the air is most unpleasantly scented at times.

It is now rumoured that the reason Sale's brigade does not come up is, that the two regiments refuse to do so. This I do not believe; they may have been annoyed at the thoughts of returning; but I will never believe they refuse to aid us in our extremity, if they have the power to do so: and I consider the report to be of a piece with Brig. Shelton's expression that Sale's brigade was safe, and would keep so.

Nooreddin Khan (the chief of the Jan Baz, who so nimbly have found their way to Cabul), was the son of an old servant of Shah Shoojah's. In consequence of the father having been faithful to him through his misfortunes, the King was anxious to provide for the son, and gave him the command of the Jan Baz. On Nooreddin's arrival, Conolly sent him a message reproaching him for the ingratitude of his conduct, to which the young scamp replied, that all he could promise in our favour was a safe retreat from the country!

The Ghoorka corps is said to be entirely cut up, and we have no longer any hopes of Rose's or Grant's escape. The men are said to have been disgusted at having persons placed over them as native officers, who were raised at the same time as themselves, and who were not of higher caste.

We have as yet no news from Candahar, from whence we expect to hear of a similar rising to that here.

Walker succeeded in throwing in ammunition into the Bala Hissar early this morning, as also 30,000 rupees, each horseman carrying a small bag of coin.

To-day part of the ammunition was removed into Westmacott's house; some put under sheds, and the rest was left in the square: it seems there was fear of its being blown up by the enemy!

21*st.*— The enemy uncommonly quiet; said to be employed in manufacturing powder and shot, and hammering such of our shot as they pick up to fit their guns.

Some servants of Skinner's have gone to the Bala Hissar to Conolly; they report that their master is still safe in the city. Capt. Drummond is under Zeman Shah Khan's protection.

Shumsuddeen Khan is said to be dying of his wounds.

At dinner time Brig. Shelton sent to Mr. Eyre, stating that the Envoy had information that 80,000 foot and 10,000 horse were coming to set fire to our magazine with red-hot balls! How these balls were to be conveyed here red hot is a mystery, as the enemy have no battery to erect furnaces in: but nothing is too ridiculous to be believed; and really any horrible story would be sure to be credited by our panic-struck garrison.

It is more than shocking, it is shameful, to hear the way that officers go on croaking before the men: it is sufficient to dispirit them, and prevent their fighting for us.

There is said to be a kind of republican council in the city, composed of twelve chiefs, to whom the people at present pay obedience. I wonder what the new King, Zeman Shah Khan, and his Wuzeer think of this new power.

A man of Warburton's artillery has deserted, as also a havildar of Hoskins' regiment; the latter was received by Zeman Shah Khan with great honour, and told that all good Mussulmans were welcome. A house and shawls were given to him.

Our useless expenditure of ammunition is ridiculous. At the captured fort last night the garrison popped away 350 rounds at shadows, probably of themselves: however, we have plenty of it; 13 lakhs made up, and 900 barrels of powder, shot, bullets, &c. in store in profusion.

Shelton croaks about a retreat; and so much is openly said of our extremity, that were we obliged to fall back on Jellalabad, it is more than probable that there would be much desertion amongst the Mussulmans.

It is difficult to ascribe the just cause to the inactivity of the enemy: if they feared us, they would disperse; and if they mean to starve us, why do they allow us to get in supplies in the quantities they do? That something is in agitation there can be no doubt; and the most plausible idea is, that the enemy think that by keeping us on the alert so long for nothing, that we shall all relax in our vigilance, and give them the opportunity to attack the cantonments with success.

Sturt has in vain suggested that a picket of infantry and cavalry with a couple of guns be sent at daybreak up the hill towards Siah Sung, to cut off the supplies we see daily going into the town.

By purchasing them, we might induce the people to supply us largely, and at all events prevent the enemy obtaining them. I have no patience with those who say, " Oh, it is not ottah, it is only charcoal." Now our foes require charcoal as much as we do food, for they cannot make their gunpowder without it; and wood is very scarce in the city, for the poor people who used to bring it in on donkeys have ceased to do so, lest it should be taken for nothing.

22*d*. — At two o'clock this morning Walker took the bedding for the artillery to the Bala Hissar.

This being considered a propitious day, the enemy lined the heights towards the lake. A party was sent to occupy the friendly village of Behmaru; but, as usual, delay was the order of the day, and it was deferred until the enemy had taken possession, though not in great force.

On the troops arriving there under Major Swayne, of the 5th, the enemy evacuated it: he, instead of allowing the men (as they themselves wished) to enter the village, kept them under hedges firing pot shots, on which the enemy re-occupied the position. The force sent out was 1 horse artillery gun, 1 mountain train ditto, 1 ressalah of Anderson's horse, 1 ditto Walker's, 1 ditto 5th cavalry, 400 5th N. I.; the whole under Major Swayne, 5th N. I. In the evening a reinforcement was sent of the remainder of the 5th, under Col. Oliver. Lieut. Eyre wounded severely in the hand. The troops returned, having done nothing.

The Ghilzye chiefs say they have sworn on the Koran to fight against us; and so they must fight, but that they will not fight hard. This is what they have told Sir William through their emissaries. He is trying to treat with all parties: but the sanctity of an oath is evidently but little regarded; and what faith can we put in their assertions?

We have just heard that Capt. Woodburn, with 130 men, returning to India, was enticed into a fort at Shekoabad, a few marches on this side of Ghuznee, where they swore on the Koran to be our friends, and where the whole party were massacred. Poor Woodburn was represented as a strong man, who took four or five Golees to kill him! There is a report to-day that two regiments coming from Candahar have been cut up.

Grand dissensions in military councils. High and very plain language has been this day used by Brig. Shelton to Gen. Elphinstone; and people do not hesitate to say that our chief should be set aside — a mode of proceeding recommended a fortnight ago by Mr. Baness, the merchant.

The poor General's mind is distracted by the diversity of opinions offered; and the great bodily ailments he sustains are daily enfeebling the powers of his mind. He has lost two of his best advisers in Paton and Thain; the former confined by his wound, the latter declining to offer advice, from disgust at its being generally overruled, by the counsel of the last speaker being acted on.

There is much reprehensible croaking going on; talk of retreat, and consequent desertion of our Mussulman troops, and the confusion likely to take place consequent thereon. All this makes a bad impression on the men. Our soldiery like to see the officers bear their part in privation; it makes them more cheerful; but in going the rounds at night, officers are seldom found with the men. There are those that always stay at their posts on the ramparts, and the men appreciate them as they deserve. To particularise them would be too openly marking the rest; but their names will, I trust, be remembered to their honour and advantage hereafter. Amongst these, Capt. Bygrave, the Paymaster-General, was conspicuous: he never slept away from his post (the battery near his house) for a single night, and took his full share of fatigue, without adverting to his staff appointment.

Col. Oliver is one of the great croakers. On being told by some men of his corps, with great *jee*, that a certain quantity of grain had been brought in, he replied, "It was needless, for they would never live to eat it." Whatever we think ourselves, it is best to put a good face on the business.

The enemy are erecting sungahs on the heights above Behmaru.

23*d.* — We had firing of one sort or other all night. From the Bala Hissar they were shelling the city, and there was much firing from our ramparts.

At about two in the morning, in consequence of a resolution arrived at the preceding evening to submit no longer to the insults of the enemy, (who by occupying Behmaru greatly annoyed our foraging parties, and almost precluded our attempting to drive them off the hill immediately above that village, whither they were accustomed to resort in great numbers for the purpose of bravado, and also probably to prove our strength or weakness,) Brig. Shelton marched out of cantonments with seventeen weak companies: I believe many of them did not muster above forty men. Those from the 44th were under the command of Major Swayne of the 5th N. I.; those from the 37th and Shah's 6th, under Major Kershaw of the 13th. All the 5th were employed under their own colonel (Oliver). One squadron of regular cavalry, and two detachments of irregular horse; one six-pound gun under Sergt. Mulhall, and 100 sappers and miners under Lieut. Laing.

This force ascended the hill immediately above Behmaru, dragging the gun with them with great difficulty, and thence up on the knoll overhanging the village. From hence they perceived that the village was in the possession of the enemy, who were discernible as they slept around their watch-fires. A few rounds of grape from the gun quickly aroused them; and they sought cover in the houses and towers, from which they replied to our cannonade and musketry by a sharp and pretty well-sustained fire of juzails. Both officers and men were most anxious to be led against the village, to take it by storm, but the Brigadier would not hear of it; and our men were helplessly exposed to the fire from behind the walls, which the enemy quickly loopholed for that purpose. After waiting until day dawned, and losing the opportunity of taking the enemy by surprise, a party was ordered under Major Swayne of the 5th, who, instead of at once leading his men through the principal entrance into the village, went to a small kirkee, which he reported himself unable to force, though this was afterwards done by a few men pulling it down with their hands and kicking at it; and after remaining there a considerable time came back, having lost several of his men killed and wounded.

The enemy (as daylight dawned) were seen leaving the village in small parties: to cut these off, Walker was sent down to the plain, on the north-west side of the hill leading to the lake, with his irregular horse. At this time large bodies of the enemy were descried ascending the hill, near the road by which they used to issue from the city, and separated from that occupied by our troops only by a narrow gorge leading to the plain and lake beyond. To meet and oppose these, Brig. Shelton, leaving three companies of the 37th, under Major Kershaw, to maintain their original position, marched the remainder of the force along the ridge towards the gorge, taking with him also his solitary gun!

I had taken up my post of observation, as usual,

on the top of the house, whence I had a fine view of the field of action, and where, by keeping behind the chimneys, I escaped the bullets that continually whizzed past me. Brig. Shelton having brought forward skirmishers to the brow of the hill, formed the remainder of his infantry into two squares, the one about 200 yards in rear of the other, the intervening space being crammed with our cavalry, who, from the nature of the ground, were exposed to the full fire of the enemy without being able to act themselves.

The number of the enemy's foot men must have been upwards of 10,000 (some say 15,000), and the plain, on the N.W. of the hills, was swept by not less than 3000 or 4000 Affghan cavalry, whose rapid advance obliged Lieut. Walker to retreat up the hill, by which the enemy were enabled to throw fresh reinforcements and ammunition into the village of Behmaru; a circumstance which rendered it difficult for him to hold his ground.

The fight continued till about 10 o'clock, by which time our killed and wounded became very numerous. In spite of the execution done by our shrapnell, the fire of the enemy told considerably more than ours did, from the superiority of their juzails and jingals over our muskets.

They also fought from behind sungahs and hillocks, whilst our men were perfectly exposed; our troops also labouring under the disadvantage of being drawn up in square, from an apprehension of an attack from the Affghan cavalry.

The vent of the gun became too hot for the artillerymen to serve it.

At this time, that is at about half-past 9 or 10, a party of Ghazeeas ascended the brow of the hill, by the gorge, where they planted three standards close to each other, a red, a yellow, and a green one. It is possible that the Brigadier might not have seen their advance; but when they had nearly attained the summit, they had an evident advantage over us, as their shots generally told in firing up at our men, whose persons were wholly exposed, whilst only a few of their heads were visible to our troops, and the old fault of firing too high most probably sent all our shots harmlessly over their heads, for to hit them it was requisite to fire on the ground. When they fairly appeared above-ground, it was very evident that our men were not inclined to meet them. Every field-glass was now pointed to the hill with intense anxiety by us in cantonments, and we saw the officers urging their men to advance on the enemy. Most conspicuous were Mackintosh, Laing, Troup, Mackenzie, and Layton; who, to encourage the men, pelted the Ghazeeas with stones as they climbed the hill; and, to do the fanatics justice, they returned the assault with the same weapons. Nothing would do,—our men would not advance, though this party did not appear to be 150 in number. At length one of the Ghazeeas rushed forward, waving his sword over his head: a Sipahee of the 37th darted forth and met him with his bayonet; but instead of a straight charge he gave him a kind of side stroke with it, and they both fell, and both rose again. Both were killed eventually; the Ghazeea was shot by another man. It was very like the scenes depicted in the battles of the Crusaders. The enemy rushed on; drove our men before them very like a flock of sheep with a wolf at their heels. They captured our gun. The artillerymen fought like heroes; two were killed at the gun; Sergeant Mulhall received three wounds; poor Laing was shot whilst waving his sword over the gun and cheering the men. It was an anxious sight, and made our hearts beat: it lasted but for a few minutes.

(Brig. Shelton says, that when our men ran, he ordered the halt to be sounded, at which the troops mechanically arrested their flight, and fell into their places!)

They ran till they gained the second square which had not broken; and the men finding a stand, turned about, gave a shout, and then the the Ghazeeas were, in their turn, panic-struck, abandoned the gun, but made off with the limber and horses.

On this we retook the gun without resistance. One of the artillerymen had a wonderful escape; he had clung on to, and under the wheels, and never quitted it. Once more in our possession, the gun was instantly re-opened on the enemy; but our men had an antipathy to the brow of the hill, and would not advance as quickly as they might have done, until some successful shots from the gun, and three splendid ones which were made by Serjeant Wade from the Kohistan Gate; one of which struck Abdoollah Khan's horse, and caused him to fall off, on which the people surrounded their chief, and were occupied in carrying him off; they fled to the other hill, and I believe never stopped until they got into the city. All appearing to be over, I hastened home to get breakfast ready for Sturt, every one supposing that the enemy were routed, and that Brig. Shelton was coming back with the troops.

At this time I was standing on the ramparts, and heard the Envoy, in my presence, ask the General to pursue the flying troops into the city, which he refused, saying it was a wild scheme, and not feasible.

Had Shelton returned to cantonments, or

thrown his force into Behmaru, all had gone well, and we had remained masters of the field.

The enemy had, as I before mentioned, a large body of cavalry on the other side of the hill, on whom our men kept firing.

At about half past twelve, just as we had finished our breakfast, the enemy gradually came up the hill; and their fire was so severe that our men in square could scarcely fill up the gaps as their comrades fell, and our whole force, both horse and foot, were driven down the hill, and our gun captured — a regular case of *sauve qui peut*.

All would have been sacrificed but for four circumstances; first, a well-directed fire kept up from the Mission Compound by part of the Shah's 6th. A charge made by Lieut. Hardyman, with a fresh troop of the 5th Cavalry, being joined in it by Walker, who had collected about twenty of his Irregulars. It was in going too far across the plain, in driving the Affghan horse back towards the hills, that poor Walker received his mortal wound in the abdomen. Major Swayne was wounded in the neck while in the square. A party of about fifty of Mackenzie's Juzailchees, under Capt. Trevor, lined some low walls on the plain in front of and to the left of the old Musjeed, whence they kept up a steady discharge. Two of these men, seeing a wounded Sipahee wave his arm for help, gallantly dashed into the midst of the enemy, and brought him off.

Perhaps the greatest safeguard of our troops was the conduct of Osman Khan, who suddenly stopped the pursuit and led his men back.

Perceiving our defeat on the hill, the troops at the captured fort and those at the Musjeed deserted their posts, and were with difficulty persuaded to go back to them. The troops all scuttled back as hard as they could. The General went outside the gate (and took great credit to himself for doing so) to rally them, as he called it; but there was little chance of doing that while they were under our walls. I was amused at hearing him say to Sir William, " Why, Lord, sir, when I said to them ' Eyes right,' they all looked the other way."

Our friends in the Bala Hissar did not tamely look on. Conolly got the King to order eight of his suwars to go and give information to Sir William of their having observed a body of 5000 men passing round to the back of Behmaru; and afterwards his Majesty ordered the whole of the Ressallahs and 100 Juzailchees to go on to the Siah Sung hill, and try and create a diversion in our favour by drawing away some of the troops who were engaged with ours on the Behmaru hill. It certainly had some effect; for immediately on their forming on the summit, a large body of men under Mahommed Shah Khan, a principal Ghilzye chief, sallied out from Mahmood Khan's fort, and advanced to the attack, which now, however, they were not imprudent enough to await, but immediately took to flight. By desire of the Wuzeer, Lieut. Melville was then sent out with a party of Juzailchees, and five sections of N. I., to keep a body of them in check who had boldly advanced within gunshot of the Bala Hissar: but after a little skirmishing the enemy retired to the Siah Sung hill.

The Affghans appear to have but one plan of attack. They go up the further hill to the extreme left near the city, and spread along the ridge, and the horsemen conduct the infantry to the gorge. The horsemen then some of them come up with the infantry to the brow of the right hill, the larger body of horse going behind it; this they did the second time in one day.

Shelton, in taking up his position as before described, had both his flanks exposed, as also his rear. The men were formed in two large squares when attacked by infantry, and in these squares were men of different regiments all mixed up together: they had never been practised to it: no man knew his place.

Whilst in this square a reward of ten rupees was offered by the Brigadier to the first man who volunteered to go with him to take the enemy's flag in the gorge; Captain Mackenzie shouted 100 for the flag. After some hesitation, a havildar of the 37th came forward; but as no other followed him, he was told to return to his place. The enemy then came on, and the whole square rose simultaneously and ran. The 44th had, I believe, fifty-eight wounded; the loss of the 5th I did not ascertain; the 37th had eighty killed, and ten wounded. Of officers, Col. Oliver, Capt. Mackintosh, and Lieut. Long were killed; Walker mortally wounded; Swinton, Evans, Major Swayne, Hawtrey, Bott, and Mackenzie wounded.

The three companies of the 37th that were out under Major Kershaw suffered severely: they were amongst the last to leave the hill. The grenadier company returned with only a Naick and two men!

The misfortunes of the day are mainly attributable to Shelton's bad generalship in taking up so unfavourable a position, after his first fault in neglecting to surprise the village, and occupy it, which was the ostensible object of the force going out.

Had he remained above Behmaru, he might have retreated into and occupied that place, in which the enemy had but few men at first, and who might have been easily dislodged. Shelton tries to lay all the blame on the Sipahees. He says they are timid, and that makes the Europeans timid also; but he has been told some home truths. On asking Capt. Troup if he did not think that the 44th had behaved nobly, that officer plainly told him he considered that all had behaved shamefully.

The troops certainly were wearied out; and, having been out since two in the morning, it appears wonderful to me that at half-past twelve they were not too weary to run; however, they had one great inducement to do so. Osman Khan was heard by our Sipahees to order his men not to fire on those who ran, but to spare them. A chief, probably the same, rode round Kershaw three times, when he was compelled to run with his men; he waved his sword over his head, but never attempted to kill him; and Capt. Trevor says his life was several times in the power of the enemy, but he also was spared.

Another great fault committed was in taking only one gun; a second would have supported the first: with only one, as soon as it was fired the enemy could rush upon it; as they did.

The enemy assembled on the Siah Sung hill, and attacked eighty horsemen sent in with letters by the King; they proved to be from Jellalabad. Our people at first fired on the sikhs, but fortunately did no harm. The enemy's cavalry then came down the Siah Sung hill, and escorted their infantry into the forts beyond the river, which we had dismantled a few days since. Our troops were in by two o'clock; before five, not an enemy was to be seen, and our people were out searching for the dead. The magazine being dropt within range of our guns was safe, and has been brought in. Abdoollah Khan is supposed to have been killed. No particular news from Jellalabad, where all was going on well. There was no letter for me; but Lawrence came to tell me that Sale was well, and busy getting in provisions.

24th.— A letter has come in, supposed to be a forged seal, from Zeman Shah Khan: it has been cautiously and courteously replied to.

A person has come in from Osman Khan (who is a nephew of the Ameer Dost Mahommed) and Shumshir deen Khan, offering us terms: they propose that we should leave the country, giving hostages that we will send the Dost back to them. They say they do not wish to harm us, if we will only go away; but that go we must, and give them back the Dost; that Mahommed Akbar Khan (his son) will be here to-morrow with 6000 men; and that if we do not come to terms, they will carry the cantonment; and that they are ready to sacrifice 6000 men to do so.

What Sir William and the General's council of

war (Shelton, Anquetil, and Chambers) mean to do we know not; but our situation is far from pleasant.

Gen. Elphinstone has written to the Envoy to-day; requesting him to negotiate with the enemy, in consequence of the impossibility of our going to the Bala Hissar, and Shelton concurs in opinion that we cannot fight our way in: also stating we have upwards of 700 sick, and the scarcity of provisions.

Last night an attempt was made to dismantle the bridge leading towards Siah Sung, which succeeded partly: it is now made a flying bridge.

Sturt proposed to destroy the Rikabashees' fort, and throw a party that was in it into the small fort near the bridge; but it was disapproved by the Envoy, who said he would place a moollah he had confidence in, in it, as the General said he could not afford twenty men to garrison it.

A boy of the Syce order, who had been a prisoner twenty days, has made his escape from the city. He tells us, that Amenoollah Khan of Logur is the chief who was killed by a grape-shot in the head yesterday.

Mahommed Akbar Khan has directed, that when the cantonments are taken, the officers, their wives and families, are to be made prisoners, as hostages for his father. If once in his power, we might be safe; but these Ghazeeas are fanatics, and would cut us into mince-meat.

Poor Oliver's head and one hand were cut off when his body was found: the latter was probably done to obtain a diamond ring which he always wore. The heads of all the Europeans were taken away, and will no doubt be exhibited as trophies!

25th. — The Big-wigs are angry at any thing having transpired regarding the letters that have come in from the chiefs; and say it is all a mistake. Be that as it may, a guard of honour was turned out, on the arrival of two men who refused to parley with Lawrence and Trevor, and said they must see the Envoy and the General. At first they were said to be Zeman Shah Khan and Osman Khan; then Jubhar Khan; and at last it proved to be Sultan Khan and his private meerza. They held their conference with the Envoy in the officer's guard-room of the rear gateway.

The new king, Zeman Shah Khan, has written to the Envoy to say that he has accepted the throne, not from his own wish, but to prevent greater ills arising.

There was a very long and unsatisfactory conference with the ambassador. He and his secretary rode sorry yaboos, and were only attended by their saces. If their array was thus humble, their demands were sufficiently exorbitant; and the terms they offered such as could not be accepted, even by persons in our condition. They require that Shah Shoojah be given up to them, with his family; demand all our guns and ammunition; and that Gen. Sale's force should move to Peshawer before we march from this place.

Mahommed Akbar Khan has arrived: we heard the firing in honour of his arrival in the city. He is reported to have brought in an accession of 6000 men to the force, which was before estimated at 10,000 horse and 15,000 foot. The new arrivals are probably Uzbeks, and not far removed from rabble; but even a mob may from numbers succeed against us.

The subadar of the native artillery has gone off, as also three of Skinner's horse : these men are all said to have families in the city.

In the evening there was a great crowd of Affghans; some hundreds of them, all armed to the teeth, round the cantonments. They came in the most friendly manner, saying all was settled, *jung-i-kalūs*. The men of the 44th went out of cantonments amongst them unarmed, were shaking hands with them, and receiving cabbages from them, unchecked by Lieut. Cadett, the officer on duty on that face, who seemed to think this friendly meeting a very fine affair : however, the circumstance got reported, and the adjutant got the men in.

This appears very like a ruse on the part of the enemy, to throw us off our guard, and surprise us. It was suggested to the adjutant to examine the cabbages; as it was possible that outer leaves might cover bladders of spirits; and that, having intoxicated the men, they would when they were drugged make an attack on us: however, nothing suspicious was discovered.

We saw a fire on the hill this evening, supposed to be a party watching our movements, towards the Bala Hissar.

There can be no doubt that the enemy have spies in cantonments; and there are so many Affghan servants, that it is perhaps difficult to prevent their passing in and out.

Two men of suspicious appearance were prowling about the Envoy's tent, and Lawrence desired a chuprassy not to molest them, but quietly to dodge them, and to report progress. This he did, and stated that the men walked all over the cantonment, looked at every thing, and then walked out at the gate! So much for surveillance.

It is now said that Abdoollah Khan was wounded by a grape shot on the 23d, and that there is no truth in the report of Amenoollah

Khan, of Logur, having been stabbed in a dispute in the council regarding terms to the Feringhees.

Poor Walker was buried to-day. He died of his wound last night. He is greatly regretted from his amiability; and, as a right gallant soldier, his loss is doubly felt in the present crisis.

The Shah Razee (Moyen oo deen's father) commanded the troops in Behmaru. He says, had we taken possession of the village in the outset, the day would have been ours on the 23d. We have also heard that so great was the alarm in Cabul, when the Affghans fled on Abdoollah Khan's being wounded, that the women were sent away out of the city in great numbers; and many in such haste, that they did not even wait to mount them on yaboos, but sent them away on foot, expecting to see our troops in the city immediately.

Great care is taken of the fire-wood in store in cantonments, and much discontent prevails because fires are not allowed. The Hindostanees feel the severity of the weather, to which they are exposed night and day; and the want of fuel adds much misery to their privations in being put on short allowance of food. There is at this time a complete winter stock of firing laid in; added to which, on emergency, the trees of the orchard might be cut down.

Capt. Sturt was urgent, both with Gen. Elphinstone and Brig. Shelton, that the men might have fires at night to enable them to warm themselves and dry their frosted clothes when coming off duty: but no order was given in consequence of his suggestions.

26*th*.— Negotiations with the enemy broken off.

Accounts received from Sale up to the 21st; from Macgregor to the 23d. The Khyberries up. Capt. Fenis and his family had fled, and got safe to Peshawer. Lieut. Mackeson was still in Alimusjid in rather a critical position. To-day the Affghans lined the hills; some thousands of them, with many horsemen. They afterwards came down to the plain, and we expected an attack upon the cantonments. On their nearer approach, they were found to be mostly unarmed; some had sticks, some sticks with a knife tied on the end of them: they were merely the shopkeepers, come out to look at us. The Affghan knife is a very formidable weapon, about two feet long, and thicker, stronger, and broader than a sword, and as sharp as possible.

Some of these men went up to the breach of the captured fort, and asked, as the *jung* was over, if they might not return, and live there. And on being told, "No," they said, "Very well; we will go away to-day, and come again to-morrow, and see if we may come then."

One well-dressed man inquired if the volunteer regiment (37th) was there; and being replied to in the affirmative, said, "I want my horse back that I lost the other day; have I any chance of getting it?"

All this coming close to our works, and spying, ought to have been stopped.

Sturt called out to them in Persian, and warned them off, or he would open the guns upon them. Some respectable people begged, for God's sake, he would not do so; for they were not warriors, but had come out to see sights and amuse themselves.

Sturt saw a man meanly dressed on foot stealing up close to the walls, and called out "*Pēsh Burrō;*" on which he raised his hand, telescope fashion, to his eye, and showed the end of a note. He was passed on to the gate, and admitted into cantonments; and was said to be the bearer of a letter from Mahommed Akbar Khan. However, this is denied, or even that any letter came.

Whenever the political horizon clears a little, mystery becomes the order of the day. "Out of the abundance of the heart the mouth speaketh;" and when overwhelmed with perplexity, the directors of events here are not so close. However, events do transpire, and we know that treaties are on foot with the Ghilzye chiefs; though that too is denied to-day.

Meer Musjudee is dead. Some say he has been poisoned; others that he died in consequence of the wounds he received last year in the Kohistan. A number of this chief's followers have gone off with the body to the Kohistan, there to attend his funeral obsequies.

A report has come to us through the enemy, that three regiments, from Kandahar, have got beyond Ghuznee, somewhere about Shecoabad; that there has been an engagement; and that though the Affghans could not conquer them, they still have been able to prevent their progress.

Sleet in the morning; and in the afternoon snow, which soon froze.

27*th*. — We had a quiet night; and it continued tranquil till the middle of this day; when the horsemen again took post on the hills, and escorted infantry to the right, and down into the village of Behmaru, into which we threw some shells.

The negotiations are now come quite to a close. The enemy's demands were modest, considering that they were the first to treat, it is said. They require, in addition to giving up the King and his family into their hands, all our guns and ammunition, muskets, bayonets, pistols, and swords.

The married men, women, and children, to be given as hostages; and then—we are to trust to their generosity! To this the Envoy sent a chivalrous reply,—That death was preferable to dishonour,—that we put our trust in the God of battles, and in His name bade them come on.

The King is in an awful state of alarm; for he has been told that we have been making terms for our free exit out of the country, paying for the same five lakhs of rupees; and leaving him to his fate, poor man! He is certainly to be pitied (if not at the bottom of it all), fallen from his high estate, and believing us to have abandoned him.

Jan Fishan Khan is the only chief who stands by him; and he has had his forts and property destroyed: his wives and children, he hopes, may have been saved by some of his neighbours; but, as yet, he only knows the fate of one young boy, who was burnt alive. He had one wife with him in Cabul when the insurrection broke out, and urged her to fly to Pughman for safety; the old chief told me, her reply was worth a lakh of rupees, "I will not leave you; if you fall, we die together; and if you are victorious, we will rejoice together!"

Some say that Mahommed Akbar Khan is now King, and Zeman Shah Khan his Wuzeer: others state that the latter refuses to give up his lately acquired power.

Ishmatoolah (the Akhoonzada or old moollah from Kandahar, who was to have gone with Sir William to Bombay), has taken himself off, leaving a message for the Envoy to say that he was gone to the city. A messenger was sent to his son, Khojeh Meer, in Behmaru; who stated that two respectable persons came to fetch the moollah, reporting that they did so by order of Mahomed Akbar Khan, who required his immediate attendance, as Lawrence and Trevor were both with him, and the Envoy coming. Whether the father and son are in league or not, remains to be proved; but this man's secession (who was much in Sir William's confidence) has caused us all to be on the alert, expecting an attack, or mischief of some kind.

There was an absurd report to-day, that the enemy had sent us back the gun they captured on the 23d, with the horses; and the gullibility of John Bull was proved by many persons leaving an auction of some of the deceased officers' property, to go to the Kohistan gate, and find it was all nonsense.

28*th*. — Shelled the village of Behmaru, whence the enemy annoyed us by firing on our yaboos sent out to endeavour to procure grain.

This day we had both rain and snow. Mahommed Shah Khan Ghilzye is come into Cabul, and therefore we think there must have been a fight below, in which he has had the worst.

A Hindu merchant has offered to bring grain, and lay it at the gate of Mahommed Shureef's fort in the night. We are not to speak to his people; and are eventually to pay him at the rate of one Cabul seer for the rupee, and we are bound to take 200 kurwars. Also on every hundred maunds being delivered, we are to lay down a bag of 1500 rupees as a present. He says many would assist us, but are afraid; that as he is the first in the market, he expects to make his fortune.

29*th*.—The enemy are not showing any cavalry to-day; and there is a rumour that they have gone to meet the corps coming in from Ghuznee — there was only infantry on the hill-side; however, some alarmists fancied that they were coming down, which they never do without horsemen: the bugles sounded, there was a great bustle, and all ended in nothing.

We shelled Behmaru and the hill above it; and also the two shops close to the village, one on either side of the road, where there is a little bridge, and the trees form an archway.

Ammunition was sent to the Bala Hissar.

The horses are hard up for grain: those for the artillery have not been much looked after since Lieut. Waller was wounded; and one of them is averred to have eaten his comrade's tail! That he bit it off there is no doubt.

30*th*.—Abdoolah Khan's death has, it is said, created some confusion in the city. Whilst still living a report was spread of his decease; and, like Alexander, he mounted his horse, and showed himself to his followers; but the exertion was too great for him, and he shortly after expired.

Amongst other political barometers, the manner in which persons are spoken of indicates whether affairs are going on well or ill: just now, things are looking up again. A few days ago people spoke of "The Macnaghtens;" then they became again "Sir William and my Lady;" and to-day they have left their refuge in a tent in cantonments, and are gone into the great house again, which they think will have a good effect, and tend to quiet people's minds.

The politicals are again very mysterious, and deny that any negotiations are going on, &c.; but letters come in constantly; and we know they are treating with the Ghilzyes.

A new arrangement is made with Khojeh Meer regarding grain: formerly he received fifty rupees daily as bukshees, whether grain was procured or not; now he is to have 500 rupees given him on delivery of every hundred khurwars.

Sturt proposes to hut the men on the ramparts,

and give them plenty of firewood. As yet they are not allowed any fires, except for cooking their food. He also wishes to have the city shelled, both from the Bala Hissar and the cantonments, particularly to annoy the quarter where the gunpowder-makers reside.

Early this morning a party of horsemen left the city in the direction of Bhoodkhak, and another towards the Kohistan.

Treaty is certainly going on; and we think that the confederacy may be breaking up. Humza Khan of Tezeen is said to be sending his women away from Cabul, and many have been seen mounted on yaboos going away on the road leading to Bhoodkhak.

1st December. — Mohun Lull writes that the enemy will show in force to-day, and attack us to-morrow. The firing we heard in the night was an attack on the patrol, who got in safe.

A cossid reported yesterday that he had been with his letter to Kelat-i-Ghilzye, but he brought no letter back. He said that the force had left the place; and as he could not give any account of, or letters from Ghuznee, we suspect that he never went at all.

A report to-day that the Hindu merchant had commenced his supplies of grain is contradicted: but a small quantity was got in to-day.

We sent to get some barley for our horses; but the enemy were hovering about the villages, and prevented us.

It is reported that the garrison at Ghuznee have blown up the bastions, and joined General Nott's force.

More treaty going on. Firing at night, said to be an attempt to blow up the Bala Hissar gate, which was repulsed. A good deal of firing during the night, and also shelling into the town.

2nd. — Last night's firing was an unsuccessful attempt of the enemy on the Bourj above the Bala Hissar.

I counted this morning 49 horsemen on the Siah Sung Hill, who were reported to the General at 300! We did not fire at them, as they were seen to come from Mahmood Khan's Fort, where the Ghilzyes reside who are now treating with us.

Mohun Lull's information was incorrect; the enemy did not show in force yesterday, neither have they to-day made their intended attack on the captured fort and that of the magazine. The person who succeeds in taking the latter is promised 40,000 rupees, and the rents of the adjacent lands.

The enemy's confederacy is said to be breaking up: they are now quarrelling regarding the partition of power which as yet they have not. One says he will be chief of Cabul, another of Jellalabad, &c. The plan proposed for the capture of cantonments by the enemy is, to send 200 bildars in front to cut down the ramparts; next come the infantry, and then the horse. I suppose we are to stand still and look on.

Mahommed Akbar Khan is said to be very ill.

There is a report that a man has come in from Gen. Nott's camp at Urghundee, eighteen miles off; that the enemy had attacked him, placing two guns in position, both of which we are said to have captured. We fear this news is too good to be true. These reports are disseminated by the enemy; and the only motive to which I can attribute them is a wish to lull us into security by reports of aid coming to us, until starvation prompts acquiescence in their demands, be they what they may.

A man of the Ghoorka corps has come in. He says the men are wandering up and down the country, and that some have taken refuge in forts; that poor Rose, in a fit of despair, put an end to his existence by shooting himself; and that Dr. Grant, when he last saw him, was wounded in the leg.

Ishmatoolah is said to be imprisoned in the city.

The Parsee merchant is also in prison until he pays a ransom of 10,000 rupees: his property has all been taken away.

The people of the city are said to be discontented. They have no firewood; the people who used to bring it in are afraid to do so lest they should be plundered.

3rd.—The attack intended for yesterday has been postponed to to-day, we hear; but there seems to be little likelihood of one.

Khojeh Meer says that he has no more grain: we only got 50 maunds in to-day. He also says that the moollahs have been to all the villages, and laid the people under ban not to assist the English, and that consequently the Mussulman population are as one man against us. He says he expects himself to have to run for his life to Peshawer whenever we go away. Khojeh Meer has a difficult part to play: his pecuniary gain in siding with us is great; but being the father-in-law of Meer Musjudee, who married the Khojeh's daughter, he of course lets the enemy occupy the village whenever they please. As far as we are individually concerned, Khojeh Meer has been very civil to us: he sells us grain whenever we can manage to send an Affghan servant on a yaboo to purchase it. Sturt has been kind to the man; and he evinces his gratitude by writing to say that he will get us what supplies he can. Much more grain might have been procured, had we not foolishly tried to drive hard bargains with Khojeh Meer. It has been intimated to the Envoy that the enemy's troops, who lately got one rupee daily for each horseman, and eight anas for each foot soldier, have not had any pay for four days, and that they are grumbling at it.

We saw a party leaving Cabul towards Bhoodkhak with two women on one horse riding with them.

A cossid came in from Jellalabad; no letter for me. He had been detained five days in the city, and his intelligence only reached to the 21st. Khojeh Meer says that the villages to our rear (from whence the grain was brought to Behmaru) are occupied; and that the only place which could have given us grain, and where we might have obtained six months' supply, was Khojeh Rewash, which is at present occupied by Sekundu Khan with 500 men.

In the evening about seven o'clock there was firing on the southern face, and towards the Magazine fort, which continued until past ten o'clock. The enemy appear to be trying to mine that fort, and Sturt saw about ten men close up under the walls of it.

The enemy seem to be on the alert; however there was no firing at night of any consequence: we shelled the city from the Bala Hissar as usual.

Orders were this day issued, that the arms and accoutrements, discipline, &c. of the various corps, should be attended to! Consequent on this order the 5th have been very busy cleaning their musket barrels,—a most unusual exertion. The arms used to be placed against the rampart, and of course the barrels were rusty and the powder damp.

A committee is ordered to assemble to-morrow to value all useless horses in the Bazaar, which are to be destroyed; so there will be plenty of cheap meat, as tattoos and camels have for some time past been eaten: even some of the gentlemen ate camel's flesh, particularly the heart, which was esteemed equal to that of the bullock. I never was tempted by these choice viands; so cannot offer an opinion regarding them.

Brig. Shelton sent to tell Sturt that one of the bastions of the captured fort was on fire, and to request he would send bildars to dig the place and lay on fresh earth. He went accordingly to see what was the matter, and came back very angry, as the guard had been burning the defences he had put up.

4*th.*—Two chiefs have been treating with the King: they propose that he throws off the Feringhees, on which they will render their allegiance to him. His Majesty, however, thinks it unsafe to break with us. Gen. Nott's brigade is now supposed to be at Shekoabad, about six marches from Cabul. The enemy assembled in numbers on the heights, and planted two guns in the gorge; from which they discharged 144 shot at us (said to have been scored on the wall of the Mission Compound). They had three other guns out, which were placed on the road behind a trench they had dug, and a kind of breastwork they had thrown up across the road, near the Shah Bagh.

In front of this they had another for their men to fire from behind it. Another party took post in the Nullah, near the bridge going to Siah Sung. A man mounted on a grey horse came down apparently to see if they were properly posted: he had a *foot* man with him. A shot was taken at the latter, who, being beyond its range, ran a few yards backwards and forwards, dancing, jumping, and cutting capers in derision.

Just as it was getting dark the fight commenced in earnest: the enemy made a rush at the captured fort. They had placed a bag of powder at the wicket, and must have been greatly astonished at finding it produced no effect in consequence of Sturt having filled the place up.

They were received with a sharp fire, which was kept up for a long time, both of musketry and guns. Lieut. Cumberland, of the 44th, was on duty there with 100 men. He sent for a reinforcement, and Sturt took fifty men to him under a very heavy fire. (Observe the wisdom of unnecessarily risking the life of our only engineer officer.)

Notwithstanding that the enemy opened five guns on us, our loss was very trifling: as yet I have heard only of one man, an artilleryman, killed; and a sergeant of Sturt's (Williams) was wounded whilst digging with the sappers. A few horses and camels were killed, as also one or two camp followers in the Mission Compound.

Some of the cannon shot went clean over the cantonments (those fired from the gorge): one fell between the legs of Mr. Mein's mule in Sturt's compound, near the rear gate, without doing any damage.

To-day Sturt came home with his clothes singed, having been nearly blown up by an explosion of powder in one of the batteries, when a man got his pouch ignited by the port-fire; he was much hurt: at 10 o'clock the shots were dropping quickly.

I can scarcely believe that this is the grand attempt at capturing cantonments; and therefore am expecting another, and wish it may occur by daylight.

The enemy's idea of blowing open a gate is excellent. They filled the bag with powder, applied and lighted a slow match, and then threw it at the gate! so that, when it exploded, of course it did no harm.

5th.—The enemy assembled in small parties on the Siah Sung Hill; also, but not in great force, on the other hills.

In the morning they attacked a foraging party sent by the cavalry, and surrounded them in a fort. At length they took an oath on the Koran not to hurt them; and a trooper, notwithstanding the remonstrances of the rest, came out: he talked with them, shook hands with them, and they seemed very friendly. They then desired the camp followers to come out; but they distrusted them, and called to the trooper to return to them: as he was doing so they shot him. The grass-cutters had amongst them one old musket, with which they shot two of the enemy: further operations were suspended by the arrival of a reinforcement, when the enemy disappeared *instanter*.

Some ottah has been said to have been dropped at the Musjed; but this has been contradicted, and I believe no grain has been brought in to-day.

The chief of Khojeh Rewash says that we must

send a force, to make it appear that we force it from him; and then he will sell us grain.

The proprietor of Kella Bolund offers 1000 kurwars of grain if we will send for it, and has given the Envoy an order for its delivery; but the difficulty lies in getting at it.

Major Kershaw has sent to announce that the enemy are coming out of the city gate with their guns.

There has been firing all day, but I believe only a bheestee of Mr. Eyre's killed, just behind our compound.

In the evening, about five o'clock, there was very quick firing about the Bazar village.

The enemy have burnt the bridge, and commenced mining one of the bastions of the captured fort.

A strong reinforcement has been sent there; and Sturt is gone down again, at nine at night, to look to its defences.

Sturt has again to-day narrowly escaped being shot. The enemy seem to know and to lie in wait for him, and he never shows his head above the rampart without a ball whistling close to it. The Affghans are good shots when they fire from their rests; and as the ammunition is the property of each individual, they do not throw it away as we do ours. Their gunners appear to be inferior, as they fired at the captured fort at a distance of 300 yards, yet did not hit it.

6th.— Sturt was out till one o'clock this morning. Between twelve and one he crept round the fort and got into the enemy's mine: they had worked in about eight feet. He blew up the mine, which fell in and destroyed the covered way they had made, and shook down part of the garden wall.

News from the Bala Hissar that the enemy are evidently thinning their numbers; and a Ghilzye chief who has been wounded is gone home.

A cossid, who was sent by the King to Ghuznee, has returned. He says he was stopped half way and put in kyde; that during the time he was a prisoner another cossid arrived, sent to Amenoollah Khan from the Kelat-i-Ghilzye chiefs with a letter. This man told him that he was the bearer of a request for troops and guns, without which they could not prevent the Feringhee King reaching Cabul; and that four regiments of infantry, 100 horse, and five guns were already at Karabagh, two marches from Ghuznee: that this occurred five days since (about the 1st). The cossid took his oath on the Koran, before four moollahs, to the truth of his statement; desired he might be put in prison (in which he was accommodated); and further begged if the force did not arrive they would put him to death! So after all this asseveration he was, of course, implicitly believed.

At daybreak not a vestige remained of the bridge; which, however, the General is still very anxious to rebuild, and has sent to inquire if Sturt can do so. Without materials or workmen, and the enemy on the spot, it is as impossible as useless to attempt it.

The General refused to have a party stationed in the small fort to defend this same bridge, and now it is gone. He seems more bewildered than ever, and says if the force arrives there will only be more mouths to eat up our provisions; and we have only eight days', this inclusive; but we have not a man to send out to forage.

The enemy were out to-day, but not in great force. They have got a Russian seventeen-pounder of brass, which they have brought in from the Kohistan, and have planted it in the road, near and on this side of Mahmood Khan's fort. From this they have been firing at us all day, and the balls fall many of them in the gardens of Messrs. Eyre and Sturt's house. We have picked up three cannon balls close to the door of the verandah.

Lieut. Hawtrey of the 37th N. I. was on duty at the captured fort to-day with 100 men — forty of these were of the 44th, the rest from the 37th. Suppose this to be the fort: * a small room up stairs, to which there was no outlet, the window being blocked up with mud. In this room were six of the 44th. The Affghans planted their crooked sticks, which served them for scaling ladders; got up one by one; pulled out the mud, and got in. A child with a stick might have repulsed them. The Europeans had their belts and accoutrements off, and the Sipahees the same. They all ran away as fast as they could! The 44th say that the 37th ran first, and as they were too weak they went too. Hawtrey says there was not a pin to choose, —all cowards alike. After he was deserted by the men, he himself threw six hand grenades before he followed them. One man of the 44th was an exception, and he was shot whilst assisting Hawtrey in throwing these missiles.

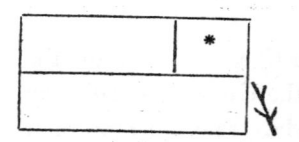

Lieut. Gray, 44th, was wounded in the arm earlier in the day, by a man who climbed up and fired through a loophole at him: he thoughtlessly left his post to return to cantonments and get his wound dressed; and the men endeavoured to excuse themselves by saying their own officer was not there to direct them. It was the most shameful of all the runaways that has occurred. The men (all agree) were not dressed when the enemy entered. The 37th had three men left dead in the breach, and two were wounded, which certainly looks as if they had defended themselves. We lost 6000 rounds of ammunition in this fort.

Brig. Shelton wished that the garrison who had evacuated the fort should retake it. For this purpose he got the men under arms as soon as they could be collected together, and kept them, regardless of the inclemency of the weather, with snow lying on the ground, until three or four o'clock in the morning; when they were eventually dismissed, nothing being attempted.

The least thing seems to-day to create alarm. The following note, accompanied by a six-pound shot, was sent by order of Brig. Shelton to Sturt:

"Dear Hogg—The enemy have planted a gun in a bastion of one of their forts, near the road leading to the Kohistan gate of the city, and have been firing it at the Magazine fort since one o'clock. Two or three shots struck the rear face. I send you one that fell in the room above the gateway, after passing through the wall.

"Yours, W. GRANT."

Gen. Elphinstone wrote again to the Envoy to-day, urging him to treat for terms with the enemy.

At near 9 A.M. Sturt left us with an intention of blowing up the captured fort, which the men seem to have taken a dislike to, and to be determined not to defend it. He had not been gone more than a few minutes when quick firing commenced: the enemy had come down evidently in force along the south-eastern face of cantonments. There was a blaze of light from Mahmood Khan's fort to our rear gate: it did not last long, but it was a very anxious time; for our north-eastern portion of rampart is occupied by the 5th, and I distinctly heard Bygrave using no gentle language whilst he kicked the men up and out of their tents. Lieut. Mein (13th) was also active in assisting to do the same, but with very little success; though the drums beating to arms, and the hallooing and shouting for the General and the Brigadier, were noise enough to have aroused the dead. Lieut. Deas was on the rear gate guard; and had a rush been made at it by the enemy, there did not seem to be any one to oppose them.

Yesterday when Sturt was talking to the General and the Brigadier about the captured fort, he mentioned that Capt. Layton commanded there that day, and that he wished he should remain and retain it as a permanent command, it being a place for which an officer should be selected, and he considered him as well fitted for the command. Shelton, with a sneer, asked if Layton would like to stay there? To which Sturt replied, "I do not know what he would like, but I know that I should wish him to do so." Capt. Layton's courage and steadiness were too unimpeachable for the sneer to affect his character as a soldier. The Brigadier's dislike to him arose from his not being a man of polished manners, and rather ungrammatical in his language.

After all had gone wrong, the Brigadier told Sturt that he had told him to order Capt. Layton to remain, and appealed to the General whether he did not; to which Elphinstone hesitatingly replied, yes. On Sturt saying that he never understood such an order, and that their recollections of the conversation were different from his; that he would not give up his own reminiscence of the business; that he (Sturt) was wide awake at the time; the Brigadier lying on the floor rolled up in his bedding, and either really or affectedly half asleep. On this the General hedged off evasively by saying, he did not think what was said amounted to an order!

Now when Sturt mentioned the circumstance to me yesterday, I asked him whether he thought they would select an officer as a permanent commandant, and his reply was, "God knows." Besides if it was to be, it would have been notified in Orders, being a decided innovation on the daily relief of the fort.

"One example is as good as a million:" these circumstances show how affairs are carried on. The General, unsettled in his purposes, delegates his power to the Brigadier, and the Brigadier tries to throw off all responsibility on the General's or any body's shoulders except his own: and the General is, as in the present instance, too gentlemanlike to tell him that he deviates a little from the exact line, and thus takes on himself the evasion.

Sturt came home quite disgusted; vowing that if those dear to him were not in cantonments, they might blow them up for what he cared.

I heard a piece of private intelligence to-day, —that three of the Envoy's Chuprassies and a Duffodar of the 4th Ressallah, with two other persons whose names have not transpired, are in connection with the enemy; and this treasonable correspondence has been discovered by some intercepted letters. The men had been disposing of their property two days previous to the discovery. The three Chuprassies are in confinement, and the Envoy talks of asking the General for a court-martial on them. The chances are they will escape punishment: whereas were they hanged as traitors at once, it might be an useful lesson to others. We have a Fakir and some Affghans in confinement also, who are suspected of being spies.

The General peremptorily forbade the camp followers trying to take away the piles of the bridge that remained; so the enemy, who are hard up for wood, came down in great numbers, and did it for us. To-day we have seven days' provisions left.

7th. — Sturt was anxious to take the *re*captured fort; and as it appears that the men are determined not to keep it, he proposed to blow it up, and to call for volunteers for that purpose.

The 44th say they wish to wipe out the stain on their name, as do the 37th. Hawtrey's company volunteer to go with him, and take it without the assistance of any other troops.

In sending the Sipahees to that fort, the sixty men were taken six from each company, so that very few could have had their own officer, European or native, havildars, jemadars, or even their own comrades. It was certainly a particularly bad arrangement.

The General wished to know from Sturt whether the fort was practicable and tenable; at least this was the message brought by Capt. Bellew: to which Sturt said but one reply could be made — " Practicable if the men will fight : tenable if they do not run away!"—but that he considered that the great object was to destroy it; as he more than doubted the willingness of the troops to garrison it, although daily relieved.

Objections were raised as to any other measures being taken than firing at it to batter it down, which was accordingly done all day. The enemy showed again; but their numbers are thinning: they fired at us all day; and the balls from the brass seventeen-pounder just opposite came whizzing over and about Sturt's house and garden.

Our chiefs are very anxious regarding three galleries that the enemy are said to be running from various points to the Bazar bastion. They are said to have mined 100 yards towards it from the captured fort. Hadjee Mahommed, the famous miner from the Kohistan, has twenty men with him; and the enemy have great confidence in his skill, and have given him 12,000 rupees.

I wonder if they paid the conquering hero of the captured fort their promised reward of 4000 rupees?

The report is, that the Affghans have sworn on the Koran to take the Bazar fort and the Magazine fort: for the latter they are to receive 10,000 rupees.

The Envoy is in hopes to get in five days' provisions from the Bala Hissar.

Mahommed Akbar Khan sent in, offering us terms to go out, bag and baggage: but this was before the fort was taken, and he will now probably rise in his demands, which have not transpired. No reply has yet been given, as hopes are entertained of the arrival of Gen. Nott's force before we are quite starved: besides, as Zeman Shah Khan has not given up the power to Mahommed Akbar Khan, he may not be able to guarantee our safety.

8th. — The first news of the day was, that the ammunition destined for the Bala Hissar during last night set out, eighty yaboos, escorted by some of Skinner's horse, under Capt. Hay: when they got to the camel sheds they found themselves between two fires, of which, however, but one shot hit a trooper. On the first shot being fired, many of the saces threw off their loads, and galloped as hard as they could. Only forty-four laden yaboos arrived: five were lost altogether, with many yaboos and loads of private baggage; for there was (now, when the enemy's suspicions were raised) an idea of trying to throw ammunition into the Bala Hissar, and of eventually endeavouring to force our way there: and a good deal of private property was attempted to be sent in with it.

We did not send any thing, expecting that our goods would never reach their destination.

Had Sturt's wish been complied with, long ago we should have been safe in the Bala Hissar, with plenty of provisions, and might have set all Affghanistan at defiance until an army could arrive from the provinces.

The orders given to the reserve last night were, to go to the rescue if the convoy was attacked on its return; but as there was no order to defend the animals laden with ammunition when going, they waited until Brig. Shelton should arrive, and when of course it was too late, and all was over.

Conolly and Jan Fishan Khan have come in, I believe to press the subject of our all going to the Bala Hissar.

The General now says that it was Sturt who objected to the attempt on the Captured fort: — rather an odd assertion, as he was not likely to object to his own proposition!

There is a report that the Wallee of Khoolloom is coming to our assistance. To-day there has been much firing in the city; and Dr. Duff says he saw with a glass the people in the Kuzzilbash quarter fighting from the tops of the houses.

Yesterday the servants of Mr. Steer and of some other officers asserted that they heard distant firing of artillery across the gorge behind Cabul, but no one gave much credit to it. This morning both Sturt and Warburton heard the booming of very distant artillery, and several other persons did the same. Ghuznee is only about eighty miles from us: so that the firing might be from thence: but it is confidently asserted that the Kandahar force must be near; and three days are given as the period for their arrival.

Great anxiety, occasioned by a new mine reported to be commenced at the mill, which Kershaw has examined, as also Sturt and his sergeants, and there does not happen to be any such thing!

Two days since we saw a funeral procession, with about fifty followers, going away by the road leading towards the ground lately occupied by the Shah's camp.

To-day we saw a number of laden camels and yaboos, and sheep, and people, all going away: they were escorted off in safety by horsemen, who returned as soon as they were out of sight of cantonments. A number also went off towards the Kohistan; and we think the confederacy must be breaking up, as we see very few of the enemy now, either horse or foot; and the information from the Bala Hissar now rates their numbers at 2500 fighting men.

A letter was sent by the General to the Envoy, finding fault with the site of cantonments, adverting to our want of provisions, &c.; and also urgently pointing out the necessity of the Envoy's negotiating with the enemy for the best terms he could get from them. This letter was signed by the four members of the council of war,—Major-Gen. Elphinstone, Brig. Shelton, Brig. Anquetil, and Col. Chambers. Anquetil appended to his signature, " I concur in this opinion in a military point of view."

9th.—Another letter, much of the same tenor, from the General to the Envoy.

Letters received from Jellalabad, but not by me. I wrote to Sale by the return cossid, from the 18th inclusive. Mackeson had thrown provisions into Alimusjid; and 400 Usutzyes were raising for its defence. The Afreedees' allegiance was doubtful, and they were likely on any reverse to become our open enemies.

Sale had written to the Commander-in-chief to say that reinforcements for this country must be much greater than those now on their way; that there must be a strong siege train, engineer officers, with all *materiel*—light infantry, British infantry, and dragoons; and had stated that the whole country was in insurrection, and up against us. In a postscript he mentions that on the day he wrote the first, they had sallied and entirely defeated the enemy.

Treating is still going on. We have only three days' provisions! The Ben-i-shehr is rich in grain. Conolly at the Bala Hissar offers to take it with the escort, but is not permitted; and to send a force from cantonments it would require a much larger one than we can afford; the same misfortune attaches to Killa Bolund and Khojeh Rewash.

The King wrote to say that John Conolly and Jan Fishan Khan, who came into cantonments, must not return to the Bala Hissar last night, as there were Juzailchees out for the purpose of cutting them off. They therefore went in at five this morning. They got in safe, though their escort was fired upon.

We had Sturt's yaboo paraded this morning, who did not seem to feel the smallest inconvenience, notwithstanding that he had been knocked down by a nine-pounder shot yesterday. The ball struck the rampart and rebounded on to his neck, which was protected by such a mane as would not be believed on description, being of the very shaggiest of those in this country.

At one this morning Sturt was roused up to examine a wall that Brig. Shelton wished to have pulled down, and was kept out, with Capt.

Hawtrey and fifty men, for an hour. It proved to be a mare's nest, and the party were sent on a harassing duty for no purpose!

The 44th have asked for a court of inquiry, and it is to sit to-morrow: but there is but too much evidence to prove that the Europeans were the first to run away from the Captured fort. The artillerymen in the bastions all assert that they were so, and also the first into cantonments; and the rest of the regiment have *cut* that company; and men are generally good judges of their comrades' conduct.

Capt. Trevor was sent by Sir William to meet several Ghilzye chiefs who had volunteered to enter into terms with him, on payment of two lakhs of rupees, which sum was taken by Trevor that night, but only one person met him, who said that the others had seceded from the engagement, and they would not receive the money. They had declared that, although connected by marriage with Mahommed Akbar Khan, they had no regard for him, and would, if Sir William wished it, bring his head; but he replied, assassination was not our custom.

The alarm was sounded, and at the same time there was a signal flying from the Bala Hissar, of the enemy being in force in the Shah's garden. They were making a place to fire behind; from which we drove them. We had the usual firing all day, and dismounted one of their guns.

Early this morning I was awakened by firing, proceeding from a party under a Duffodar, in charge of twenty yaboos, with 100 sacks to be filled with grain at the Bala Hissar. They were fired on by the enemy; and came scampering back without their bags, and having lost six ponies.

Capt. Hay was this day sent with a message of consequence to the King, attended by an escort of fifty horse. He went out of cantonments at a brisk trot, and forded the river. The enemy kept an excellent look-out; they were immediately in pursuit, but our party got safe into the Bala Hissar. It was a beautiful sight to see Hay with his cap pulled down on his brows, his teeth set, neither looking right nor left, but leading his men with the air of a man ready and expecting to encounter the worst, and fully determined to do his *devoir*. We were all very anxious about him, and were delighted to hear that he had got back safe, for they were fired on in returning, and ten horses without riders were the heralds of their return. One man only is missing, and we hope he may yet find his way in, as it is very dark, and the enemy may miss him.

To avoid the enemy, they had to make a *détour*

out of the road some miles, and the men got dismounted by their horses stumbling and falling into ditches, &c. There was much anxiety relative to the purport of the message. It was supposed to be an urgent entreaty from the Envoy to the King, that the latter would come into cantonments for the purpose of retreating with the army to India: whatever it was, it produced an order for the immediate evacuation of the Bala Hissar by our troops.

The enemy have been busy to-day making a platform (said to be 12 feet by 4) behind the commissariat fort.

It is surmised that this is a contrivance to cross the ditch with; but, as that is 20 feet wide, it is not likely to succeed. They are said to have appeared to be trying its strength by walking over it.

This day orders have been issued to deprive all camp followers that are not mustered of their grain rations; but those who will take meat are permitted to have it in lieu. We have commenced giving our servants two sheep a day. Between Sturt's servants, mine, and Mr. Mein's (who is staying with us), we muster forty.

Sturt was told yesterday that two of his sappers were going to desert, and he had the circumstance reported; but the General and Capt. Bellew would not put them into confinement, because their plan being overheard was not considered as a sufficient proof of their intentions : so they ordered them to be watched; and the end of the story is, that to-day they are not be found. A second case of most excellent surveillance.

11*th*. — Early this morning, a convoy went to and returned from the Bala Hissar, having conveyed bags there to be filled with grain.

An armistice; and chiefs came to treat with the Envoy: they met on the plain; and whilst the negotiations (which were lengthy) were carrying on, the enemy were busy throwing up works and placing guns in position.

A letter was received last night from Ghuznee: that place was invested; and Col. MacLaren was marching up with troops, who were somewhere between Candahar and that place.

As we have only two days' provisions, terms have been accepted. As far as I can learn, four political hostages are to be given — Pottinger, Trevor, MacGregor, and Conolly — to insure the return of the Dost.

Mahommed Akbar Khan is to go down with us. They say they will give us carriage, and we are to be off on Tuesday. The 54th from the Bala Hissar are to come in to-morrow morning.

12*th*. — The troops from the Bala Hissar have

not come in, at the desire of the chiefs; who have now decided that they wish the Shah to remain, and only require us to go. They wish the King to strengthen their allegiance by giving his daughters in marriage to the chiefs, and receiving theirs in return.

They were anxious to have our ladies as hostages, but it was refused.

The Kuzzilbashes have every thing to lose, should the Dost return, and the Barukzye power come in.

13*th.* — Another letter from Gen. Elphinstone, urging the Envoy to treat with the chiefs.

A report prevalent that it is wished the force should remain; which is, however, discredited.

The Kohistanees are in great numbers in Behmaru, the Shahbagh, &c.; and unless the chiefs take possession of the forts *near*, and probably have a party *in* cantonments, they will certainly get in, and loot immediately on our going out.

A curious scene occurred to-day. The men are to leave their old muskets, and take fresh ones out of the magazine. Without any order or arrangement the Europeans, Sipahees, and camp followers all got into the midst of the stores, and helped themselves to whatever came in their way; it was a regular scene of plunder.

CABUL. 175

14*th*.—The troops left the Bala Hissar last night, but it was considered unsafe for them to come on here on account of the lateness of the hour. Immediately on their getting outside the gate, a rush was made by Mahommed Akbar Khan's men, that chief wishing to seize on the Bala Hissar, and the person of the King. His majesty had the gates shut, and in so doing shut in the quarter guard, with some prisoners of the 54th. Finding that the force could not come on, Conolly returned to the gate to ask to be re-admitted, at which time he was saluted with a discharge of grape, had one horse shot under him, and another wounded. This was afterwards explained away as having been intended for the King's and our mutual foes: if so, they were not very particular as to which party they fired at. Our troops remained out all night; and this morning had to fight their way in, against a mixed rabble of Ghilzyes, Logurees, and Cabulees.

The bullock drivers ran away from the nine-pounder gun; of which the enemy took possession. They carried off the bullocks; but being near cantonments, fresh animals were sent out (it was on this side of the Siah Sung Hill), the gun was soon recaptured; but not till an unfortunate artilleryman, who being sick rode on it, had been cut to pieces.

Osman Khan sent to say that if one of the three lakhs promised to him was sent this evening, he would send in provisions, of which we are in great need, having only sufficient for to-day and to-morrow's consumption. In the evening three and a half lakhs were sent.

15*th.*—There is a very evident change in politics. " The good King," as Sir William used to call him, is now thrown over by us, as he refused to deviate from his accustomed hauteur towards his nobles, or to admit of his daughters marrying the chiefs as they proposed.

Shah Shoojah has also set his seal to a proclamation calling on all true Mussalmans to fight against the Feringhees.

A small quantity of ottah was brought in to-day.

Negotiations are still going on.

The chiefs are very anxious to have all the married men and their families as hostages for the Dost's safe return.

Two days since the King was to have come into cantonments, in rather light marching order, to accompany us to the provinces. At that time it was decided that Osman Khan (head of the Barukzyes now in the country, and at present

Vizier) should remain at Cabul: and it being expected that the expulsion of our force would be a scene of bloodshed and disaster, a running fight all the way down, Sturt said, that if he could see Osman Khan himself, and make his own terms with him for our safety and protection in his own house, he would not object to being one of the hostages, and keeping his wife and mother with him: he authorized Capt. Lawrence to say as much to the Envoy. To his great astonishment he heard that his name had been proposed to the chiefs without any further communication with him, and with a state of politics wholly different from those under which he would have acquiesced in the proposition. In the first place, Shah Shoojah is not going with our army; but is doing all he can to raise a party against us, and sits at a window of his palace in the Bala Hissar, whence he distributes shawls, khelluts, and bhood-khees to the Ghazeeas. In the second place, Osman Khan is one of the chiefs who it is now decided are to go down with the Envoy.

Sturt's having talked imprudently to a friend, and its being taken advantage of, prevents his interfering in the affair; but *I* am not so tied, and have represented (through friends) to the General in a military point of view that he ought to object to Sturt's being taken as a hostage, on the plea that should there be any thing to do on the way down, through the Khyber or in the Punjab, he is the only engineer officer we have; —a circumstance which the General acknowledges escaped his recollection, but he quickly remedied the ill by writing to the Envoy on the subject; and time must show the result.

Determined not to put his wife and myself in the enemy's power, he wrote to the Envoy as follows: —

" My dear Sir William,

" Within the last hour a report has reached me, that myself, Lady Sale, and Mrs. Sturt, had been proposed to the Cabul chiefs as hostages, in exchange for Capt. Trevor.

" I have a very distinct recollection of having told Lawrence to mention to you, that I had no objection to such an arrangement *under certain terms;* but not having been made acquainted with the fact of such a proposition having been made, or further consulted on the subject, I write in much anxiety to inquire if there is any foundation for the report, and if there is, to be made acquainted with the arrangements proposed, under which I can be expected to acquiesce in them as far as regards Lady Sale and Mrs. Sturt; for myself I am ready for any circumstances likely to benefit or aid in bringing negotiations to a satisfactory conclusion. I trust you will ease my mind upon this point, for reports have reached me from several quarters, all of which are more vague than satisfactory.

"Very truly yours,
"J. L. D. STURT.

"15th December, 1841."

This elicited a reply from Sir William stating that he was much hurried by business, and did not recollect whether Sturt's name had been mentioned to the chiefs or not; but it was of no consequence, as no ladies were to be sent as hostages, &c. The letter was evasive and diplomatic; and did not inform us whether Sturt was to be sent from us or not. It was, I believe, unfortunately thrown amongst a heap of papers which Sturt was destroying, for I could not find it afterwards.

16th.—The impudence of these Affghans is very great! Yesterday some men who were looting our people close to the gates were warned off, and they replied, that we might keep within our walls; all *without* belonged to them.

To-day a well-dressed man, one of Mahommed Akbar Khan's personal attendants, was attacked by them close to the walls, and stripped of his garments.

Mr. Baness, the merchant, was standing talking to some of the Affghans by the gate; a man snatched his watch from him, ran up to a suwar, knocked him off his horse, mounted it, and galloped off.

This day Sturt was fortunate in purchasing a bag of otta sent in to him by Taj Mahommed; whose man brought another which our servants were purchasing.

In a moment there was a cry of otta! and the garden was filled with camp followers and Sipahees. I never saw such a scene: the joy of those who got a handful for a rupee, the sorrow evinced by those who were unsuccessful, and the struggles of all to get close to the man! The gentlemen had to stand with thick sticks to keep the people off. There was no weighing; at first the man gave two handsful for a rupee, but the quantity soon diminished in consequence of the great demand for it.

To prove our good faith and belief in that of the chiefs, we are to-day placed entirely in their power.

They know that we are starving; that our horses and cattle have neither grain, bhoosa, nor grass. They have pretty well eaten up the bark of the trees and the tender branches; the horses gnaw the tent pegs. I was gravely told that the artillery horses had eaten the trunnion of a gun! This is difficult of belief; but I have seen my own riding-horse gnaw voraciously at a cart-wheel. Nothing is *satisfied* with food except the Pariah dogs, who are gorged with eating dead camels and horses.

This evening the Rikabashees fort, Zulfa Khan's fort, and the Magazine fort, were given up to the chiefs.

Misseer Aollah Khan, brother of Nawaub Zeman Shah Khan, came in as a hostage.

In the Magazine fort our allies are said to have placed 4,000 men. The chiefs promised, as soon as they were in possession of our forts, to give us grain; and about half an hour after our garrisons were withdrawn 155 maunds of otta and a small quantity of bhoosa was brought in.

They have also promised to procure us 2,000 camels and 400 yaboos.

To show how strangely military matters are conducted at present; we were taking our evening walk on the ramparts, when a Sipahee quite out of breath came up, and asked for the Brigade Major, saying that he was sent from the Rikabashees fort to ask for the order to give it up, as the men were waiting outside the gate ready to march off, and the Affghans were also waiting to march in; as we plainly saw, when we stood near

Bygrave's bastion. I do not attach any blame to the General in this; but to those whose duty it was to issue the orders and see them executed.

At eleven P.M. heard some firing, and began to think there was going to be some treachery.

Our allies, as they are now called, will be very magnanimous if they let us escape, now that they have fairly got us in their net. It is said the Bala Hissar will be attacked to-morrow by those who are neither the King's nor our friends; though they are now termed allies instead of enemies.

17*th*.—There has been news from Jellalabad to-day up to the 7th. I hear that Sale and all are well there; but it came out by accident. The Sikhs have refused to assist us, which is breaking their treaty, and portends military movements in the Punjab;—an additional reason why our only engineer should not remain in Cabul.

Accounts from Candahar and Khelat-i-Gilzie. All is right again, they say, at the former place; that prompt measures were taken; a chief seized and blown from a gun, which terrified the rest into subjection. No further news from Ghuznee; which, by the last accounts, was invested.

Both otta and bhoosa brought in to-day; but not more than for the day's consumption, and only for the commissariat. Camels were brought in, and some sold to the commissariat for 140 and

150 rupees each. We offered 1000 rupees for eight camels; but for so few they insisted on receiving 200 for each. The plunderers were, as usual, outside attacking all who passed, friend or foe, and were fired on from the magazine fort: the garrison there were also firing.

Sturt was standing at the rear gate, when a man inquired if he was an officer; and, on his asking why he wished to know, and what he wanted with him, said, half drawing his sword, " to fight."

It is said that our departure depends on the King's reply, which was expected to be given to-day. He is either to go with us to Loodianah, to remain here, or to go on a pilgrimage to Mecca.

In the city Zeman Shah Khan now reigns.

The people say that, as soon as we go, there will be dreadful fighting; not such as they have had with us, but chupaos on each other's houses, sword in hand, and cutting each other's throats: that we shall be attacked all the way to Khoord Cabul, but not after that, as that part of the country belongs to Ameenoollah Khan, whose son goes with us.

Nothing decided regarding Sturt, but it is said he will have to remain.

18*th*.—When we rose this morning the ground

was covered with snow; which continued falling all day.

A very strange circumstance occurred last night. Some persons were endeavouring to remove the barricade at the gate of the mission compound: on being discovered, two Europeans galloped away, who were not recognised. The third, ——, a writer in Capt. Johnson's office, was taken prisoner: he refuses to name his companions, and says they were going to Mahommed Akbar Khan to obtain provisions for the army. —— is a man of bad character; he has lately got himself into bad repute by writing letters in the newspapers under the signature of " Sharp." He was also connected with a man of the name of O'Grady Gorman in a correspondence with the Russians; which was proved by letters found amongst the papers of the latter after he was murdered at Candahar.

Two men of the 54th have made their escape out of the Bala Hissar; they passed a rope through one of the loopholes and let themselves down. They say the King has been tampering with them, offering to give them 15 rupees a month, and to promote all the non-commissioned officers; but that not one has accepted his offers.

This day we bought camels at 150 rupees each.

19*th*. — More strange things have occurred.

Brig. Shelton wrote privately to Mahommed Akbar Khan for forage for his own use, and obtained ten loads of bhoosa. He made the man who brought it a present (writing to Sir William that he wished to have a pair of pistols or a chogah of small value from the Tosha Khana to present to a respectable native), and the present was sent with a bill attached to it for 30 rupees. On its arrival, Shelton left the room to receive it, and during his absence the Affghan appropriated to himself a sword which had been a gift to the Brigadier from Shah Shoojah. On this he applied to the Envoy for its restoration, which brought the whole story to light; and occasioned the Brigadier to receive an admonition for having, unknown to the Envoy, entered into correspondence with one of the chiefs. The General, having heard the former part of the above story, wrote to the Envoy to ascertain if he also could not obtain forage from Akbar direct; but Sir William was extremely indignant at any attempt at correspondence being entered into with any of the chiefs by individuals, and peremptorily forbade it; having the courtesy to add, that he was in expectation of obtaining some for himself, of which he would permit Gen. Elphinstone to have a part.

The chiefs are evidently fearful that we are

getting in supplies to a greater extent than they wish.

We had been fortunate enough to purchase some otta and barley for our servants and cattle. A servant of Mahommed Akbar Khan's came into our verandah and wanted to take it away by force; but I saw what was going on, and called Sturt, who took him by the collar, and expedited his departure by a kick; to the great astonishment of sundry Affghans at such indignity being offered to the servant of a sirdar.

Snow again fell to-day.

In a letter from Gen. Elphinstone to the Envoy to-day, he observes, " that the force is not in a state to act in any way necessity might require; but he hoped that it would be better disposed to-morrow!"

20*th*. — Taj Mahommed Khan came again to see Sturt; and through his servants we got some new cheese. He told us that Shamsuddeen's brother died last night.

Taj Mahommed assures us of the intended treachery of Akbar; and says the force will be annihilated, and is most anxious that we should accept such protection as he is willing to afford us somewhere in the hills until the return of the English; — for that a strong force will be sent to retake Cabul, and avenge the meditated destruction of our army, is a general opinion amongst the thinking Affghans, several of whom, as well as Taj Mahommed Khan, obtained written testimonials of their friendship towards the English, that they may hereafter produce them for their advantage. We can only thank him for his good intentions. It is difficult to make these people understand our ideas on military subjects; and how a proceeding, which was only intended to save a man's life, conjointly with that of his wife and mother, can in any way affect his honour. Certain it is that we have very little hope of saving our lives.

The Envoy seems to fear treachery on the part of the chiefs; and evidently wishes to break the treaty. If he does so, it must be by a simultaneous attack on the three forts we have given up to our "allies," and also on Mahommed Khan's fort. It would, if successful, give us a decided advantage, and perhaps alarm many into siding with us; but the plan is too late a one. Sturt was applied to for a sketch of operations, which he gave, for the attack on Mahommed Khan's fort, but was of opinion we were too weak, and our men too dispirited, to attempt it. On this subject he received a letter from the General, of which the following is a copy:—

"My dear Sturt,

"I do not know whether Thain has written to you the substance of a conversation I had this day with the Envoy. He thinks it possible we may be driven to hostilities, and asked, with the view to the recapture of the magazine (fort omitted), whether we had ladders, or the means of making them. I hope they will not drive us to this, although things look very ill and very like treachery.

"Yours,
"20th Dec." "W. K. E."

The Envoy had a meeting with the allies this evening: he says they have not broken their treaty, but are fearful we shall break ours. The chiefs rise daily in their demands; and to-day required that we should send the guns and ammunition that were to be left at once into Mahmood Khan's fort.

They now will not give up Trevor; because, as the Envoy wishes to get him back, they take it for granted he is a person of consequence. The affair of the sword has made the same impression regarding Brig. Shelton, whom the chiefs have demanded, with Captains Grant and Conolly. Trevor is with them, and Drummond and Skinner are still detained in the city.

Chiefs, or their deputies, daily come in to negotiate; but we have only Moussa Khan with us as an "honoured guest."

Sturt has proposed to the General that we break off all treaty, and openly retreat to Jellalabad; directing Sale to remain there, and the whole force to await the arrival of troops either at Jellalabad or Peshawer; not to leave our sick, as was intended, with Zeman Shah Khan, but to take all officers' and other private baggage for them, and the ammunition, allowing a small portion for women and children. The staff and sick officers to be allowed a riding horse, the others to march with their men. This is a public-spirited proposition of his; for we had succeeded, at great expense, in obtaining carriage for his most valuable property, which, by this arrangement, must be abandoned, and for which it was possible he would not receive any recompence.

We hear that the inhabitants of the fortress of Ghuznee communicated with the enemy without; and by a coalition have driven our troops from all other parts than the citadel and the Cabul gateway. Now, had we retreated to the citadel in the Bala Hissar, as Sturt recommended before the Rikabashees' fort was taken, and often afterwards, we should not now be in the humiliating situation that we are.

The troops sent to the relief of Ghuznee only got two marches beyond Khelat-i-Ghilzie: their further progress is said to have been prevented, not only by the overpowering numbers of the enemy, but also by the snow, which rendered the passes impracticable; they fell back upon Candahar, leaving reinforcements in Khelat-i-Ghilzie.

Orders were despatched yesterday to Ghuznee, for the surrender of that place The troops will have to march through the Zoormut country, and go down by Dera Ismael Khan.

Thursday is at present said to be the day for our departure.

21*st.* — The hostages are decided on, — Airey, Pottinger, Warburton, and Conolly, who are to start immediately for the city.

The Envoy met Osman Khan and Mahommed Akbar Khan in conference.

22*d.* — The waggons, ammunition, &c., given up to our "allies."

Lady Macnaghten's carriage and horses given to Mahommed Akbar Khan.

The troops were kept under arms for two hours about nothing. Some cavalry horses were sent out to be shot: the Affghans wished to take them away, but the guard (37th) bayoneted one man, and shot another; on which they dispersed.

The Affghans say, that if, when we retook the

gun on the hill, on the 23d of last month, we had pursued to the gates of Cabul, they would never have made head against us again. They say they cannot understand Shelton's conduct on the hill on that day; and that, if our generals can do no more, the Affghans have nothing to fear from them. This is nearly verbatim what has been remarked before, but I am not attempting to shine in rounded periods; but give every thing that occurs as it comes to my knowledge: and this was the saying of an Affghan gentleman, and also of several of the lower classes, who came both to-day and often, to see Sturt, to give him warnings, which, alas! were by those in authority slighted.

A general opinion prevails amongst the Affghans that a force will be sent up against them; and many persons are getting letters to prove who are our friends.

Macgregor writes that for reasons of the utmost consequence, it is impossible for Sale's brigade to leave Jellalabad. Yesterday there was a grand discussion in the chiefs' durbar. One party objected to the departure of the English, urging that, *coute qui coute*, they should be killed: the Nawaub Zeman Shah Khan said, "If that is your opinion, I shall go into cantonments; after that, do as you will: for me, I will never lend myself to any act that is contrary to good faith." Our friends in the city seem to think that this chief's character is not understood by our chiefs in cantonments. Zeman Shah Khan does not wish our departure; but he fears his followers, and dares not openly say what he thinks.

The Envoy, in taking the part of Mahommed Akbar Khan, and in giving him money, has given him the means of doing much harm. Before he received money from us he had no power, and was not a person of any consequence; now he is in force, with the disadvantage of possessing a very bad disposition; and until the Nawaub said, "if you put difficulties in their route to Jellalabad I shall go into cantonments," he did every thing in his power to embarrass the council. At present, all appears *couleur de rose*.

It is said that yesterday Mahommed Akbar Khan went to Osman Khan's house, and swore on the Koran that he would do whatever the Nawaub desired. This act they say decided every thing; and it was settled that the troops should march on Tuesday the 4th, Osman Khan to go with the army; he appears to be a good and an intelligent person. The son of the Nawaub also goes, but he is not considered a shining character, though a good person. It is believed that Shah Shoojah will have a strong party after the English depart; but the Nawaub's faction treat this opinion with ridicule.

23*d.* — Humza Khan is a Ghilzye chief, now in Mahmood Khan's fort. He was the governor of the Ghilzye country; and, when the insurrection broke out in the end of September at Bhoodkhak, he was sent by the King to suppress it: instead of which he organised the rebel force.

On the return of this chief to Cabul he was put in irons in prison, and was to have been sent to the fortress of Ghuznee; he obtained his release when the insurrection of the 2d of November took place. This said Humza Khan has proffered to the Envoy, for a large consideration, provisions, if we will hold out; but his reputed bad character for faith renders him perhaps unsafe to deal with: besides, it may be a mere *ruse* to ascertain whether we are sincere or not in regard to the treaty we have made. There are said to be 2000 men in Mahmood Khan's fort at present.

Our sick men were placed in doolies to-day, preparatory to their removal to Zeman Shah Khan's house in the city; but their departure was delayed.

Some of our ammunition waggons were taken away by the allies; as also shrapnell and eight-inch shells.

Capt. Skinner came in at eleven last night with two Affghans; one, I believe, was a half brother of Mahommed Akbar's, by name Sultan Khan. At one this morning they returned to the city on important business. Moussa Khan was also sent into the city early this morning on some affair connected with negotiations.

The 54th, Shah's 6th, and some guns are ordered for a secret service; which the staff officer who gave the order said was to attack Mahmood Khan's fort, and from thence to bring away Amenoollah Khan, dead or alive. This force was ordered on an especial requisition of the Envoy's: I was present at mid-day, when Capt. Lawrence told Capt. Boyd that he was to purchase any quantity of grain and provision in his power, even to the extent of fifty days' supplies; and if it was not required, the loss would fall on the Government, should we go away and leave it behind. This conversation took place just previous to the Envoy going out to meet Akbar Khan, on the plain between the cantonments and the Siah Sung Hill.

I remarked that Lawrence styled the chiefs rebels instead of allies; which, coupled with the order to the commissariat officer to lay in provisions, looked very suspicious.

About two o'clock we suddenly heard firing, and all went to the rear gate to see what the matter was; when I met Mr. Waller, who informed me that the Envoy had been taken away by the chiefs.

The clearest account we have yet obtained was from Le Geyt, who accompanied the Envoy. It seems, when he arrived at the burnt bridge, the Envoy sent back all his escort except ten men.

Brig. Shelton having expressed a wish to be present at the conference, and not having joined the party, Le Geyt was sent back to hasten his arrival. The Brigadier said he was occupied, and could not go; and when Le Geyt returned it was too late, and he met the escort, who said that Lawrence and Mackenzie had ordered them back.

Many shots were fired, and some of them came into cantonments. Le Geyt's saces, who had been desired to remain when his master returned to cantonments, now came up; and reported that on the Envoy's arrival he found the chiefs seated on a loonghee on the ground; that he sat there with them and discoursed, whilst Trevor, Mackenzie, and Lawrence remained on their horses; that after a time two sirdars came, and stood behind the Envoy, who rose, as did Akbar Khan; that the Ghazeeas came and cut in between them and the cantonments, and firing commenced; that one of them drew Lawrence's sword from his side; that Akbar Khan took the Envoy by the hand, and led him, and all the gentlemen dismounted, towards the Yaghi fort; but it is generally believed that they are all safe, but taken into the city; however, great anxiety prevails regarding their fate, and that of Skinner, Conolly, and Airey, who are in the city as hostages.

The regiments were got under arms, the walls manned, &c.; but nothing was done. Grant declared that it was impossible to say whether it was a piece of treachery on the part of the chiefs, or friendship to save the party from an attack by the Ghazeeas. The only certain thing is, that our chiefs are at a nonplus.

The Affghans are greatly alarmed at a letter they have intercepted from Major Leech, political agent: this letter was of an old date, in which he tells the Envoy to hold out, that reinforcements are coming from Candahar, and that by hook or by crook he will obtain other aid from Hindostan.

There is also a native report, that four regiments are between this and Jellalabad. A cossid has come in from Macgregor; where he has been detained we know not; but the letters he brought were of the 16th of November. There is a general opinion in cantonments that faith has been broken on both sides, and that the Affghans have made the cleverest chupao.

Boyd has seven days' provisions; and says the bazaar can furnish seven more.

The bridge is taken up at the rear gate, and the camels that came in with grain have not been allowed to go out again. Neither is egress permitted to any respectable-looking Affghan who is in cantonments. The Meerakhor (one of the hostages, and the general go-between in our negotiations) has promised to get a letter conveyed to Sir William in the morning and to obtain a reply: he says there are too many Ghazeeas about to attempt it to-night.

The plain was at one time covered with people; but the horsemen seemed wending up and down trying to quiet them, and they gradually dispersed.

There was a great crowd about a body, which the Affghans were seen to strip: it was evidently that of an European; but, strange to say, no endeavour was made to recover it, which might easily have been done by sending out cavalry.

A red flag, said to be Amenoollah Khan's, went with about thirty men to reinforce the Rikabashees fort; and subsequently a greater number.

The Magazine fort was crowded with men.

24*th*. — I received a note from Lawrence, enclosing one from Conolly (Sir William's nephew) to Lady Macnaghten, and had the sad office imposed on me of informing both her and Mrs. Trevor of their husbands' assassination: over such scenes I draw a veil. It was a most painful meeting to us all.

Numerous reports are current. That of to-day is, that Sir William was taken to the city, and arraigned before a tribunal there for want of faith; and that Trevor suffered from the assiduity with which he executed the Envoy's orders. All reports agree, that both the Envoy's and Trevor's bodies are hanging in the public chouk: the Envoy's decapitated and a mere trunk; the limbs having been carried in triumph about the city.

A fallen man meets but little justice; and reports are rife that the Envoy was guilty of double-dealing, treating with Akbar Khan and Amenoollah Khan at the same time. In justice to a dead man, it should be remembered that the only person supposed to know the object of the Envoy's going out on the 23d was Skinner; who is now in the city. Sultan Khan was, I believe, the name of the person who came in with him, with a letter from Akbar Khan, on the night of the 22d. In that letter, which was read by a friend of mine, Akbar proposed that he should be made wuzeer to Shah Shoojah; he was to receive thirty lakhs of rupees, down, and four lakhs per annum: our troops to remain eight months; and then only to go if the King wished them to do so. He urgently requested the Envoy to come and talk it over with him.

We must hold in mind that, although we had performed all promises made on our part, given up our waggons, ammunition, forts, &c., the treaty had never been signed by the chiefs; nor had they fulfilled a single condition which had been specified verbally, beyond giving us grain in small quantities. The sequitur is, that the Envoy was perfectly justified, as far as keeping good faith went, in entering into any arrangement by which the condition of the troops could be ameliorated and the honour of our country be insured. He only erred in supposing it possible that Akbar Khan, proverbially the most treacherous of all his countrymen, could be sincere.

It was a part of Akbar Khan's plan to have Amenoollah Khan seized and brought to cantonments as a hostage.

It was a most decided piece of treachery on the part of Akbar. They were seated on a bank together: Lawrence, a very spunky active man, felt as if something was wrong; and when urged to sit, only knelt on one knee, that he might start up on occasion: but his pistol and sword were seized and his arms secured instantaneously, which rendered him powerless, and he was hurried away behind a chief on horseback; as was Mackenzie.

At that time Mahommed Akbar Khan had seized the Envoy by his left wrist, and Sultan Jan held him by the right; they dragged him down the bank, he exclaiming, "Az burai Kodar!" (For the love of God!) At the moment he was laid hands on, Mackenzie, Trevor, and Lawrence were disarmed, and forced away *en croup* behind different chiefs. They saw no more of the Envoy alive. Sultan Jan uttering an opprobrious epithet, calling him a dog, cut poor Trevor down, as did also Moollah Momind. Mackenzie would have shared the same fate had not Mahommed Shah Khan, behind whom he rode, received the cut on his own arm, which went through his postheen. Lawrence's life was saved by hard galloping: but he received some blows. This account I had from the surviving principals in the tragedy; so it may be depended on as the true account. The body we saw from the rear gate was that of the Envoy.

A letter has this day been received, signed by several Kohistanees, of no great consequence, setting forth that they do not care for either party; that they can muster 400 men, and are ready for a handsome consideration to escort us down safe to Jellalabad. No notice was taken of this letter, but the idea was laughed to scorn.

The original treaty between Sir William and

the chiefs has been sent in again; with three additional clauses:—

To leave all our treasure:

To leave all our guns excepting six:

To exchange the present hostages for all the married men and their families; and General Sale's name particularly mentioned. No doubt he was not forgotten by Mahommed Shah Khan the Ghilzye, whom he defeated at Jellalabad, and 500 of whose followers were killed.

General Elphinstone said he might give the officers as hostages; but that their wives and families were not public property: and, unless the husbands consented, he could not send them.

Major Thain was accordingly sent round to ask all the married officers if they would consent to their wives staying; offering those who did so a salary of 2000 rupees a month. Lieut. Eyre said if it was to be productive of great good he would stay with his wife and child. The others all refused to risk the safety of their families. Capt. Anderson said he would rather put a pistol to his wife's head and shoot her; and Sturt, that his wife and mother should only be taken at the point of the bayonet: for himself, he was ready to perform any duty imposed on him.

There certainly appears to have been a fatality about the events of yesterday. I have mentioned that Sir William applied to Gen. Elphinstone for two regiments and two guns for a secret service, which were in readiness, but never went out of cantonments: had they done so, it is more than probable that the surprise never would have occurred. Added to this, with his usual vacillation, Gen. E. wrote a note to the Envoy, which never reached him, as it arrived at his house after his departure, and was not even opened at the time. In this note he stated that we were too weak to send two regiments out of cantonments; particularly as the magazine fort was now garrisoned by 400 men instead of 40, the number the allies had stipulated should be thrown into it: and that if two regiments and two guns were to go out, the safety of the cantonments would be endangered. The Envoy had only ordered ten of his escort to attend him. Lawrence had taken sixteen; but a part of these returned of their own accord, feigning orders from Lawrence and Mackenzie. They probably had some knowledge of what was in contemplation; for there can be no doubt that the Envoy was surrounded by spies and traitors. Persian notes, that have arrived, have on different occasions been offered for perusal by his chuprassies—who were unable to read themselves, and anxious to know the contents—to Capt. Trevor's elder boys, who could read the characters; but they, imagining it was pure curiosity, and having no turn of a diplomatic description, refused to read them; and the notes were probably taken to others who did so, and made bad use of what intelligence they contained.

As it appears extremely uncertain whether we shall get on with the treaty or not, we are busy making up hammocks to carry the sick. They are making up in Sturt's compound; so light that two men can carry a heavy man in one easily.

Reports are assiduously spread that the Envoy's and Trevor's deaths were the act of the Ghazeeas; and that Mahommed Akbar Khan greatly regrets all that has passed.

25th. — A dismal Christmas-day, and our situation far from cheering. A letter brought in from Conolly to say, that the Nawaub Zeman Khan had interested himself greatly in the cause; and had procured the two bodies to be stolen, and that they hoped to be able to send them in at night. Trevor's had not been mutilated. It appears probable that the Envoy's death was not contemplated. Akbar wished to seize him, in hopes, by making him a hostage, to obtain better terms: but he is a man of violent passions; and, being thwarted, the natural ferocity of his disposition was evinced.

At night there was some firing, and the bugles sounded: all went to their respective posts, but the party of about 200 Affghans went away.

There was evidently great commotion in the city at the same time.

A cossid came in from Jellalabad; but no news later than the 7th.

26*th*. — The bodies were not sent in. The city is in great excitement; the Affghans fearing we shall not make the treaty good and force our way down.

It seems that the original treaty insured to the chiefs thirteen lakhs of rupees; and they insist on having it paid; not, as was stipulated, on our safe arrival at Peshawer, but to be given now in bills on Government, which there are people here who will cash for them on the spot. We are to be allowed to keep six yaboo loads of treasure; and all the rest is to be given to them before we go; or else the chiefs fear they will not get it, as their people would *loot* it all.

However, we are informed that the chiefs do not mean to keep faith; and that it is their intention to get all our women into their possession; and to kill every man except one, who is to have his hands and legs cut off, and is to be placed with a letter *in terrorem* at the entrance of the Khyber passes, to deter all Feringhees from entering the country again. A Persian note, without signature or address, was brought by a common-looking man to the officer on duty at the rear gate; giving information that the cantonments are to be attacked to-night. We have also information that the road to Jellalabad is clear; as the Ghilzyes are all come into Cabul to exterminate us and *loot* the cantonments.

The chiefs wish to force us to go down by another route, where our people say we are sure to be opposed.

Letters received from Capt. Mackeson, P.A. at Peshawer, state that the advance with ammunition had reached Peshawer, and the 16th Lancers, the 9th, and 31st, were close behind: it is, however, impossible that they can arrive here in time to save us from either a disgraceful treaty, or a disastrous retreat.

27th. — The Council — Elphinstone, Shelton, Anquetil, and Chambers, with Major Pottinger — have ratified the treaty. No one but themselves exactly knows what this same treaty is; further than that it is most disgraceful! $14\frac{1}{2}$ lakhs to be given for our safe conduct to Peshawer; all our guns to be given up save six; and six hostages to be given on our part; and when they are sent Lawrence and Mackenzie are to return.

28th. — Lawrence has come in, looking haggard and ten years older from anxiety. It appears that the Envoy, when Mahommed Akbar Khan took hold of him, grappled with him and threw him on the ground. Akbar fired his pistol at him, and wounded him; and afterwards he was cut to pieces.

There has been great excitement in the city. Khan Shereen Khan refused to attend the Durbar; and Akbar's conduct has been generally condemned by the chiefs.

Naïb Shureef paid for the interment of Sir A. Burnes's body; but it was never buried; and part of it, cut into many pieces, is still hanging on the trees in his garden.

The Envoy's head is kept in a bhoossa bag in the chouk: and Akbar says he will send it to Bokhara; to show to the king there how he has seized the Feringhees here, and what he means to do to them.

Our guns are brought down to the gate, to be ready for the Affghans to carry off to-morrow.

Conolly, Airy, and Skinner are in the city; and Warburton, Walsh, and Webb have been sent as the other three hostages, to make up the number, although the treaty is not yet signed by the chiefs. There is much doubt whether Mackenzie will be given up to us.

It was reported that the Meer Wallee of Khoolloom was expected with reinforcements to Akbar to-day; but we have not heard whether he has arrived or not.

Many routes have been named for our downward march this morning. We were to go by Zoormut; but I believe we still go by Jellalabad.

Amenoollah Khan is now represented as our best friend amongst the chiefs.

Whether we go by treaty or not, I fear but few of us will live to reach the provinces.

Although there is plenty of carriage for the sick, it is to-day decided that they are to be left behind; and the medical men drew lots who were to stay: they fell upon Primrose of the 44th, and Campbell of the Company's service: the former exchanged with Dr. Berwick, the late Envoy's medical staff, who, with Mr. Campbell of the 54th, are to go to the city with the sick men.

Snow all day.

29*th*. — Mackenzie and Skinner came in, in handsome dresses presented to them by Mahommed Akbar Khan, who professed to them he had no hand in the Envoy's death; and, to prove his sincerity, wept for two hours.

Brig. Shelton has again had recourse to Mahommed Akbar; and has obtained carriage from him.

It is said it was the Envoy's intention to have superseded Gen. Elphinstone, had Gen. Nott arrived: but no such measure would have been requisite, as the General had summoned Nott to take the command, and had, in fact, given it over to him from the 1st of November: so that it is a point to speculate upon as to who is our military chief; and whether, under existing circumstances, Gen. Elphinstone is empowered to treat with the chiefs regarding the troops.

To give an instance of the strange way in which matters are conducted here: Serg. Deane came and reported to Sturt that he had received orders to slope the banks of the canal, &c., without any reference to Sturt; who, of course, ordered his sergeants not to undertake any work without his orders. Sloping these banks would facilitate the passage of the enemy; who otherwise must cross the canal at the usual spots, either the ford or bridge.

Our sick sent to the city.

Snow all day.

30*th*. — 500 Ghazeeas made a rush at the rear gate; and only desisted on finding the port-fire ready, which would have sent grape in amongst them. In revenge, they tore up the small bridge over the canal.

More of our guns were sent to the chiefs, who now dictate to us, delaying our departure, which is to be postponed according to their pleasure.

More sick men sent to the city to-day. As the

camels and doolies that conveyed them there returned, they were attacked and plundered; the men were stripped, and had to run for their lives without any clothing, their black bodies conspicuous as they ran over the snow. The doolies and camels were all carried off. One of the hostages has written to me, dated midnight of the 29th, and tells me that they are all well in the city, and that, from the appearance of affairs, we shall most likely go down unmolested: that the Nawaub Zeman Khan is very kind; and he or one of his sons is with them nearly all day: the room they inhabit is eighteen feet by ten, and all the hostages are together: it is very uncomfortable, being thus confined; this, however, must be the case for some time: even the court-yard below is not free from vagabonds. The night the Envoy was killed the Ghazeeas rushed even up to the door, determined on Conolly's and Airy's death; and it was difficult to get rid of them. The poor Envoy's hand was held up to the window, to show it to Conolly! Ameenoollah Khan seems to be well pleased. The King went to them the night the letter was written, and took his musicians with him, who played and sang till eleven o'clock: he is represented as a most fatherly old gentleman. This alludes to Zeman Shah Khan, and not to Shah Shoojah.

The Nawaub's second son, Soojah ool Dowlah, is to go down with us: he is represented as a very nice fellow, about twenty-two years old. A postscript, added this morning, informs me that the chiefs are very well pleased; and do not wish us to go till all our arrangements are comfortably made, for their suspicions are now at an end.

Sturt received instructions from Capt. Bellew to scarp the banks of the canal, by way of rendering them easier for the camels to get over. "To slope, I suppose you mean?" said Sturt. "You may suppose what you please," replied Bellew; "but the General's orders sent by me are, to scarp the banks;—and now do as you like: and you are also to cut the rampart down, to make a free passage for the troops; as, there being but one gateway on the face, it would take a long time for the troops and baggage to pass out."

When Sturt was first desired by the General to cut an opening, he proposed making two of twelve feet each, with twenty feet between: this was objected to, as being too small; and he then said he would throw down the rampart between, which would make an opening of forty-four feet: but of course such a breach (for the rampart was to be thrown in to fill the ditch, twenty feet wide) was a work only to be undertaken at the last hour; unless the General could give guns and additional troops to defend it.

In consequence of these messages, Sturt wrote to Grant to say, that unless we were to start instanter after the breach was made, or the General had the necessary means for its defence, it would risk the safety of the cantonments; particularly after what had occurred this morning. Grant, by the General's desire, wrote to know what did occur; and then Sturt wrote an account of the attack of the Ghazeeas at the rear gate, our cattle having been carried off and the bearers plundered, &c.: upon this Grant, by the General's desire, wrote to say they did not know any of the circumstances; and begged nothing might be done to injure our defences.

Snow all day.

Dec. 31*st.*—The chiefs say they have no control over the Ghazeeas; that when they offend we may fire on them; that they will have the camels, taken from us yesterday, restored.

Now did they give us even camel for camel, it would be another matter: but, instead of that, fifteen of the worst of our own were brought back out of thirty-six; and a present of 100 rupees was made to them for the trouble they had taken.

This morning a number of camels laden with

grain, &c. were plundered close to the rear gate. Verbal orders were sent by Brig. Shelton to fire on these people if absolutely requisite: but no written order to that effect has been given, and no one will take the responsibility upon his own shoulders. No orders of any import are transmitted in writing. Some one, any one, is sent, with a verbal message to the officer it concerns; and, if any thing goes wrong, what has he to show as his authority for acting as he has done? Amongst other orders, there is one not actually to fire, but to make believe they are going to do so; which has occasioned some ridiculous and harmless flourishes of port-fires.

There is still negotiation going on; and there seems to be some hints regarding Shah Shoojah's abdication. The Affghans do not wish to put him to death, but only to deprive him of sight.

The chiefs are, we hear, to come into Mahmood Khan's fort with a large force to-morrow, to be ready to protect cantonments, and we are to march out the next day.

Thus ends the year. The bodies of the Envoy and Trevor have not been brought in; and we hope that the Nawaub Zeman Khan may be able to get them privately interred in his own garden.

Sergeant Williams, who died in consequence of

his wound, was placed in the coffin and buried in the grave prepared for the Envoy behind the barracks.

Snow has lain on the ground since the 18th of December.

Jan. 1*st,* 1842. — The Naïb Meer came in: negotiations are still going on.

The Nawaub Zeman Shah Khan and Osman Khan appear to be honourable men; as also Mahommed Shah Khan Ghiizye: the former, or his son, sits with the hostages day and night to insure their protection. The latter is the person who received the sword-cut on his arm intended for Mackenzie, and thereby saved his life, on the 23d of last month.

A party of fifty Affghan workmen, magnified by the General into 500, have been sent to work on the banks of the canal: they soon said they were cold and tired, and would finish the rest tomorrow.

Two men came in to-day with a Koran to Sergeant Deane (who, from having an Affghan wife, has many acquaintances and friends amongst the people of Cabul): they report that Mahommed Akbar Khan is false; that 10,000 Kohistanees are to attack us at Tézeen, and all the Ghilzyes at Soorkhab.

Offers have been made of provisions; but it is

suspected that it is only to try our faith, and see if we will lay in provisions on the sly.

2d.—Before breakfast Sturt received the following note from Gen. Elphinstone:—

"Dear Sturt,

"Are we to have the Affghan Bhildars again to-day? If so, they had better be employed on the other side of the river. Pottinger proposes our taking on the planks to cross the streams in the Khoord Cabul pass. He says 250 planks would do. He will explain this to you after breakfast. Let me hear what was done yesterday. We shall march on Tuesday, I think: that is the present arrangement. You must settle with Boyd about the bullocks for the bridge, which we must take on to the Loghur.

"Yours,
"W. R. E."

There have been so many clever propositions during the siege, that, if I succeed in saving my papers, many of the original letters will require to be appended, to prove that I do not use the traveller's privilege! To-day's is this. We make a bridge to cross the Cabul river; and carry on planks to the Loghur, in case that bridge should have been destroyed. Major Pottinger proposes that we carry 250 planks, to be laid down in the

Khoord Cabul, for crossing the streams, which occur on an average every 100 yards. Could we afford transport for these planks, the delay occasioned would render the journey through that pass one of about three days, as the stream is crossed about thirty times. One word regarding the carriage of these said planks. A camel would only carry two; thus, 125 animals would be required; and we are unable to take the requisite quantity of ammunition, for want of carriage. Besides, why is this stream not to be frozen, as it is but a few inches deep any where?

There appears to be much commotion amongst the chiefs regarding the Envoy's death, and Akbar's conduct; who still repeats that he did not kill the Envoy, but that it was done by the Ghazeeas. He threatens to attack us on the road; and Osman Khan says if he does he will fight him all the way down, taking, as his own party, 1000 horse and 500 foot.

Aziz Khan is to be at Soorkhab ready to exterminate us. We hear from the city that Sale has been taking forts, carrying off women and provisions, and greatly annoying the good people about Jellalabad.

3*d*.—The march, which was fixed for to-day, is again postponed. The Kohistanees have not received any part of the money given to the chiefs.

They have sent an agent to Sturt to say that, if we wish it, they will bring the chiefs of Kardurrah into cantonments, with four others, as hostages; that we need not give them any money now, they know that we have none, and are content with our promise. They wish us to remain quiet. They will give us provisions; and attack and fire Cabul within three days. They will also go down and bring up reinforcements for us from Jellalabad. They assure us that the chiefs are false, and mean to attack us on the road. All this was represented to our chiefs by Sturt. The reply he received was, "It was better to keep the matter quiet; as in the present state of things it might, if known, cause excitement."

Shah Shoojah is said to have a strong party: and all the roads leading to the Bala Hissar are watched, to prevent persons joining him; though Nooreddin has succeeded in doing so, with twenty followers.

The 40,000 rupees given by us to the chiefs, to raise 2000 men, at twenty rupees each, to protect us to Jellalabad, have not succeeded. They have kept the money, of course; but say they cannot get men to go at this season; and even if they could, the chiefs cannot afford to weaken their party by sending their followers away.

The thermometer to-day at sunrise was below

zero; in the sitting room, with an enormous blazing fire, at noon, 40°. Yesterday, with the same good fire, at 9 A.M., 11°.

Another excellent project of Major Pottinger's. Among our various vacillatory measures, there is again a thought, now that the time for action is long past, to force our way into the Bala Hissar: but how are we to get our ammunition in? Erect a battery on the Siah Sung Hill (of course to be the work of fairies during the night), fire our shot from cantonments into the battery, where of course guardian sylphs would protect the lives of our men, who were quickly to pick them up, and send them on, in like manner, into the Bala Hissar! No arrangement made for transporting the powder. The tale was told from where the conversation had taken place — at the General's. The narrator was Capt. Bellew. Both Sturt and I taxed him with joking; but he assured us it was all true, and only another of the many strange events constantly occurring. Then ensued a long parley and military discussion on the point, its feasibility, and its having been tried in some peninsular warfare. But I never could get Bellew to explain how our men's lives in the battery were to be saved.

4th. — I heard from Sale, dated 19th December. He acknowledged the receipt of my note, giving an account of operations up to the 9th instant. He was doubly anxious relative to our situation, from having heard only the day before that the Kandahar troops were near us, and all the cossids telling those at Jellalabad that we had plenty of provisions; and he still trusts in God that the Kandahar force may arrive in time to save us; and prevent the necessity of terms disgraceful to our reputation in India. He informs me of the arrival of the advanced guard of our cavalry at Peshawer with ammunition; and that the 3d Buffs and 9th Foot had marched; with altogether six regiments of N. I., and some artillery, sappers, and engineer officers. The news from Cabul had not then had any effect on the chiefs about Jellalabad, whose followers are daily diminishing. Our troops were, nevertheless, as hard at work as ever, making the place as strong as possible. At that time Mackeson had not sent them any money; of which they were in great want, not having a rupee to give to the troops, and three months' pay nearly due. Extracts from my letter had been sent to Government and to the Commander-in-Chief. The original has been sent to my son-in-law, Capt. Bund; as Sale writes me that no other person gives them any idea of our real position at Cabul.

The Affghans still tell us we are doomed; and

warn us to be particularly cautious of our safety in going out of cantonments. Taj Mahommed says that Mrs. Sturt and I must wear neemchees over our habits — common leather ones — and turbans, and ride mixed in with the suwars; not to go in palkees or keep near the other ladies, as they are very likely to be attacked.

The chiefs are to come in to-morrow to take charge of cantonments before we leave them. Nawaub Zeman Shah Khan is also to come in to see the General.

Orders for the first bugle at 6, the second at 7. Sturt inquired if he was to make the breach, and, when made, who were to guard it, &c.: to which the following is the reply: —

"My dear Sturt,
"If it is as well as before, the General thinks you need not turn out the sappers. The Brigadier says you are the best judge as to whether it is defensible or not.
"Yours truly,
"4th Jan. 7 P.M. "WM. THAIN.

"The General wants to know if the planks which were sent have been removed. The troops are not to turn out at 6 in the morning as ordered, but wait till further orders.
"W. T."

January 5th. — Sturt employed in making the breach. The chiefs say we shall go to-morrow. Orders out for 7 and 8 o'clock.

Shah Shoojah has sent a message to ask if not even one officer of his force will stand by him. This message was, I know, delivered by Sturt himself to several; but circumstances admitted not of their further adherence. Indeed it is more than doubtful that the King was at the bottom of the insurrection, never dreaming that it would go so far.

THE RETREAT FROM CABUL.

Thursday, 6th January, 1842. — We marched from Cabul. The advanced guard consisted of the 44th Queen's, 4th Irregular Horse, and Skinner's Horse, two H. A. six-pounder guns, Sappers and Miners, Mountain Train, and the late Envoy's escort. The main body included the 5th and 37th N. I.; the latter in charge of treasure; Anderson's Horse, the Shah's 6th Regiment, two H.A. six-pounder guns. The rear guard was composed of the 54th N. I., 5th Cavalry, and two six-pounder H. A. guns. The force consisted of about 4500 fighting men, and 12,000 followers.

The troops left cantonments both by the rear gate and the breach to the right of it, which had been made yesterday by throwing down part of the rampart to form a bridge over the ditch. All was confusion from before daylight. The day was clear and frosty; the snow nearly a foot deep on the ground; the thermometer considerably below freezing point.

By eight o'clock a great part of the baggage was outside the cantonments. It was fully expected that we would have to fight our way out of them, although terms had been entered into with the Sirdar for our safe escort. Bills were granted on India for fourteen and a half lakhs of rupees, by the political authority (Major Pottinger) to the Cabul Shroffs, to be paid to the following Sirdars, who were, on their part, to protect the force as far as Peshawer:—

Mahommed Zeman Shah Khan, three lakhs:

Amenoollah Khan, six lakhs:

Khan Shireen Khan, head of the Kuzzilbashes, two lakhs:

Mahommed Akbar Khan, one lakh:

Osman Khan, two lakhs:

The Ghilzye chiefs, half a lakh.

We started at about half-past nine A. M. The advance party were not molested; there might have been 50 or 100 Affghans collected about the gateway to witness our departure. The ladies, collectively speaking, were placed with the advance, under the charge of the escort; but Mrs. Sturt and I rode up to Capt. Hay, and mixed ourselves with his troopers.

The progress was very slow; for the first mile was not accomplished under two and a half hours. There was only one small bridge over the Nullah, which is eight feet broad, but deep, situated about fifty yards from cantonments.

Great stress had been laid on the necessity of a bridge over the Cabul river, about half a mile from cantonments. In vain had Sturt represented over and over again, that as the river was perfectly fordable, it was a labour of time and inutility : with snow a foot deep, the men must get their feet wet. However, as usual, every sensible proposition was overruled; and Sturt was sent long before daylight to make the bridge with gun carriages. They could not be placed over-night, as the Affghans would have carried them off: he had therefore to work for hours up to his hips in water, with the comfortable assurance that, when his unprofitable task was finished, he could not hope for dry clothes until the end of the march; and immediately on quitting the water they were all frozen stiff. I do not mention this as an individual grievance, but to show the inclemency of the weather, and the general misery sustained.

The bullocks had great difficulty in dragging these gun carriages through the snow, and when the bridge was made it was proved to be an unnecessary expense of time and labour. The baggage might have forded the river with great ease, a little above the bridge, where it was not deep. Mrs. Sturt and I rode with the horsemen through the river, in preference to attempting the rattling bridge of planks laid across the gun carriages: but the camp followers determined not to go through the water, and jostled for their turns to go over the bridge. This delay was the origin of the day's misfortune, which involved the loss of nearly all the baggage, and the greater part of the commissariat stores.

The troops had been on half rations during the whole of the siege: they consisted of half a seer of wheat per diem, with melted ghee or dhal, for fighting men; and for camp followers, for some time, of a quarter of a seer of wheat or barley. Our cattle, public and private, had long subsisted on the twigs and bark of the trees. From the commencement of negotiations with the chiefs, otta, barley, and bhoosa were brought in in considerable quantities; the former selling at from two to four seers per rupee, and the latter from seven to ten; but neither ourselves nor our servants benefited by this arrangement: it came to the commissariat for the troops. The poorer camp followers had latterly subsisted on such animals (camels, ponies, &c.) as had died from starvation. The men had suffered much from over work and bad feeding, also from want of firing; for when all the wood in store was expended, the chiefs objected to our cutting down any more of the fruit trees; and their wishes were complied with. Wood, both public and private, was stolen: when ours was gone, we broke up boxes, chests of drawers, &c.; and our last dinner and breakfast at Cabul were cooked with the wood of a mahogany dining table.

When the advance had proceeded about a mile, an order was brought for a return to cantonments, as Mahommed Zeman Shah Khan had written to say the chiefs were not ready; but shortly afterwards a counter order arrived to proceed without loss of time.

When the rear guard left cantonments, they were fired upon from the cantonment then filled with Affghans. The servants, who were not concerned in the plunder, all threw away their loads, and ran off. Private baggage, commissariat, and ammunition were nearly annihilated at one fell swoop. The whole road was covered with men, women, and children, lying down in the snow to die.

The only baggage we saved was Mrs. Sturt's bedding, on which the ayah rode; and keeping her close to us, it was saved.

The Mission Compound was first vacated: and when the force from thence came into cantonments in order to pass through them, it was immediately filled with Affghans; who, in like manner, occupied the cantonments as our troops went out.

It was the General's original intention to halt at Begramee, close to the Loghur river, and about five miles from Cabul (reiterated was the advice of our Affghan friends—alas, how little heeded!— to push on at all risks through the Khoord Cabul the first day): but the whole country being a swamp encrusted with ice, we went on about a mile further, and halted at about 4 P. M. There were no tents, save two or three small palls that arrived. All scraped away the snow as best they might, to make a place to lie down on. The evening and night were intensely cold: no food for man or beast procurable, except a few handfuls of bhoosa, for which we paid from five to ten rupees. Captain Johnson, in our great distress, kindly pitched a small pall over us: but it was dark, and we had few pegs; the wind blew in under the sides, and I felt myself gradually stiffening. I left the bedding, which was occupied by Mrs. Sturt and her husband, and doubled up my legs in a straw chair of Johnson's, covering myself with my poshteen. Mr. Mein and the ayah fully occupied the remainder of the space. We only went in all six miles, and had to abandon two H. A. guns on the road: we were also much delayed by the bullocks that dragged the planks, in case the Loghur bridge should have been destroyed. We had, however, positive information that it was all right; and so it proved.

Previous to leaving cantonments, as we must abandon most of our property, Sturt was anxious to save a few of his most valuable books, and to try the experiment of sending them to a friend in the city. Whilst he selected these, I found, amongst the ones thrown aside, Campbell's Poems, which opened at Hohenlinden; and, strange to say, one verse actually haunted me day and night:—

> "Few, few shall part where many meet,
> The snow shall be their winding sheet;
> And every turf beneath their feet
> Shall be a soldier's sepulchre."

I am far from being a believer in presentiments; but this verse is never absent from my thoughts. Heaven forbid that our fears should be realized! but we have commenced our retreat so badly, that we may reasonably have our doubts regarding the finale. Nearly all Hopkins's corps, the Shah's 6th, deserted from this place; as also the Shah's sappers and miners, 250 in number.

We afterwards heard that 400 of Hopkins's men went back to Cabul the next day.

7th.—Yesterday's rear-guard did not get up to our bivouac till two this morning, as there was no attempt to form any lines. As stragglers came up we heard them shouting out, to know where their corps were; and the general reply, — that no one knew any thing about it.

During last night, or rather towards the morning, there was an alarm. Had it proved the enemy, we were perfectly defenceless; fortunately it was only camp followers, &c.

At daylight we found several men frozen to death, amongst whom was Mr. Conductor Macgregor.

The reason the rear-guard were so late was, that they did not leave cantonments till sunset. Previous to their quitting them the Affghans had entered; and set fire to all the public and private buildings, after plundering them of their contents. The whole of our valuable magazine was *looted* by the mob; and they burned the gun-carriages to procure the iron. Some fighting took place between the Affghans and our Sipahees. About fifty of the 54th were killed and wounded; and Cornet Hardyman, of the 5th Cavalry, killed. A great deal of baggage and public property was abandoned in cantonments, or lost on the road; amongst which were two Horse Artillery six-pounders, as before mentioned.

The officers of the rear-guard report that the road is strewn with baggage; and that numbers of men, women, and children, are left on the road-side to perish. Captain Boyd's office accounts, to the amount of several lakhs of rupees, have been lost.

Two or three small tents came up to-day.

The men were half-frozen; having bivouacked all night in the snow, without a particle of food or bedding, or wood to light a fire.

At half-past seven the advance-guard moved off — no order was given — no bugle sounded. It had much difficulty in forcing its way ahead of the baggage and camp followers; all of whom had proceeded in advance as soon as it was light. Amongst them there were many Sipahees; and discipline was clearly at an end. If asked why they were not with their corps, one had a lame foot, another could not find his regiment, another had lost his musket: any excuse to run off.

The whole of what little baggage was left, was not off the ground ere the enemy appeared, and plundered all they could lay their hands on.

As the mountain train, consisting of three three-pounders dragged by yaboos and mules, was passing a small fort close to our back-ground, a party of Affghans sallied out, and captured the whole. Scarcely any resistance was offered on the part of our troops, and the saces immediately absconded. Brig. Anquetil and Lieut. Green rallied the men, and retook the guns; but were obliged to abandon them, as the 44th, whose duty it was to guard them, very precipitately *made themselves scarce:* but this was not done until Anquetil and Green had spiked them with their own hands, amid the gleaming sabres of the enemy.

As the troops advanced on their road, the enemy increased considerably on both flanks; and greatly annoyed the centre and rear.

It was the General's intention to proceed through the Khoord Cabul pass to Khoord Cabul; and as it was not above one P.M. when the advance arrived at Bhoodkhak, having only come five miles, it was with dismay we heard the order to halt.

We left Cabul with five and a half days' rations to take us to Jellalabad, and no forage for cattle, nor hope of procuring any on the road. By these unnecessary halts we diminished our provisions; and having no cover for officers or men, they are perfectly paralysed with the cold. The snow was more than a foot deep. Here, again, did evil counsel beset the General: his principal officers and staff objecting to a further advance; and Capt. Grant, in whom he had much confidence, assured him that if he proceeded he risked the safety of the army!

On our arrival at Bhoodkhak, the enemy had very greatly increased around our position; and we heard that Mahommed Akbar Khan was with them. Scarcely any baggage of either officers or men now remained. In a very small pall of Johnson's we slept nine, all touching each other.

We were also indebted to Johnson and Troup for food. They had a few Cabul cakes and some tea, which they kindly shared with us.

During this short march we were obliged to spike and abandon two other six-pounders, the horses not having strength sufficient to drag them on. We have only two horse artillery guns left, with scarcely any ammunition.

Again no ground was marked out for the troops. Three fourths of the Sipahees are mixed up with the camp followers, and know not where to find the head-quarters of their corps.

Snow still lies a foot deep on the ground. No food for man or beast; and even water from the river close at hand difficult to obtain, as our people were fired on in fetching it.

Numbers of unfortunates have dropped, benumbed with cold, to be massacred by the enemy: yet, so bigoted are our rulers, that we are still told that the Sirdars are faithful, that Mahommed Akbar Khan is our friend!!! &c. &c. &c.; and the reason they wish us to delay is, that they may send their troops to clear the passes for us! That they will send them there can be no doubt; for every thing is occurring just as was foretold to us before we set out.

Between Begramee and Bhoodkhak, a body of the enemy's horse charged down into the column (immediately after the 5th and 37th had passed); and succeeded in carrying off an immense quantity of baggage and a number of camels, without experiencing the least resistance.

8*th.* — At sunrise no order had been issued for the march, and the confusion was fearful. The force was perfectly disorganised, nearly every man paralysed with cold, so as to be scarcely able to hold his musket or move. Many frozen corpses lay on the ground. The Sipahees burnt their caps, accoutrements, and clothes to keep themselves warm. Some of the enemy appearing in rear of our position, the whole of the camp followers rushed to the front; every man, woman, and child, seizing all the cattle that fell in their way, whether public or private. The ground was strewn with boxes of ammunition, plate, and property of various kinds. A cask of spirits on the ground was broached by the artillerymen, and, no doubt, by other Europeans. Had the whole been distributed fairly to the men, it would have done them good: as it was, they became too much excited.

The enemy soon assembled in great numbers.

Had they made a dash at us, we could have offered no resistance, and all would have been massacred.

After very great exertions on the part of commanding officers, portions of their corps were got together. The 44th, headed by Major Thain, drove the enemy off to a short distance, and took up a position on a commanding height. The cavalry were also employed. Bullets kept whizzing by us, as we sat on our horses, for hours. The artillerymen were now fully *primed*, by having had some brandy given them from the 54th's mess stores, which were being distributed to any one who would take them. They mounted their horses; and, with the best feeling in the world, declared that they were ashamed at our inactivity, and vowed they would charge the enemy. Capt. Nicholl, their immediate commandant, came up; abused them as drunkards, and talked of punishment: not the way, under such circumstances, to quiet tipsy men. They turned to Sturt shortly after their own officer had left them, having showered curses and abuse on them, which had irritated them dreadfully. Sturt told them they were fine fellows, and had ever proved themselves such during the siege; but that their lives were too valuable to be risked at such a moment: but, if need were, and their services were required, he would himself go with them. This, in a certain degree, restrained their ardour; yet still they kept on talking valiantly. These men listened the more readily to Sturt because they know him well: he was daily and hourly in the batteries with them, encouraging them by being ever the foremost in the post of danger; and on those dreadfully cold nights during the siege, whilst there was a bottle of brandy to be had at any price, after his own small store was expended, he gave those men on duty each one glass to warm and cheer them—a comfort they fully appreciated, as they had long been without what was now become necessary, though it is in general the soldier's bane. For myself, whilst I sat for hours on my horse in the cold, I felt very grateful for a tumbler of sherry, which at any other time would have made me very unlady-like, but now merely warmed me, and appeared to have no more strength in it than water. Cups full of sherry were given to young children three and four years old without in the least affecting their heads.

When Major Thain took command of the 44th, he took part of the 37th N. I. with him. The 44th lines were nearest to the men who were firing into our camp; which was only saved by the promptness of Thain and Lawrence, who brought up the escort at a trot in the direction of the firing. He had to pass to the right of the 44th, and there he found about 150 of that regiment falling into their ranks. Major Thain was about 200 yards in advance, apparently reconnoitring the enemy, who were creeping up under cover of the ravines and hillocks, and keeping up a desultory fire on our camp. About this time a company of the 37th N. I. formed on Lawrence's right, and on Thain making a signal all moved forward, and drove off the enemy in good style. Anderson's horse were formed on the opposite face of the camp, with orders to keep back the camp followers, who were rushing towards the entrance of the pass. Major Thain appears to have acted on the spur of the moment; which is the only reason I can assign for his commanding the 44th. Lawrence was not under any one's orders; as the General, before quitting cantonments, told him that his escort would be an independent body.

I am by no means certain that our chiefs pursued the wisest course. Had they, when the enemy first appeared, showed a good front, and dashed at them, they would probably all have scampered off as fast as they could. The Affghans never stand a charge.

The General and Major Pottinger soon discovered that Mahommed Akbar Khan was there, and entered into communication with him: he agreed to protect the troops, on condition that he should receive hereafter 15,000 rupees; and that Pottinger, Lawrence, and Mackenzie should be given over to him as hostages for General Sale's evacuation of Jellalabad; but that the troops should not proceed further than Tézeen until information be received of the march of the troops from that place. These disgraceful propositions were readily assented to; and the three officers went off to the Sirdar.

Capt. Lawrence received a note from Conolly, telling him to be cautious, to put ourselves as little as possible in Akbar's power, and above all things to push on as fast as we could: but this note did not arrive until the conference was over, and all points adjusted.

We commenced our march at about mid-day, the 5th N. I. in front. The troops were in the greatest state of disorganisation: the baggage was mixed in with the advanced guard; and the camp followers all pushed ahead in their precipitate flight towards Hindostan.

Sturt, my daughter, Mr. Mein, and I, got up to the advance; and Mr. Mein was pointing out to us the spots where the 1st brigade was attacked, and where he, Sale, &c. were wounded. We had not proceeded half a mile when we were heavily fired upon. Chiefs rode with the advance, and desired us to keep close to them. They certainly desired their followers to shout to the people on the height not to fire: they did so, but quite ineffectually. These chiefs certainly ran the same risk we did; but I verily believe many of these persons would individually sacrifice themselves to rid their country of us.

After passing through some very sharp firing, we came upon Major Thain's horse, which had been shot through the loins. When we were supposed to be in comparative safety, poor Sturt rode back (to see after Thain I believe): his horse was shot under him, and before he could rise from the ground he received a severe wound in the abdomen. It was with great difficulty he was held upon a pony by two people, and brought into camp at Khoord Cabul.

The pony Mrs. Sturt rode was wounded in the ear and neck. I had fortunately only *one* ball *in* my arm; three others passed through my poshteen near the shoulder without doing me any injury. The party that fired on us were not above fifty yards from us, and we owed our escape to urging our horses on as fast as they could go over a road where, at any other time, we should have walked our horses very carefully.

The main attack of the enemy was on the column, baggage, and rear guard; and fortunate it was for Mrs. Sturt and myself that we kept with the chiefs. Would to God that Sturt had done so likewise, and not gone back.

The ladies were mostly travelling in kajavas, and were mixed up with the baggage and column in the pass: here they were heavily fired on. Many camels were killed. On one camel were, in one kajava, Mrs. Boyd and her youngest boy Hugh; and in the other Mrs. Mainwaring and her infant, scarcely three months old, and Mrs. Anderson's eldest child. This camel was shot. Mrs. Boyd got a horse to ride; and her child was put on another behind a man, who being shortly after unfortunately killed, the child was carried off by the Affghans. Mrs. Mainwaring, less fortunate, took her own baby in her arms. Mary Anderson was carried off in the confusion. Meeting with a pony laden with treasure, Mrs. M. endeavoured to mount and sit on the boxes, but they upset; and in the hurry pony and treasure were left behind; and the unfortunate lady pursued her way on foot, until after a time an Affghan asked her if she was wounded, and told her to mount behind him. This apparently kind offer she declined, being fearful of treachery; alleging as an excuse that she could not sit behind him on account of the difficulty of holding her child when so mounted. This man shortly after snatched her shawl off her shoulders, and left her to her fate. Mrs. M.'s sufferings were very great; and she deserves much credit for having preserved her child through these dreadful scenes. She not only had to walk a considerable distance with her child in her arms through the deep snow, but had also to pick her way over the bodies of the dead, dying, and wounded, both men and cattle, and constantly to cross the streams of water, wet up to the knees, pushed and shoved about by men and animals, the enemy keeping up a sharp fire, and several persons being killed close to her. She, however, got safe to camp with her child, but had no opportunity to change her clothes; and I know from experience that it was many days ere my wet habit became thawed, and can fully appreciate her discomforts.

Mrs. Bourke, little Seymour Stoker, and his mother, and Mrs. Cunningham, all soldiers' wives, and the child of a man of the 13th, have been carried off. The rear was protected by the 44th and 37th; but as they neared the pass, the enemy, concealed behind rocks, &c. increased their fire considerably upon them. The companies that had been skirmishing on the flanks of the rear-guard closed in; and they slowly entered the pass, keeping up a heavy fire on the assailants, who had by this time got amongst the straggling camp followers and Sipahees. Owing to a halt having taken place in front, the pass was completely choked up; and for a considerable time the 44th were stationary under a heavy fire, and were fast expending their ammunition. The 37th continued slowly moving on without firing a shot; being paralysed with cold to such a degree that no persuasion of their officers could induce them to make any effort to dislodge the enemy, who took from some of them not only their firelocks, but even the clothes from their persons; several men of the 44th supplied themselves with ammunition from the pouches of the Sipahees: and many proceeded to the front owing to their ammunition being expended. Major Scott and Capt. Swinton, of the 44th, had also gone to the front severely wounded; and the command of the regiment devolved on Capt. Souter. Lieut. Steer, of the 37th N. I., with great difficulty succeeded in bringing to the rear a yaboo loaded with ammunition: but scarcely were the boxes placed on the ground, opened, and a few rounds taken out, than they were obliged to be abandoned; as, owing to our fire having slackened, the enemy became bolder and pressed upon the rear in great numbers. They had the advantage of being covered by our stragglers, which compelled our men to retire, firing volleys indiscriminately amongst them and the Affghans. At this time our men were dropping fast from a flanking fire from the heights; and, seeing it was useless to attempt to maintain a position in the rear, under such circumstances, with only about sixty men, they were withdrawn; and with difficulty forced their way through the crowd to a more commanding position, where the rear-guard of the 44th was joined by Gen. Elphinstone, Col. Chambers, of the 5th Lt. Cavalry, with some troopers, and Capt. Hay, with a few of the Irregular Horse, and the only remaining gun, one having been abandoned in the pass. The 37th and the camp followers gradually passed to the front; but the Affghans were checked from following them.

After halting full an hour to let the stragglers, &c., get well to the front, they resumed their march; but, owing to the depth of the snow, the troops were compelled to assist the gun by manual labour, the horses being unable to get it on. In this way they reached the encamping ground, without molestation from the enemy.

On leaving Cabul each Sipahee had forty rounds of musket ammunition in pouch, with 100 spare loads—we have now not three camel loads left; and many Sipahees have not a single cartridge in pouch.

500 of our regular troops, and about 2500 of the camp followers, are killed.

Poor Sturt was laid on the side of a bank, with his wife and myself beside him. It began snowing heavily: Johnson and Bygrave got some xummuls (coarse blankets) thrown over us. Dr. Bryce, H. A., came and examined Sturt's wound: he dressed it; but I saw by the expression of his countenance that there was no hope. He afterwards kindly cut the ball out of my wrist, and dressed both my wounds.

Half of a Sipahee's pall had been pitched, in which the ladies and their husbands took refuge. We had no one to scrape the snow off the ground in it. Capt. Johnson and Mr. Mein first assisted poor Sturt over to it, and then carried Mrs. Sturt and myself through the deep snow. Mrs. Sturt's bedding (saved by the ayah riding on it, whom we kept up close with ourselves) was now a comfort for my poor wounded son. He suffered dreadful agony all night, and intolerable thirst; and most grateful did we feel to Mr. Mein for going out constantly to the stream to procure water: we had only a small vessel to fetch it in, which contained but a few mouthfuls.

To sleep in such anxiety of mind and intense cold was impossible. There were nearly thirty of us packed together without room to turn.

The Sipahees and camp followers, half-frozen, tried to force their way, not only into the tent, but actually into our beds, if such resting-places can be so called—a poshteen (or pelisse of sheep skin) half spread on the snow, and the other half wrapped over one.

Many poor wretches died round the tent in the night.

The light company of the 54th N. I., which left Cabul, thirty-six hours previously, eighty strong, was reduced to eighteen files. This is only one instance, which may fairly be taken as a general average of the destruction of our force.

9th.—Before sunrise the same confusion as yesterday. Without any order given, or bugle sounded, three fourths of our fighting men had pushed on in advance with the camp followers. As many as could, had appropriated to themselves all the public yaboos and camels, on which they mounted.

A portion of the troops had also regularly moved off, the only order appearing to be, " Come along; we are all going, and half the men are off, with the camp followers in advance!" We had gone perhaps a mile, when the whole were remanded back to their former ground; and a halt for the day was ordered, in accordance with the wishes of the Sirdar; who had represented to the General, through Capt. Skinner, that his arrangements were not made either as regarded our security or provisions. Skinner urged the General to show some mark of confidence in the Sirdar's promises; which he instantly did by sending Capt. Anderson to order back the troops and baggage.

Mrs. Trevor kindly rode a pony, and gave up her place in the kajava to Sturt, who must otherwise have been left to die on the ground. The rough motion increased his suffering and accelerated his death: but he was still conscious that his wife and I were with him; and we had the sorrowful satisfaction of giving him Christian burial.

More than one half of the force is now frostbitten or wounded; and most of the men can scarcely put a foot to the ground.

This is the fourth day that our cattle have had no food; and the men are starved with cold and hunger.

Reports are prevalent in camp that the Irregular Cavalry, and the Envoy's escort, are about to desert to Mahommed Akbar Khan; and also that the Affghans are tampering with our Sipahees to leave us and return to Cabul. The Subadar Major of the 37th N. I. has deserted: he was a Subadar Bahakur of the order of British India.

Shortly after Pottinger, Mackenzie, and Lawrence arrived at the Khoord Cabul fort with the Sirdar, he turned to Lawrence and said that he had a proposal to make, but that he did not like to do so lest his motives might be misconstrued;

but that, as it concerned us more than himself, he would mention it; and that it was, that all the married men, with their families, should come over and put themselves under his protection, he gauranteeing them honourable treatment, and safe escort to Peshawer. He added, that Lawrence must have seen from the events of the day previous — the loss of Capt. Boyd's and Capt. Anderson's children, &c. — that our camp was no place of safety for the ladies and children. Lawrence replied, that he considered the proposition a most admirable one; and, Skinner coming in just then, he repeated what had passed to him, who replied, " This is just what I was thinking of suggesting." On which Lawrence begged he would go off and get the General's sanction, and bring them all without delay. Major Pottinger concurred entirely in the expediency of this measure.

Our present position is one of imminent peril. Immediately on Skinner's arrival about mid-day, we set off escorted by some chiefs to a fort about two miles distant, where Mahommed Akbar Khan had taken up his temporary residence. Capt. Troup, Brigade-major to the Shah's force, who was wounded, accompanied the party, as did also Mr. Mein of the 13th, who, having been sent back with a year's sick-leave to Cabul, after he was wounded in October, followed Mrs. Sturt's and my fortunes, not being attached to any corps, nor having any duty to perform.

There can be little doubt but that the proposition was acceded to by the General in the twofold hope of placing the ladies and children beyond the dangers and dreadful privations of the camp, and also of showing the Sirdar that he was sincere in his wish to negotiate a truce, and thus win from him a similar feeling of confidence.

Overwhelmed with domestic affliction, neither Mrs. Sturt nor I were in a fit state to decide for ourselves whether we would accept the Sirdar's protection or not. There was but faint hope of our ever getting safe to Jellalabad; and we followed the stream. But although there was much talk regarding our going over, all I personally know of the affair is, that I was told we were all to go, and that our horses were ready, and we must mount immediately and be off.

We were taken by a very circuitous route to the Khoord Cabul forts, where we found Mahommed Akbar Khan, and the hostages. Mr. Boyd's little boy had been brought there, and was restored to his parents. Mrs. Burnes and young Stoker were also saved, and joined our party. Anderson's little girl is said to have been taken to Cabul, to the Nawaub Zeman Shah Khan.

Three rooms were cleared out for us, having no

outlets except a small door to each; and of course they were dark and dirty. The party to which I belonged consisted of Mrs. Trevor and seven children, Lieut. and Mrs. Waller and child, Mrs. Sturt, Mr. Mein, and myself, Mrs. Smith and Mrs. Burnes, two soldiers' wives, and young Stoker, child of a soldier of the 13th, who was saved from people who were carrying him off to the hills, and came in covered, we fear, with his mother's blood: of her we have no account, nor of Mrs. Cunningham, both of the 13th. The dimensions of our room are at the utmost fourteen feet by ten.

At midnight some mutton bones and greasy rice were brought to us.

All that Mrs. Sturt and I possess are the clothes on our backs in which we quitted Cabul.

Here I must divide the account. I shall go on with my own personal adventures; and afterwards, from the same date, follow up the fortunes of our unhappy army, from the journals of friends who, thank God! have lived through all their sufferings.

10*th.* — Mahommed Akbar Khan left us, to escort our troops. 500 deserters are said to have come in to him. It is reported that the thieves have nearly exterminated our force; and that four of Mahommed Akbar's sirdars are killed. Akbar is expected back at night; and if the road is clear, we are to march at night and go thirty miles. Some officers are said to have taken refuge in a fort near this place. A letter came from the General, stating that he wished Capt. Anderson and Capt. Boyd to return: this was in consequence of a representation made to him that Anderson's making over the command of his corps to Lieut. Le Geyt, and going away, might have a bad effect on his men, who now showed symptoms of an inclination to leave us to our fate. But it was decided by the politicals that for those officers to return would have the appearance of their faith in the Sirdar's promises being shaken, and that it would be productive of much evil: they remained therefore with us. Here was another instance of the General's vacillation. Anderson, on his return from taking the message to bring the troops back, was ordered by the General to go off with the other married men and families. Whatever may have been his own sentiments on the occasion, his opinion was never asked; and he had but to obey.

11*th*.—We marched; being necessitated to leave all the servants that could not walk, the Sirdar promising that they should be fed. It would be impossible for me to describe the feelings with which we pursued our way through the dreadful scenes that awaited us. The road covered with awfully mangled bodies, all naked: fifty-eight Europeans were counted in the Tunghee and dip of the Nullah; the natives innumerable. Numbers of camp followers, still alive, frost-bitten and starving; some perfectly out of their senses and idiotic. Major Ewart, 54th, and Major Scott, 44th, were recognised as we passed them; with some others. The sight was dreadful; the smell of the blood sickening; and the corpses lay so thick it was impossible to look from them, as it required care to guide my horse so as not to tread upon the bodies: but it is unnecessary to dwell on such a distressing and revolting subject.

We hear that Mahommed Abkar Khan offered to escort the army down, provided the troops laid down their arms; but that the General went on, upon his own responsibility.

We arrived at the Tézeen fort, where we were well treated; and where we found Lieut. Melville, 54th. He had, in guarding the colour of his regiment, received five severe wounds. He had fortunately seven rupees about him; these he gave to an Affghan to take him to the Sirdar, who dressed his wounds with his own hands, applying burnt rags; and paid him every attention.

12*th*. — We went to Seh Baba; and thence

out of the road, following the bed of the river, to Abdoollah Khan's fort. We passed our last gun, abandoned, with poor Dr. Cardew's body lying on it, and three Europeans close by it.

During the march, we were joined by Mr. Magrath, surgeon of the 37th N. I., and six men of the 44th. He had been wounded and taken prisoner on the 10th, whilst endeavouring to rally a party of some forty or fifty irregular cavalry, and bring them to the assistance of the unfortunate wounded men, who were being butchered at the bottom of the Huft Kohtul. On his coming up with this party, and again ordering them to halt, to his great disgust he found Khoda Bukh Khan, a Ghilzye chief, amongst them; to whom they were apologising for not having gone over the day previous, as their comrades had done. Mr. Magrath had several narrow escapes; and, when surrounded by Ghilzye footmen with their long knives drawn, owed his life in a great measure to an Affghan horseman, who recognised him as having shown some little kindness to some of his sick friends at Cabul.

At night we had snow.

Our whole party, ladies and gentlemen, crammed into one room; one side of which was partitioned off with mats and filled with grain. Here an old woman cooked chupatties for us, three for a rupee; but, finding the demand great, she soon raised the price to a rupee each.

13th.—We travelled over mountain paths, where the camels found it difficult to get on with the kajavas, till we arrived at Jugdaluk: near the Ghavoy there had been fearful slaughter, principally of Europeans.

We found Gen. Elphinstone, Brig. Shelton, and Capt. Johnson here in tents.

Having brought our party safe to Jugdaluk, I now return to the proceedings of our unfortunate army; taking up the tale at the period when the ladies and their party took protection. On the 9th a round Affghan tent was pitched for the ladies; and we felt the courtesy of the sirdars, who slept in the open air to give us shelter, even such as it was, for the wind blew in in every direction.

Immediately after our departure the irregular horse, with the exception of about eighty men, went over in a body to the Sirdar; and as they were afterwards seen in company with a body of Affghan horse at about a mile distance, there was an attack from them apprehended: all was consternation. Several of our Sipahees absented themselves during the day, also a number of camp followers. A message was sent to Mahommed Akbar Khan, and a hope expressed that he would not favour the desertion of the troops; and he promised that all going over to him should be shot, which was immediately made known to the men. One of the Mission chuprassies was caught in the act of going off, and shot.

Lieut. Mackay, assistant to Capt. Johnson, was sent in the afternoon to the Sirdar (to the fort where the ladies were), for the purpose of being the bearer of a letter to Gen. Sale at Jellalabad, to order him to evacuate his position. This letter was written by Major Pottinger.

All the dhooley bearers either deserted or were murdered the first day.

The whole of the camels and yaboos have been either taken by the enemy or plundered by our no less lawless camp followers and soldiers.

The greatest confusion prevailed all day; and anxiety and suspense for the ultimate fate of the army was intense; all expecting that if in a few hours they were not deprived of life by cold and hunger, they would fall by the knives of the Affghans; which, had they been then attacked, must indubitably have occurred; for on the return of the troops after their set-out in the morning, commanding officers had great difficulty in collecting sixty files a corps: but even of these many could scarcely hold a musket; many died of cold and misery that night. To add to their wretchedness, many were nearly, and some wholly, afflicted with snow blindness.

10th. — No sooner was it light than the usual rush to the front was made by the mixed rabble of camp followers, Sipahees, and Europeans in one huge mass. Hundreds of poor wretches, unable to seize any animals for themselves, or despoiled by stronger persons of those they had, were left on the road to die or be butchered.

After much exertion, the advance, consisting of the 44th, the only remaining six-pounder, and about fifty files of the 5th cavalry, managed to get ahead of the crowd. The Affghans were appearing on the hills early: on arriving at the Tunghee Tareekee, a narrow gorge about ten feet wide and two miles distant from their last ground, Capt. Johnson was sent with the advance; the heights were taken possession of by the enemy; who fired down incessantly on the road, from which they were inaccessible. The snow increased in depth as the army advanced. There is a gradual ascent all the way from Khoord Cabul to Kubber-i-Jubhar, a distance of five miles; the progress was necessarily slow, and many poor fellows were shot.

After getting through the pass, not above fifty yards in length, they proceeded to Kubber-i-Jubhar; where they halted for their comrades.

Latterly no Affghans had been seen, except at a distance; the horror of our people was therefore the greater when a few stragglers from the rear came up, and reported themselves as the remnant of the rear column, almost every man of which had been either killed or wounded: Capt. Hopkins had his arm broken by a musket ball. There was now not a single Sipahee left of the whole Cabul force.

A desperate attack had been made by a body of Affghans, sword in hand: our men made no resistance, but threw away their arms and accoutrements; and fell an easy prey to our barbarous and bloodthirsty foe.

The rear-guard was composed of the 54th regiment. On arriving at the narrow pass called Tunghee Tareekee, or "the dark pass," a turn in the road shut out from their sight the enemy, who had followed close on their heels, but on whom they had received strict orders not to fire; although the Ghilzyes, from the heights and ravines, had kept up a sharp discharge, killing many Sipahees and camp followers, and cutting up all wounded and sick left behind. On arriving at the above-mentioned pass, the turn in the road allowed the Ghilzyes to close up; and a general attack was made on all sides: hundreds of Affghans rushing down from the rocks and hills cut to pieces their now reduced regiment. Here Major Ewart, commanding 54th, had both his arms broken by bullets from the Juzails; Lieut. Morrieson, the adjutant, was wounded; and Lieut. Weaver, of the same corps, slightly. Lieut. Melville, on observing the Jemadar, who carried the regiment's colour, wounded and dropping his charge, seized it; and, after vainly attempting to tear it off the staff, to which it was too firmly attached, made his way on foot (his horse having been killed), with the colour in his hand. This made him a mark for the enemy; and ere he had got out of the pass, being nearly, or quite, the last man of the column, or rather rabble, he received a spear wound in his back, which threw him on his face: ere well able to rise, a severe sword-cut in the head again laid him prostrate; but he contrived to crawl as far as the fast retreating column; when again the knife of an Affghan wounding him in the neck, and a spear in the chin, he gave up all for lost. He was now surrounded by a dozen Ghilzyes; and no man, save the dead and dying, near him; when the enemy, observing a box of treasure on the opposite side of the pass, left him, for the purpose of rifling the money, either supposing they had already killed him, or intending to return when they had secured the more valuable booty. This pause gave Lieut. Melville an opportunity of escaping and regaining the column; which, although weak from his wounds, he availed himself of; and by going through the snow in the ravines, he contrived to reach the column; where a pony without an owner, or saddle of any description, presenting itself, he scrambled on to it; and, with the assistance of a Mehter, gained the centre of the column, where the 44th and one gun still kept some order. Lieut. Melville was tied on the gun, and was told by Gen. Elphinstone, that he should be sent over to the charge of the Sirdar, Mahommed Akbar Khan, on reaching Tézeen, or at any opportunity of going.

On a report of a large body of horse being observed in the rear, the gun was ordered there; and Lieut. Melville was placed on a bank on the road-side. The column passed on; and he was expecting the fate of the other poor fellows who had fallen; when, providentially for him, a horseman rode up, who had known him in cantonments, and who strapped him on his horse, and took him over to the party of horsemen, consisting of Mahommed Akbar Khan and his followers; who received him most kindly, and, binding up his wounds, gave him a loonghee, his regimental cap being cut to pieces.

The loonghee is the cloth worn as a turban

commonly by the Affghans, and is generally of blue check with a red border: those worn by the Khyberries are much gayer, and have a large admixture of yellow.

Melville gave to Omer Khan, the horseman who saved his life, seven rupees, being all the property he possessed.

Every particle of baggage was gone.

The small remnant of the army consisted of about seventy files of the 44th, fifty of the 5th cavalry, and 1 six-pounder gun. Observing a body of cavalry in their rear, they determined to bring their solitary gun into position, and make a last effort for existence. Finding it was again Mahommed Akbar Khan, Capt. Skinner (Assist.-Com.-Gen.) by direction of the General, went over, under escort, to him; to remonstrate on the attack made on our troops after a treaty had been entered into for our protection. He replied, he regretted it, he could not control the Ghilzyes (the inhabitants of this part of the country) with his small body of horse, about 300; but that as the remnant of our troops was merely a few Europeans, he would guarantee their safety, and that of all the European officers, to Jellalabad, if the General would conduct them all disarmed, whilst the Affghans were to have the use of their weapons. He said his motives for this were, that should they bring their arms with them, his own followers would be afraid of treachery. To this proposition the General would not assent.

Mackay returned with Skinner from the Sirdar, as the road to Jellalabad was said to be unsafe.

The troops continued their fearful march: the remnant of the camp followers, with several wounded officers, went ahead: for five miles they saw no enemy: all who could not walk were necessarily left behind. They descended a long steep descent to the bed of the Tézeen Nullah. At this dip the scene was horrible: the ground was covered with dead and dying, amongst whom were several officers: they had been suddenly attacked and overpowered. The enemy here crowded from the tops of the hills in all directions down the bed of the Nullah, through which the route lay for three miles; and our men continued their progress through an incessant fire from the heights on both sides, until their arrival in the Tézeen valley, at about half-past four P. M.

The descent from the Huft Kohtul was about 2000 feet; and here they lost the snow.

About 12,000 persons have perished!

A quarter of an hour after their arrival, the Sirdar and a party came into the valley to a fort higher up belonging to his father-in-law, Mahommed Shah Khan. A signal was made to his horsemen to approach: two came, and Capt. Skinner, by the General's desire, accompanied them to Mahommed Akbar Khan, to devise some means of saving the remnant — about 4,000 people of all descriptions.

Skinner returned at dusk; and brought back the same message as from Kubber-i-Jubhar, regarding disarming the Europeans: and again this was refused.

The General then decided, weak and famished as the troops were, and without any prospect of procuring provisions at Tézeen, to march at seven in the evening (they had left Khoord Cabul, fifteen miles from Tézeen, half-past six A. M.), and proceed, if possible, through the Jugdaluk pass by eight or nine the next morning. In this consisted their only chance of safety; for, should the enemy obtain intimation of their approach, the pass would be occupied, and the object defeated. Johnson pointed out to the General that Mahommed Akbar Khan and his party could, by means of a short cut across the mountains, start long after them, and arrive before them, ready to oppose them.

Jugdaluk is about twenty-four miles from Tézeen; the pass about two miles long, very narrow, and commanded on both sides by high and precipitous hills.

At Tézeen Gen. Elphinstone received a note in cypher from Capt. Conolly, warning him that Mahommed Akbar Khan had quitted Cabul, with the avowed intention of getting into his hands the person of the General, and all the married people with their families.

A message was sent to Mahommed Akbar Khan that they were going to march to Seh Baba, seven miles from Tézeen (this place is sometimes called Tukeea-i-Fakeer): the road lies down the bed of a Nullah, with high hills on either side. The place is only remarkable from having a few trees and a grave or two under them; and from the latter I believe it takes its name.

The camp followers having been the bane of this unfortunate army, they hoped to move off quietly and leave them behind; but no sooner did they start, than they found that all who were able to stand were accompanying them. They left their remaining gun behind; and Dr. Cardew, who was mortally wounded at the dip into the Tézeen Nullah, was laid on the carriage to await death, which was rapidly approaching: he was found dead by Mahommed Akbar's people the next morning.

The night was fine and moonlit, and they reached Seh Baba about midnight; here a few shots were fired on them; and the rear being attacked, the whole remains of the 44th, with the exception of about nine files to form the advance, were ordered there; and thus the column remained until their arrival at Jugdaluk; their progress being again impeded by that evil which always attends Indian armies, the camp followers; who, if a shot is fired in advance, invariably fall back; and if in rear, rush to the front.

11*th*.— From Seh Baba the road turns off sharp to the right over the mountains to Jugdaluk; and across the Nullah is seen the short road to Cabul, but which cannot be travelled by guns or camels.

At Seh Baba Dr. Duff (the Surgeon-General to the forces in Affghanistan), who had had his hand cut off with a penknife at Tézeen, in consequence of a severe wound, was from weakness obliged to lag behind, and was two days afterwards found murdered.

Bareekub is three miles from Seh Baba: there is a clear stream of water, and several caves cut in the rocks. Here our force observed a number of people in the caves; with whom they did not interfere, as they did not molest them. They eventually fired some volleys on the rear.

At day-break the advance arrived at Killa Sung, about seven miles from Seh Baba, where there are some streams of water: this is the general encamping ground, though very confined, and commanded by hills all round.

They proceeded about half a mile further on, and then halted, until the rear-guard should arrive; but they, having been much molested on the road, did not arrive for two hours. On their first arrival not an Affghan was to be seen; but shortly several made their appearance on the hills, and the number continued every moment to increase. Not a drop of water was procurable; nor would they get any until their arrival at Jugdaluk. They had marched for twenty-four hours consecutively, and had still ten miles to go before they could hope for rest. On being joined by the rear-guard they continued their march; the enemy in small numbers watching every opportunity to murder stragglers from the column.

At two miles from Jugdaluk the descent into the valley commences.

The hills on each side of the road were occupied by the enemy, who kept firing from their long juzails; and again the road was covered with dead and dying, as they were in such a mass that every shot told.

On arrival in the valley, a position was taken up on the first height near some ruined walls. As scarcely any Europeans of the advance now remained, and the enemy were increasing, the General called all the officers (about twenty) to form line and show a front: they had scarcely done so when Capt. Grant, Assistant-Adjutant-General, received a ball through the cheek which broke his jaw.

On the arrival of the rear-guard, followed up by the enemy, the latter took possession of two heights close to our position: on which our force went for security within the ruined walls. The men were almost maddened with hunger and thirst: a stream of pure water ran within 150 yards of the position, but no man could go for it without being massacred.

For about half an hour they had a respite from the fire of the enemy, who now only watched their proceedings.

The General desired Johnson to see if there were any bullocks or camels procurable amongst the followers: he obtained three bullocks, which were killed, served out, and devoured instantly, although raw, by the Europeans.

A few horsemen coming in sight, they signed for one to approach: he did so, and on being questioned what chief was present, said Mahommed Akbar Khan. A message was sent to the Sirdar by the General to know why they were again molested: the chief replied, he wished to converse with Skinner, who immediately accompanied the messenger. This was about half past three P. M. of the 11th.

After marching for thirty hours they lay down on the ground worn out by cold, hunger, thirst, and fatigue: but scarcely had Skinner taken his departure, when volley after volley was poured into the enclosure where they were resting. All was instant confusion, and a general rush took place outside the walls; men and cattle all huddled together, each striving to hide himself from the murderous fire of the enemy.

At this time twenty gallant men of the 44th made a simultaneous rush down the hill, to drive the enemy off the heights they occupied: in this they were successful; for, supposing they were followed by the rest, the foe took to flight ere our men could reach their position.

In about a quarter of an hour, as so small a party would not admit of any division, this party was recalled. They again entered within the broken walls; and instantly our inveterate foes were in their former position dealing death amongst them.

About 5 o'clock Skinner returned with a message that the Sirdar wished to see the General, Brig. Shelton, and Johnson; and if they would go over to confer with him, he would engage to put a stop to any further massacre, and also to give food to our troops: and on condition of their remaining with him as hostages for Gen. Sale's evacuation of Jellalabad, he would escort all the small remaining party in safety.

Mahommed Shah Khan, father-in-law to the Sirdar, and whose daughter is with the Dost at Loodianah, is one of the principal Ghilzye chiefs: he came at dusk with an escort to receive them; and they started in the confident hope that some arrangement would be entered into to save the lives of the remainder of the army. The General and the above-mentioned officers proceeded to the top of the valley for about two miles, and found the Sirdar and his party in bivouac: nothing could exceed the kind manner in which they were received. The chief, on hearing they had not tasted food for forty-eight hours, had a cloth spread on the ground; and a good pillau and other dishes, as also tea, were quickly brought; and they formed a circle round it, and all ate out of the same dish.

Their hunger, though great, was not to be compared to their thirst, which had not been quenched for two days.

The party consisted of the Sirdar, Mahommed Akbar Khan, Mahommed Shah Khan, Abdool Ghyas Khan (son of Jubhar Khan), and a young lad called Abdool Hakeem Khan, nephew to the Sirdar. The attention of the Sirdar and his party was excessive; and after dinner they sat round a blazing fire, and conversed on various subjects. The General requested that Mahommed Akbar Khan would early in the morning forward provisions to the troops, and make arrangements for supplying them with water: all which he faithfully promised to do.

The General was anxious for permission to return to his troops; and offered to send Brig. Anquetil, should the Sirdar require an officer in his stead. Johnson, by the General's desire, pointed out to the Sirdar the stigma that would attach to him as commander of the force, were he to remain in a place of comparative security, whilst such danger impended over the troops. To this the Sirdar would not consent. At about 11 P. M., the Sirdar promised he would early in the morning call the chiefs of the pass together, to make arrangements for a safe escort: he then showed them into a small tent, where, stretched on their cloaks, they found relief in sleep.

Our unfortunate force at Jugdaluk this day consisted of 150 men of the 44th; 16 dismounted horse artillery men; 25 of the 5th cavalry. Not a single Sipahee with arms, no spare ammunition, and the few rounds in pouch had been taken from the killed.

12th.—The English officers arose at sunrise, and found the Sirdar and his party were up. They showed them the same civility as over night; two confidential servants of the chief were appointed to wait on them; and they were warned not to attempt to leave the tent without one of these men, lest they should be maltreated or insulted by the Ghilzyes, who were flocking in to pay their respects to Mahommed Akbar.

About 9 A. M., the chiefs of the pass and the country around Soorkhab arrived. Soorkhab is about thirteen miles from Jugdaluk, towards Jellalabad, and is the usual halting ground.

The chiefs sat down to discuss affairs. They were bitter in their hatred towards us; and declared that nothing would satisfy them and their men, but our extermination. Money they would not receive. The Sirdar, as far as words could prove his sincerity, did all in his power to conciliate them; and, when all other arguments failed, reminded them that his father and family were in the power of the British government at Loodianah; and that vengeance would be taken on the latter if mercy were not showed to the British in their power.

Mahommed Shah Khan offered them 60,000 rupees on condition of our force not being molested. After some time they took their departure to consult with their followers; and Mahommed Shah Khan mentioned to Johnson that he feared the chiefs would not, without some great inducement, resist the temptation of plunder and murder that now offered itself: and wound up the discourse by asking if we would give them two lakhs of rupees for a free passage. On this being explained to the General, he gave his consent; and it was made known to Mahommed Shah Khan, who went away and promised to return quickly.

The General again begged of the Sirdar to permit him to return to his troops; but without avail.

Johnson, by the General's desire, wrote early in the day to Skinner, to come to the Sirdar. This letter and two others, it is to be feared, he never received. A report was brought in that Skinner was wounded, but not dangerously; the Sirdar expressed much sorrow; poor Skinner died of his wound the same day.

Until 12 o'clock crowds of Ghilzyes with their respective chiefs, continued to pour in from the surrounding country to make their salaams to Mahommed Akbar Khan, to participate in the plunder of our unfortunate people, and to revel in the massacre of the Europeans. From their expressions of hatred towards our whole race, they appeared to anticipate more delight in cutting our throats than in the expected booty. However, on a hint from the Sirdar, they changed the language, in which they conversed, from Persian to Pushtoo, which was not understood by our officers.

The Sirdar, to all appearance, whilst sitting with Johnson, endeavoured to conciliate them; but it very probably was only done as a blind to hide his real feelings.

In two instances, the reply of the chiefs was,— " When Burnes came into this country, was not your father entreated by us to kill him; or he would go back to Hindostan, and at some future day bring an army and take our country from us? He would not listen to our advice, and what is the consequence? Let us now, that we have the opportunity, take advantage of it; and kill those infidel dogs."

At about 12, the Sirdar left them, and went on the top of a hill in rear of the British bivouac. He did not return till sunset; and in reply to the anxious inquiry when Mahommed Shan Khan would return, they were always told immediately. Frequent assurances had been given that the troops had been supplied with food and water; but subsequently they learnt that neither had been given them in their dire necessity.

The Sirdar returned at dusk; and was soon followed by Mahommed Shah Khan, who brought intelligence that all was finally and amicably arranged for the safe conduct of the troops to Jellalabad. The Sirdar said he would accompany them in the morning early. By the General's request, Johnson wrote to Brig. Anquetil to have the troops in readiness to march by 8 o'clock: he had also commenced a letter to Gen. Sale to evacuate Jellalabad (this being part of the terms). Suddenly, and before the first note was sent off, much musketry was heard down the valley in the direction of the troops; and a report was brought in that the Europeans were moving off through the pass followed by the Ghilzyes. All was consternation. At first the Sirdar suggested that he and the officers should follow them: in this the General concurred. In a few minutes the Sirdar changed his mind; said he feared their doing so would injure the troops, by bringing after them the whole horde of Ghilzyes then assembled in the valley. He promised to send a confidential servant to Meer Afzul Khan at Gundamuk (two miles beyond Soorkhab) to afford them protection; and agreed to start with them at midnight, as being mounted they would overtake the others before daybreak. When about to separate for the night, the Sirdar again altered the time of departure to the first hour of daylight. Remonstrances were of no avail; and our party were too completely in the power of the enemy, to persist in what they had not the power to enforce.

Mahommed Akbar Khan told Johnson, after Mahommed Shah Khan went out to consult with the chiefs of the pass, that the latter were dogs and no faith could be placed in them; and begged Johnson would send for three or four of his most intimate friends, that their lives might be saved in the event of treachery to the troops. Gladly as he would have saved his individual friends, he was under the necessity of explaining to the Sirdar that a sense of honour would prevent the officers deserting their men at a time of such imminent peril. The Sirdar also proposed, that in the event of the Ghilzyes not acceding to the terms, he would himself, at dusk, proceed with a party of horsemen to the foot of the hill where our troops were; and, previous orders being sent to the commanding officer for all to be ready, he would bring every European away in safety, by each of his horsemen taking up one behind him: the Ghilzyes would not then fire upon them, lest they should hit him or his men. But he would not allow a single Hindostanee to follow; as he could not protect 2000 men (the computed number).—Johnson interpreted all this to the General: but it was deemed impracticable; as from past experience they knew how impossible it was even to separate the Sipahees from the camp followers. Four or five times during the day they heard the report of musketry in the direction of our troops; but they were always told that all fighting had ceased. This was subsequently proved to be a gross falsehood. Our troops were incessantly fired upon from the time that the General and the other officers quitted them to the time of their departure, and several hundreds of officers and men had been killed or wounded. The remainder, maddened with cold, hunger, and thirst, the communication between them and the General cut off, and seeing no prospect but certain death before them by remaining in their present position, determined on making one desperate effort to leave Jugdaluk. Snow fell during the night.

My narrative now continues from information furnished by a friend remaining with the remnant of this ill-fated army.— They halted this day at Jugdaluk, hoping to negotiate an arrangement with Mahommed Akbar Khan and the Ghilzye chiefs, as before stated: but the continual firing, and frequent attempts made by the enemy to force them from their position during the day, but too well indicated that there was little or no chance of negotiations being effectual to quell hostilities, and admit of their resuming their march in safety:

on the contrary, there appeared an evident determination still to harass their retreat to the very last.

Near the close of the day the enemy commenced a furious attack from all sides. The situation of our troops at this time was critical in the extreme: the loss they sustained in men and officers had been great during the day, and the survivors had only been able to obtain a scanty meal of camel's flesh: even water was not procurable without the parties proceeding for it being exposed to a heavy fire. The men, under all this suffering, perishing with cold at their post, bravely repelled the enemy; and would then have followed them from under the dilapidated walls had they been permitted to do so. During this conflict Capt. Souter of the 44th, anxious to save the colours of his regiment, tore one of them from its staff, and folding it round his person, concealed it under the poshteen he wore: the other was in like manner appropriated by Lieut. Cumberland; but finding that he could not close his pea-coat over it, he reluctantly entrusted it to the care of the Acting Quartermaster-Sergeant of the 44th regiment.

Great anxiety prevailed amongst the troops, caused by the continued absence of Gen. Elphinstone and Brigadier Shelton, the two seniors in command. It was resolved, as they did not return, to resume their march as soon as the night should shroud them from observation; and Brig. Anquetil, now in command, ordered the troops to fall in at eight o'clock: but before the men could take the places assigned to them, the camp followers, who were still numerous, crowded upon them as usual. At length between 8 and 9 o'clock they took their departure; which was rendered a very trying scene, from the entreaties of the wounded, amounting to seventy or eighty, for whom there was no conveyance; and therefore, however heartrending to all, they were necessarily abandoned, with the painful conviction that they would be massacred in cold blood, defenceless as they were, by the first party of Ghilzyes that arrived.

The enemy, who seem to have been aware of the intended removal, soon commenced an attack upon the straggling camp followers: and a number of Affghans, favoured by the darkness of the night, stole in amongst the followers that were in column, whom they quietly despatched, and proceeded to plunder. These daring men, however, were nearly all cut up or bayonetted by the enraged soldiery; who shortly after came upon an encampment of the enemy; in passing which they were saluted with a heavy fire, followed up by a sally upon the camp followers, as usual.

They proceeded on until they came to a gorge, with low steep hills on either side, between which the road passed, about two miles from Jugdaluk. Here two barriers had been thrown across the road, constructed of bushes and branches of trees. The road, which had been flooded, was a mass of ice, and the snow on the hills very deep. The enemy, who had waited for them in great force at this spot, rushed upon the column, knife in hand. The camp followers and wounded men fell back upon the handful of troops for protection; thus rendering them powerless, and causing the greatest confusion; whilst the men, in small detached parties, were maintaining conflicts with fearful odds against them.

In this conflict the Acting Quartermaster-Sergeant fell: and in the confusion, caused by an overwhelming enemy pressing on the rear in a night attack, it is not surprising that it was found impossible to extricate the colour from the body of the fallen man; and its loss was unavoidable. The disorder of the troops was increased by a part of them, the few remaining horsemen, galloping through and over the infantry in hopes of securing their own retreat to Jellalabad. The men, maddened at being ridden over, fired on them; and it is said that some officers were fired at; but that rests on doubtful testimony. When the firing slackened, and the clashing of knives and bayonets had in some measure ceased, the men moved on slowly; and on arriving at the top of the gorge were able to ascertain the fearful extent of the loss they had sustained in men and officers. Of the latter Brigadier Anquetil and above twenty others were missing. The troops now halted unmolested for an hour; during which time a few stragglers contrived to join them.

The country being now of a more open description, our small force suffered less annoyance from the fire of the enemy: but the determination of the men to bring on their wounded comrades greatly retarded their marching; and from the troopers having proceeded onwards the wounded could not be mounted behind them: thus their pace did not exceed two miles in the hour. From time to time sudden attacks were made on the rear; particularly in spots where the road wound close under the foot of the hills, and there a sharp fire was sure to be met with. In this manner they went on till they reached the Soorkhab river, which they forded below the bridge at 1 A.M. on the 13th, being aware that the enemy would take possession of it, and dispute the passage. Whilst fording the river a galling fire was kept up from the bridge: here Lieut. Cadett of the 44th and several men were killed and wounded.

13*th.* — From Soorkhab the remnant of the column moved towards Gundamuk: but as the day dawned the enemy's numbers increased; and unfortunately daylight soon exposed to them how very few fighting men the column contained. The force now consisted of twenty officers, of whom Major Griffiths was the senior, fifty men of the 44th, six of the horse artillery, and four or five Sipahees. Amongst the whole there were but twenty muskets; 300 camp followers still continued with them.

Being now assailed by an increased force, they were compelled to quit the road, and take up a position on a hill adjoining. Some Affghan horsemen being observed at a short distance were beckoned to. On their approach there was a cessation of firing: terms were proposed by Capt. Hay, to allow the force to proceed without further hostilities to Jellalabad. These persons not being sufficiently influential to negotiate, Major Griffiths proceeded with them to a neighbouring chief for that purpose; taking with him Mr. Blewitt, formerly a writer in Capt. Johnson's office, who understood Persian, that he might act as interpreter.

Many Affghans ascended the hill where our troops awaited the issue of the expected conference; and exchanges of friendly words passed between both parties. This lasted upwards of an hour; but hostilities were renewed by the Affghans, who snatched at the fire-arms of the men and officers. This they of course resisted; and drove them off the hill: but the majority of the enemy, who occupied the adjoining hills commanding our position, commenced a galling fire upon us. Several times they attempted to dislodge our men from the hill, and were repulsed: until, our ammunition being expended, and our fighting men reduced to about thirty, the enemy made a rush, which in our weak state we were unable to cope with. They bore our men down knife in hand; and slaughtered all the party except Capt. Souter and seven or eight men of the 44th and artillery. This officer thinks that this unusual act of forbearance towards him originated in the strange dress he wore: his poshteen having opened during the last struggle exposed to view the colour he had wrapped round his body; and they probably thought they had secured a valuable prize in some great bahadur, for whom a large ransom might be obtained.

Eighteen officers and about fifty men were killed at the final struggle at Gundamuk. Capt. Souter and the few remaining men (seven or eight) that were taken alive from the field were, after a detention of a month in the adjoining villages, made over to Mahommed Akbar Khan and sent to the fort of Buddeeabad in the Lughman valley, where they arrived on the 15th of February.

THE CAPTIVITY.

We must now return to the General and his party. At daybreak on the 13th the Sirdar had again changed his mind; and instead of following up the troops, he decided to move to the position they had vacated, and remain there during the day; and should the ladies and officers left at Khoord Cabul arrive in the evening, that all should start the next morning over the mountains to the valley of Lughman, north of Jellalabad. At 8 A. M., they mounted their horses; and with the Sirdar and his party rode down the pass, which bore fearful evidence to the last night's struggle. They passed some 200 dead bodies, many of them Europeans; the whole naked, and covered with large gaping wounds. As the day advanced, several poor wretches of Hindostanees (camp followers, who had escaped the massacre of the night before) made their appearance from behind rocks and within caves, where they had taken shelter from the murderous knives of the Affghans and the inclemency of the climate.

They had been stripped of all they possessed; and few could crawl more than a few yards, being frostbitten in the feet. Here Johnson found two of his servants: the one had his hands and feet frostbitten, and had a fearful sword cut across one hand, and a musket ball in his stomach; the other had his right arm completely cut through the bone. Both were utterly destitute of covering, and had not tasted food for five days.

This suffices for a sample of the sufferings of the survivors.

About four o'clock Sultan Jan (a cousin of the Sirdar) arrived with the ladies and gentlemen; also Lieut. Melville of the 54th, and Mr. Magrath, surgeon of the 37th, both of whom had been wounded between Khoord Cabul and Tézeen. A large party of cavalry accompanied Sultan Jan, both Affghan and our irregular horse, who had deserted, as before mentioned.

14*th*. — We marched twenty-four miles to Kutz-i-Mahommed Ali Khan: started at about 9 A.M.; the Sirdar with Gen. Elphinstone; Brig. Shelton, and Capt. Johnson bringing up the rear.

We travelled over a dreadfully rough road: some of the ascents and descents were fearful to look at, and at first sight appeared to be impracticable. The whole road was a continuation of rocks and stones, over which the camels had great

THE CAPTIVITY.

difficulty in making their way; and particularly in the ascent of the Adrak-Budrak pass, where I found it requisite to hold tight on by the mane, lest the saddle and I should slip off together.

Had we travelled under happier auspices, I should probably have been foolish enough to have expressed fear, not having even a saces to assist me. Still I could not but admire the romantic tortuous defile we passed through, being the bed of a mountain torrent, which we exchanged for the terrific pass I have mentioned, and which was rendered doubly fearful by constant stoppages from those in front, which appeared to take place at the most difficult spots.

At the commencement of the defile, and for some considerable distance, we passed 200 or 300 of our miserable Hindostanees, who had escaped up the unfrequented road from the massacre of the 12th. They were all naked, and more or less frostbitten: wounded, and starving, they had set fire to the bushes and grass, and huddled all together to impart warmth to each other. Subsequently we heard that scarcely any of these poor wretches escaped from the defile: and that driven to the extreme of hunger they had sustained life by feeding on their dead comrades.

The wind blew bitterly cold at our bivouac; for the inhabitants of the fort refused to take us in;

stating that we were Kaffirs. We therefore rolled ourselves up as warm as we could; and with our saddles for pillows braved the elements. Gen. Elphinstone, Brig. Shelton, and Johnson considered themselves happy when one of the Affghans told them to accompany him into a wretched cowshed, which was filled with dense smoke from a blazing fire in the centre of the hut. These officers and Mr. Melville were shortly after invited by Mahommed Akbar Khan to dine with him and his party in the fort. The reception room was not much better than that they had left: they had, however, a capital dinner, some cups of tea, and luxurious rest at night; the room having been well heated by a blazing fire with plenty of smoke, with no outlet for either heat or smoke, except through the door and a small circular hole in the roof.

15th January.—A bitterly cold wind blowing, we started at 7 A.M.; crossed two branches of the Punjshir river, which was not only deep, but exceedingly rapid. The chiefs gave us every assistance: Mahommed Akbar Khan carried Mrs. Waller over behind him on his own horse. One rode by me to keep my horse's head well up the stream. The Affghans made great exertions to save both men and animals struggling in the water; but in spite of all their endeavours five unfortunates lost their lives. We passed over many ascents and declivities; and at about 3 P. M. arrrived at Tighree, a fortified town in the rich valley of Lughman; having travelled twenty miles over a most barren country, without a blade of grass or drop of water until we approached Tighree. Our route lay along a tract of country considerably higher than Lughman, with scarcely a footpath visible the whole way. The road was good for any kind of carriage. We passed over the Plain of Methusaleh; and saw at a short distance the Kubber-i-Lamech, a celebrated place of pilgrimage, about two miles from Tighree and twenty-five from Jellalabad.

The Sirdar desired the General, the Brigadier, and Johnson to take up their quarters with him, whilst the ladies and the other gentlemen were located in another fort.

A great number of Hindu Bunneahs reside at Tighree. We went to the fort of Gholab Moyenoodeen, who took Mrs. Sturt and myself to the apartments of his mother and wife. Of course we could not understand much that they said; but they evidently made much of us, pitied our condition, told us to ask them for any thing we required, and before parting they gave us a lump of goor filled with pistaches, a sweetmeat they are themselves fond of.

16th. — Halted. They tell us we are here only thirty miles from Jellalabad. It being Sunday, we read prayers from a Bible and Prayer Book that were picked up on the field at Bhoodkhak. The service was scarcely finished when a clannish row commenced. Some tribes from a neighbouring fort who had a blood feud with the chiefs with us came against the fort: a few juzails were fired; there was great talking and noise; and then it was all over.

17th. — Early in the morning we were ordered to prepare to go higher up the valley. Thus all hopes (faint as they were) of going to Jellalabad were annihilated; and we plainly saw that, whatever might be said, we were virtually prisoners, until such time as Sale shall evacuate Jellalabad, or the Dost be permitted by our government to return to this country.

We had a little hail this morning; and shortly after, at about nine o'clock, we started, and travelled along the valley, which was a continuation of forts, until we arrived at Buddeeabad (about eight or nine miles): it is situated almost at the top of the valley, and close to the first range of hills towards Kaffiristan.

Six rooms, forming two sides of an inner square or citadel, are appropriated to us; and a tykhana to the soldiers. This fort is the largest in the valley, and is quite new; it belongs to Mahommed Shah Khan: it has a deep ditch and a faussebraye all round. The walls of mud are not very thick, and are built up with planks in tiers on the inside. The buildings we occupy are those intended for the chief and his favourite wife; those for three other wives are in the outer court, and have not yet been roofed in. We number 9 ladies, 20 gentlemen, and 14 children. In the tykhana are 17 European soldiers, 2 European women, and 1 child (Mrs. Wade, Mrs. Burnes, and little Stoker).

Mahommed Akbar Khan, to our horror, has informed us that only one man of our force has succeeded in reaching Jellalabad (Dr. Brydon of the Shah's force: he was wounded in two places). Thus is verified what we were told before leaving Cabul; " that Mahommed Akbar would annihilate the whole army, except one man, who should reach Jellalabad to tell the tale."

Dost Mahommed Khan (the brother of Mahommed Shah Khan) is to have charge of us. Our parties were divided into the different rooms. Lady Macnaghten, Capt. and Mrs. Anderson and 2 children, Capt. and Mrs. Boyd and 2 children, Mrs. Mainwaring and 1 child, with Lieut. and Mrs. Eyre and 1 child, and a European girl, Hester Macdonald, were in one room; that adjoining was appropriated for their servants and baggage. Capt. Mackenzie and his Madras Christian servant Jacob, Mr. and Mrs. Ryley and 2 children, and Mr. Fallon, a writer in Capt. Johnson's office, occupied another. Mrs. Trevor and her 7 children and European servant, Mrs. Smith, Lieut. and Mrs. Waller and child, Mrs. Sturt, Mr. Mein, and I had another. In two others all the rest of the gentlemen were crammed.

It did not take us much time to arrange our property; consisting of one mattress and resai between us, and no clothes except those we had on, and in which we left Cabul.

Mahommed Akbar Khan, Sultan Jan, and Ghoolam Moyen-oo-deen visited us. The Sirdar assured me we were none of us prisoners; requested that we would make ourselves as comfortable as circumstances would admit of; and told us that as soon as the roads were safe we should be safely escorted to Jellalabad. He further informed me that I might write to Sale; and that any letters I sent to him he would forward. Of this permission I gladly took advantage to write a few guarded lines to say that we were well and safe.

19*th*.—We luxuriated in dressing, although we had no clothes but those on our backs; but we enjoyed washing our faces very much, having had but one opportunity of doing so before, since we left Cabul. It was rather a painful process, as the cold and glare of the sun on the snow had three times peeled my face, from which the skin came off in strips.

We had a grand breakfast, dhall and radishes; the latter large hot ones that had gone to seed, the former is a common pulse eaten by the natives: but any change was good, as we find our chupatties made of the coarse ottah anything but nice. Ottah is what in England is called pollard; and has to be twice sifted ere it becomes flour. The chupatties are cakes formed of this ottah mixed with water, and dried by standing by the fire set up on edge. Eating these cakes of dough is a capital recipe to obtain the heartburn. We parch rice and barley, and make from them a substitute for coffee. Two sheep (alias lambs) are killed daily; and a regular portion of rice and ottah given for all. The Affghans cook; and well may we exclaim with Goldsmith, " God sends meat, but the devil sends cooks; " for we only get some greasy skin and bones served out as they are cooked, boiled in the same pot with the rice, all in a lump. Capt. Lawrence divides it; and portions our food as justly as he can. The chupatty is at once the plate and bread: few possess other dinner-table implements than their fingers. The rice even is rendered nauseous by having quantities of rancid ghee poured over it, such as in India we should have disdained to use for our lamps.

21*st.* — The weather cleared up at noon. Major Pottinger is said to have received information that Zeman Shah Khan and all the Dooranees have surrendered to Shah Shoojah; and that his Majesty was at the bottom of the whole affair to turn us out of Affghanistan.

22*nd.* — I heard from Sale, dated the 19th. Our force can hold out at Jellalabad for six months. It is calculated that Col. Wylde must be at Jellalabad to-day with 5000 men. Gen. Pollock is coming with an army across the Punjab.

We hear that Mahommed Akbar has been offered the Sirdar-i-sirdaranee; but has refused it. He is said to be gone, or going, to the Khyber.

23*rd, Sunday.* — After prayers Mahommed Akbar Khan and Sultan Jan paid us a visit: the latter took charge of a letter from me for Sale. He told me that Abdool Guffoor Khan says that Sale is quite well.

They say that Shah Shoojah demanded Conolly and three other hostages to be given up to him to put them to death; but Zeman Shah Khan refused.

24*th.* — A day or two ago the Sirdar sent some chintz to be divided amongst us. A second quantity was to-day given out; and we are working hard that we may enjoy the luxury of getting on a clean suit of clothes. There are very few of us that are not covered with crawlers; and, although my daughter and I have as yet escaped, we are in fear and trembling.

It is now said that the General gave Anderson's horse permission to go over to the enemy: a circumstance that does not at all agree with his conduct on the day following our taking protection; when he wished for Anderson's return lest the men should desert.

Dost Mahommed Khan took Mrs. Trevor's boys and some of the gentlemen out walking in the sugar-cane fields near the fort, which they enjoyed very much.

25th.—The Sirdar sent eight pieces of long cloth to be divided amongst us. I fancy he is generous at little cost; and that it is all a part of the plunder of our camp. He is said to have received letters from the Khyber stating that our force has been defeated there; two guns taken, and some treasure: and that Mackeson is shut up in Ali Musjid with 300 men.

26th.—As soon as the Bukhraeed is over, Shah Shoojah is to send 4000 men, and all the guns we left in Cabul, against Jellalabad. A Mussulman force is also now at Balabagh.

Mahommed Akbar Khan has had a private conference with Major Pottinger; of which no account has transpired. We had two shocks of earthquake at night.

27*th*.—A report that Sale has made another sally, and has taken a number of prisoners. I heard from him to-day: he has sent me my chest of drawers, with clothes, &c.: they were all permitted to come to me unexamined. I had also an opportunity of writing to him by Abdool Guffoor Khan, who brought them to me. I was rejoiced to see any one I had known before; and especially one who was well inclined towards the English, though nominally on the side of Akbar.

4*th*.—The irregular cavalry have had their horses and everything taken away from them; and have been turned adrift. I wrote to Sale, ut my note did not go.

5*th*.—My note to Sale was sent to-day. I got another from him dated the 29th, and replied to it.

9*th*.—We hear that all our horses are to be taken away; as also our servants. Rain to-day, as if the clouds wept for our misfortunes.

10*th*. — I received boxes from Sale, with many useful things; and also books, which are a great treat to us. I wrote to him, but fear my letter will not reach him, as all notes that came for us

THE CAPTIVITY.

were kept back by the Sirdar; who is very angry, having detected a private cossid between Capt. Macgregor and Major Pottinger: if we behave ill again, the Sirdar says, woe will betide us. Abdool Guffoor again came to see us; and I had again the comfort to hear that Sale was well. We had rain to-day. Major Griffith arrived, with Mr. Blewitt.

Major Griffith tells me, that on the morning of the 13th, at daylight, the miserable remains of the force, reduced to about 100 Europeans of all ranks, including 20 officers, worn out with fatigue and hunger, and encumbered with very many wounded, some on horseback and some on foot, were, when within four miles of the bridge of Gundamuk, surrounded by a considerable number of the enemy both horse and foot. They had only thirty-five muskets and but little ammunition remaining; finding it impossible to proceed further, a position was taken up on a hill to the left of the road; and a parley opened with the enemy by means of waving a white cloth. This produced a cessation of the firing; and brought four or five men up to ascertain the cause. It was unanimously agreed that he (Major Griffith), as senior officer of the party, should go to the chief, and endeavour to make some terms for the peaceful march of the party to Jellalabad. He accordingly went, accompanied by Mr.

Blewitt as interpreter, escorted by one or two of the enemy. On reaching the chief, they were hurried off without his giving them the opportunity of making any proposal. The last sight Major Griffith had of the party he had left, they appeared to be engaged in hostilities with the Affghans, whose numbers had gradually increased. He afterwards understood that the waving of a loonghee is considered by them as an act of unconditional surrender; and as our party would not give up their arms, the Affghans resorted to force; but were driven off the hill for the time. The few natives who had accompanied us so far did not go up the hill; but kept the road, and were seen to be plundered by the enemy. This he was afterwards told by Capt. Souter; who was brought to the village of Tootoo some hours after Major Griffith was taken there. This village was between two and three miles to the right of the scene of action. The same evening Major Griffith and Mr. Blewitt were taken to the Khan's fort, four or five miles further on the hills; where they found three or four European soldiers, who had escaped from the slaughter, wounded and taken prisoners. Some days after five more Europeans were brought in, who had proceeded in advance of our party. Major Griffith opened a communication with Jellalabad; and was in great hopes of effecting the release of the prisoners on ransom : but, owing to the jealousy and suspicion of the Khan Ghobam Jan Uzbezee, in whose power they were, nothing could be arranged. At last, after twenty days' confinement, he allowed one of their party, Serg.-Major Lisson, 37th N. I., to proceed to Jellalabad, and endeavour to explain matters. The party in all consisted of ten : two of these died, and Capt. Souter was left wounded at Tootoo.

The man who accompanied the Sergeant-Major returned the third day, and told them all was right. He was understood to have received 500 rupees as the ransom of the Sergeant-Major, who remained at Jellalabad. The party had strong hopes of liberation : but unfortunately the Sirdar, Mahommed Akbar Khan, heard of their being prisoners and sent to demand them. After some hesitation it was agreed to; and they were marched off to Charbagh to the Sirdar, and from thence to Buddeeabad.

Major Griffiths was severely wounded in the right arm on the 8th of January, just at the entrance of the Khoord Cabul pass; and, from want of dressing, the wound had become very painful the day he was taken prisoner.

11*th*. — Rain. We hear that the force under Col. Wylde have fallen back on Peshawer; that

Gen. Avitabile, the Sikh General with them, has been obliged to retreat to Attock.

I had again an opportunity, and wrote to Sale.

To-day all arms have been taken from the officers, on a promise that they shall be restored when we go away. I took poor Sturt's sword myself and begged that the Sirdar would keep it himself; that we might be sure of its restoration, as being invaluable to his widow. Dost Mahommed Khan, Abdool Guffoor Khan, &c., desired me to keep it myself; acting in the handsomest manner, and evincing much feeling on the occasion.

12*th*. — The snow at Tézeen is reported to be knee-deep. A very dismal day, with gentle rain at night. The Europeans, who have arrived, are all full of tales regarding each individual's escape. Six of them, amongst whom was Serg.-Major Lisson, of the 37th N. I., at daylight on the morning after the final struggle at Gundamuk, found themselves about a mile and half on the Jellalabad side of Gundamuk; and perceiving some Ghilzyes coming over the edge of a hill, they betook themselves to a cave in the neighbourhood, where they contrived to conceal themselves until about 11 A. M.; when their retreat was betrayed by the neighing of a horse belonging to one of the men, which caused them to be discovered by a party of the enemy who were passing near the mouth of the cave. These men came up, and told them to come outside; which they refused to do: the Ghilzyes then offered them bread, provided they would pay for it; and they thus procured three nans for forty-six rupees! The enemy then again ordered them to come out of the cave; and they replied, "In the evening, when it gets dusk, we will come outside." They were watched till then; and at that time gave themselves up. They were immediately rifled of all the money, &c. they possessed; and then taken to a fort in the neighbourhood, and afterwards transferred to another, where they found Major Griffiths; and from whence Lisson was despatched to Jellalabad, to treat for terms of ransom, as before mentioned.

13*th.* — A fine day. Not content with the arms given up, they pretend our servants have others, and a general search took place to-day; when all the poor wretches were fleeced of the few rupees they had succeeded in securing on their persons.

14*th.* — This is the day that Mahommed Akbar Khan is to go over the river towards Jellalabad to attack it. The 13th sent a quantity of clothes for distribution amongst the gentlemen. I received a large packet of letters, both from my family in the provinces, and also from England, but no note from Sale; so the Sirdar is still angry about the private correspondence. It was a very foolish attempt, for there was no news of consequence to send; and rousing the Sirdar's suspicion is not the way to make him kind to us.

15*th*. — Firing of heavy guns distinctly heard to-day; supposed to be a salute at Jellalabad. Shah Shoojah is said to be still in the Bala Hissar; and Zeman Shah Khan with Amenoollah Khan in the city. They are said to be raising a force to be sent by the former against Jellalabad; which force is to be commanded by his son Futteh Jung. To-day we hear that our horses are not to be taken away from us; and every thing is to be done to make us comfortable. There is an old adage, that "Fair words butter no parsnips."

17*th*. — The ground was covered with snow at daybreak; which continued to fall all day, and also at night. At breakfast-time we distinctly heard the report from three guns; and about half an hour afterwards three or four heavy discharges of musketry.

18*th*. — Dost Mahommed Khan came with his son; the family have all arrived at a neighbouring fort in this valley. There is a report that Sale has chupaoed Mahommed Akbar Khan's camp at Charbagh, and cut up fifty of his men.

19th. — I heard from Sale. A friend writes me that there will be no relief before April. At noon I was on the top of the house; when an awful earthquake took place. I had gone up stairs to see after my clothes; for, servants being scarce, we get a sweeper, who also acts as saces, to wash for us; and I hang them up to dry on the flat roof: we dispense with starch and ironing; and in our present situation we must learn to do every thing that is useful. But to return to the earthquake. For some time I balanced myself as well as I could; till I felt the roof was giving way. I fortunately succeeded in removing from my position before the roof of our room fell in with a dreadful crash. The roof of the stairs fell in as I descended them; but did me no injury. All my anxiety was for Mrs. Sturt; but I could only see a heap of rubbish. I was nearly bewildered, when I heard the joyful sound, "Lady Sale, come here, all are safe;" and I found the whole party uninjured in the courtyard. When the earthquake first commenced in the hills in the upper part of the valley, its progress was clearly defined, coming down the valley, and throwing up dust, like the action of exploding a mine.—I hope a soldier's wife may use a soldier's simile, for I know of nothing else to liken it to. Our walls, and gateways, and corner towers, are all much shaken, or actually thrown down. We had at least twenty-five shocks before dark; and about fifteen more during the night, which we spent in the courtyard. The end wall of the room Lady Macnaghten and party were in has sunk about two feet, and all the beams have started.

20*th.* — I wrote to Sale, to tell him we were all safe. At 3 in the morning we had a pretty smart shock; and constant ones, some severe, and many very slight, on an average every half hour all day, and five or six slight ones at night. The gentlemen gave up their largest room to my party, who were utterly roofless. Nearly all the others slept outside: but we had only one crack in the roof of our room, caused by part of the wall falling on it. The cold outside was intense; and the dew completely saturated the bed clothes last night: added to which, should the buildings come down, we were safer above, for the yard was so crammed that, in case of accident, half the people below must be crushed.

21*st.* — At 1 in the morning a sharp shock made us run to the door. We had numerous slight, and three or four pretty good shocks: they became more frequent in the evening. Part of our party made awnings in the court-yard to sleep under; but Mrs. Sturt and myself still preferred the house as safest.

Dost Mahommed Khan brought workmen to clear away the *débris*. He tells us our fort is the best of forty that have suffered in this valley; and that many are entirely thrown down. In one, a tower fell, and crushed five women and a man: others have not a wall remaining.

We have various reports regarding Jellalabad; — that it has been taken, that the walls and all the defences are thrown down, &c.

Dost Mahommed says that a man was sent as a spy to Jellalabad: that Macgregor sent for him; and, with Sale, took the man round to show him the state of the place: that two bastions had sunk a little; but that they were not only able to withstand Mahommed Akbar, but, if he came against them, they would meet him in the plain. It is said that Mahommed Akbar intends sending Gen. Elphinstone away if he can get a palkee. Lady Macnaghten has requested she may go with him; being, she says, differently circumstanced from the rest, who have most of them their husbands with them. Not even an animal's life was lost in our earthquake (I mean at our fort). Lady M.'s cat was buried in the ruins, and dug out again.

22*d.* — My wounds are quite healed. We had earthquakes day and night; less severe, but equally frequent. A prop was put up in our room to support the broken roof. We experienced a curious shock in the evening like a heavy ball rolled over our heads. Some large pieces of hills have fallen, and immense masses of stone. I miss some large upright stones on the hills that divide us from Kaffiristan, and that looked in the distance like large obelisks.

23d. — This has been a very close and gloomy day; earthquakes frequent, and some very sharp ones. We hear that, at Charbagh, 120 Affghans, and 20 Hindostanees were buried in the ruins.

Capt. Bygrave arrived, with one of his feet severely frost-bitten: we were all rejoiced to see him, having long supposed he had shared the fate of the many. On the 12th of January, perceiving that our army was utterly annihilated, he left the road at midnight, turned to the left, and took to the mountains; where he was out seven days and six nights. During a part of this time he was accompanied by Mr. Baness, the merchant from Delhi, who had with him a small bag containing coffee: on this they subsisted, taking each about six grains a day. When this was spent Baness proceeded on; and we afterwards heard that he got to Jellalabad, but so worn out with fatigue that he only arrived to die. Capt. Bygrave suffered greatly from having his feet frost-bitten: he however contrived at daylight in the morning of the 19th to reach Nizam Khan's village, called Kutch Soorkhab, about four miles north of Gundamuk, and twenty-eight from Jellalabad. Here he remained (plundered of course of what little money he had about him) until the 14th of February; when he was sent for to the Indian camp, then about six miles from Jellalabad. He had been demanded some days previously; but Nizam Khan refused to give him up until the arrival of the second messenger, accompanied by two mounted followers, when he was obliged to comply. Bygrave reached the Sirdar's camp in the afternoon of the 15th, and remained there with him till the 21st, on which day he started for Buddeeabad; and has, as before remarked, this day joined the other prisoners.

24th.—Very few shocks, and those gentle ones: but all last night, and great part of to-day, particularly late in the evening, there was a tremulous motion as of a ship that has been heavily struck by a sea, generally feeling as if on the larboard quarter, and accompanied by a sound of water breaking against a vessel. At other times we have just the undulatory motion of a snake in the water: but the most uncommon sensation we have experienced has been that of a heavy ball rolling over our heads, as if on the roof of our individual room, accompanied by the sound of distant thunder.

Abdool Ghyas Khan came to Buddeeabad. The report is, that Sultan Jan was sent the day before yesterday with 1000 men to make a false attack on Jellalabad; in which, on retreating, he lost three men. Yesterday he was sent to repeat the experiment, an ambuscade being planted by Mahommed Akbar's order; and it is said that our troops were led on to the spot in pursuit of the fugitives; and that the enemy lying in ambush attacked them, and cut up a whole regiment, of which only three men escaped to tell the tale at Jellalabad.

General Pollock with 5000 men is said to have arrived at Peshawer, as commander of the forces in Affghanistan, and with full political power. The news came from a merchant, who has just arrived from Peshawer.

25*th*. — The earth is still unquiet, constantly trembling, with reports like explosions of gunpowder, but no severe shocks.

We hear that the camp followers we passed on the road are eating the bodies of those that die: eventually they must take their turn; for frostbitten as they are, they never can leave the places we saw them at.

27*th*. — A man has arrived who confirms the report of a fight, four days ago, at Jellalabad: and says four of the 13th are killed, and four taken prisoners; but they do not know whether they are officers or men. Sultan Jan is said to have had a narrow escape, all his men having been cut up.

Earthquakes very frequent, but not severe, though worse than yesterday. The Ameer Dost Mahommed is reported to be on his way up from the provinces with the army; others say he has escaped from Ferozepore.

28*th*.—In consequence of a message from the Sirdar, our guards are doubled. The Mirza Bowadeen Khan is to go to him to-morrow. It is said 8000 men are coming from Cabul. A smart shock of an earthquake about 9 o'clock in the evening; and during the night several slight ones.

March 1*st*.—The Mirza went to the Sirdar. Nothing has transpired. A smart double shock in the morning, with slight tremulous motion.

3*rd* & 4*th*.—Earthquakes as usual. To-day every servant that is frost-bitten or unable to work has been turned out of the fort: they were stripped first of all they possessed. I received two notes from Sale, dated the 11th and 16th.

5*th*.—At 3 A.M. turned out of bed by a smart shock of an earthquake. Three continuous ones at breakfast-time. Futteh Jung is reported to be at Tighree.

8*th*.—A letter arrived from Mahommed Akbar Khan; stating that the King has written to desire that the force at Jellalabad may be withdrawn, and that Futteh Jung is on his way down with 8000 men. It is stated that Macgregor has refused to receive the King's messenger; and that our force have arrived at Jumrood.

9*th.* — Several slight shocks at night; after which, great screaming and alarm. Husnoo, a sweeper, being a disappointed man, attempted to strangle Rookeria, a woman of the same cast. The gentlemen searched every corner; and the delinquent had to jump down the wall; in doing which he seriously injured his back. There was no other mode of escape, as we are always locked into the square at night.

10*th.* — The Affghans gave Mr. Husnoo a desperate flogging; and had it not been for the officers, would have hanged him afterwards: he was, however, stripped, and turned out of the fort.

11*th.* — Dost Mahommed Khan came. Khoda Bukeh, the half-brother of Mahommed Shah, has, we are told, left the Sirdar, whose party is breaking up; and he is supposed to be trying to get Major Pottinger to make some terms for him with Macgregor, and for him to join the English against the King. Col. Palmer has sent down to Macgregor the terms on which he will surrender at Ghuznee; but Macgregor refuses to ratify them; and has forwarded them to Gen. Pollock, through the Sirdar, who has sent them here to Pottinger. Meantime the garrison at Ghuznee are to be provisioned by the chiefs. Dost Mahommed says that the King has written to Macgregor to vacate Jellalabad; and at the same time sent, by the bearer of the letter, a verbal communication not to do so. The messenger had a long conversation with Macgregor, and then started sharp for Cabul, passing Mahommed Akbar Khan's camp at night; who, on his part, was expecting to catch him in the morning, and possess himself of the letters.

The Mirza Bowadeen Khan is getting a paper signed by us all, to say he has treated us well: from whence we suspect he thinks our party will eventually gain the ascendant.

The Sirdar sent to Lady Macnaghten to say that if she did not require the services of three Hindostanee saceses that are in another fort, he will send them, with the Resallah, to Peshawer on rafts, the day after to-morrow: a demonstration of civility without meaning. The saceses are useless at a distance; and she does not require grooms for the horses that have been taken from her, either by him or Mahommed Shah Khan.

13*th*. — Earthquakes as usual. There has been a fight at Jellalabad. A party were sent out to mine: Sale, having intelligence of their intention, planted an ambush. The enemy were first attacked from the fort; and when they fled, they fell into the ambuscade, and were cut to pieces. Numbers of wounded Affghans have come into this and the neighbouring forts.

14*th.*—Earthquakes in plenty. Mrs. Boyd was confined early this morning; adding another to our list of female captives. In the evening Affghans came in with many reports; confirming the account that there have been three fights, in which the Affghans have been worsted; that after the last battle Mahommed Akbar Khan in his retreat was fired at by an Affghan, and wounded in the body and arms.

The Affghans tell two tales: one, that Shah Shoojah had bribed a man with a lakh of rupees to assassinate Akbar; the other, that Capt. Macgregor gave Abdool Guffoor Khan (Akbar's cousin) the same sum to procure the like effect; and that Abdool and all his family have been put to death.

They say that Mahommed Akbar Khan chafes like a lion taken in the toils, with his three wounds, —for he was previously wounded in the thigh. He allowed no one but Mahommed Shah Khan to enter his tent.

15*th.*—I was made very anxious by a report that Jellalabad had been taken: it proved to be a piece of wit, to impose on those who were eager for news. The Mirza, as soon as he heard of it, left his tent to come and assure me that it was false, and to request I would not make myself unhappy about it.

Of authentic accounts the last are, that there was a burj between the Sirdar's camp and Jellalabad, which Mahommed Akbar wished to establish as an outpost, and intended taking possession of. "Fighting Bob" (as Sale is called), having got intelligence of their intentions, sent a party of sappers and miners with supports during the night, who destroyed the work and returned; and on the Sirdar's party's arrival, they found their intended post annihilated.

Further accounts regarding the Sirdar's wound state, that it was purely accidental. A favourite Pesh Khedmut, who had accompanied Mahommed Akbar Khan to Bokhara, and had been with him in all his changes of fortune, was assisting him to dismount from his horse, when some part of his dress catching upon his fire-arms, they went off, and the Sirdar was wounded through the arm and lungs. One account states, that the unfortunate man was instantly cut to pieces; another, that he was burnt alive; and that to the last he took his oath on the Koran that the act was an accident. There is nothing too brutal or savage for Akbar to accomplish: he is known to have had a man flayed alive in his presence, commencing at the feet, and continuing upwards until the sufferer was relieved by death.

The Mirza has sent for nalbunds to shoe our horses; and there seems to be an idea that we shall not long remain here. We have lately made ourselves more comfortable: a temporary shed or two, composed of mats, have been erected since the great earthquake for the accommodation of those who were turned out of their rooms at that time, all of course at their own expense. We have also got stools to sit upon, and charpoys instead of lying on the ground; and a cujava, with boards nailed on it, serves me for a table — a decided luxury, there being but one other here. *Mirza*, in this man's case, denominates a secretary: he is a kind of under-jailor (Dost Mahommed Khan being the principal one), who issues out our allowance of food: to some he is civil, and has been so to me: to some very rude; and has even drawn his knife on one of the officers.

18*th.*— We had two slight shakes, with reports like distant guns or thunder in the morning; and another during prayers at night. The Mirza Bowadeen Khan is to leave us the day after tomorrow. The servants have a report that there have been several engagements, in which Sale has been victorious; that the Sirdar is wounded in two places; and that the married people are all to be sent to Jellalabad, and the bachelors to Cabul.

19th.—No earthquake to-day. The Mirza is ordered off; and the Nazir of Mahommed Shah Khan is come in his place: that is, he is to be our sub-jailor, Dost Mahommed Khan being the principal one, and answerable for our safe custody to Mahommed Shah Khan, his brother, who rules all Mahommed Akbar Khan's councils.

The Nazir begins well: says the Mirza cheated us of our allowance; that two sheep and twenty fowls are to be distributed daily, one seer of ottah, and one of rice to each room, with ghee in proportion; and that we are to have keshmish, sugar, and tea, monthly.

It is further reported that the Sirdar never intended the servants to be sent away; and that it was done by the Mirza in hopes of obtaining plunder. However, to do him justice, he sent to Capt. Lawrence, desiring him to make it known that the servants' money was unsafe; and that those who had any had better intrust it to the keeping of their masters. Now this he never would have done had he intended to fleece them. For myself I regret his going away; as he was always very civil to me, getting me any little thing I required.

20th. — During prayers (it being Sunday) about one o'clock we felt three distinct shocks.

Numbers of cattle are being driven off towards the hills. The people are sending their families and property away from the villages. The Affghans say that it is only the wandering Ghilzye tribes returning, as is their wont in the spring of the year, towards Cabul; having, as usual, wintered their flocks in the warmer climate of the Lughman valley.

21st. — The no-roz, or vernal equinox. Mr. Melville brought us a bouquet of narcissuses, which we highly prized, for it is long since we have seen even a blade of grass.

The report of to-day is, that troops have at length arrived at Jellalabad; having lost 1000 out of 3000 men in forcing the Khyber pass. All the forts about this place are filling fast with wounded men of Akbar's army; and skirmishes are said to take place daily at Jellalabad, in which we never hear of the Sirdar being victorious.

A nalbund is come to this fort, and is shoeing all our horses, we paying for the same. This looks like preparation for a move; but we trust it will not be a precipitate flight to Khoolloom with Mahommed Akbar Khan, as we have heard it hinted.

Mr. Clarke is stated to have arrived at Peshawer. He is an active political functionary, and just the man to set things to rights.

Mahommed Akbar Khan sent 800 men to watch the proceedings at Jellalabad. Sale is said to have attacked them, and cut them to pieces. This is the Affghan report of to-day.

23*d*.— A report that the Sirdar is willing to go over to the English; but that Mahommed Shah Khan is averse to the measure.

Another report, that all the horses and ponies are sent for by the Sirdar, has caused a great commotion; which, however, has subsided, on the discovery that the Sirdar had sent to claim a blue horse he had lent Mr. Ryley on the march, which he requires for his artillery: it was an iron grey.

An earthquake early in the morning, and many slight ones at night.

Mahommed Shah Khan's people are sounding us, to ascertain whether we shall be ransomed or not; talking of a lakh and half as our value: the General, Major Pottinger, and Capt. Lawrence to remain until we are in safety, and their rupees in hand. A council of officers was held at the General's regarding this same ransom business: which they refer to Macgregor. I protest against being implicated in any proceedings in which I have no vote.

25th.— The Nazir says it was only a feeler, and it was a lakh and half each that Mahommed Shah Khan required from us. Perhaps this is only a piece of Affghan wit.

26th.— Letters from Jellalabad. The 31st, and 9th Queen's, a regiment of Dragoons, two of Native Cavalry, eight of Infantry, three eighteen-pounders, three nine-pounders, and six six-pounders, are expected there on the 1st of April. Gerard has been wounded. Abbott hit by a spent ball: all well, thank God!

This news is very different from what we heard this morning, which was that those left at Cabul and Ghuznee have been sent to Bokhara to be sold as slaves; and that our turn would come next.

The thermometer of our spirits has risen greatly. We hear from Jellalabad that all at Cabul are well, and that Ghuznee has been obliged to surrender; but that the officers are all well, safe, and taken care of, as we are here.

Earthquakes in the usual number.

27th.—*Easter Sunday.* I wrote to Sale. Four earthquakes before breakfast, and more at night.

28th.— We hear from an Affghan, just come from Jellalabad, that two regiments have left

Peshawer, and advanced two marches; that Capt. Mackeson, political agent, has bought over the Khyberries; but that Gholab Sing, the Sheikh general, has claimed the honour of keeping the pass open for us.

29*th*. — An Affghan reports that our troops have arrived at Lallpoorah. A trifling earthquake at sunset; the hills enveloped in clouds, which suddenly assumed a lurid hue, and one sharp clap of thunder much resembling a gun was heard; after which they cleared off. A little rain about 8 P. M. when it became very warm, and we experienced a very hot night.

30*th*. — Sultan Jan and Mahommed Shah Khan are (we hear) gone with 3000 men to oppose the troops coming up. This force might annoy ours very much in the Cholah Khyber, between Lallpoorah and Hazar-i-now.

Another report is current to-day, that we are to be off on Sunday for Jellalabad.

Heavy rain in the evening and at night, with rumblings and trifling shocks.

31*st*. — The weather has cleared up again. To-day's report is, that we go on Monday to Tagow or Kaffiristan. The people are becoming very civil; ask if we will spare their lives, and are sending their women away. We tell them that all who behave well to us will have their property respected, and be well treated.

They say that Sultan Jan is really gone with 3000 men to the Cholah Khyber; that our force coming up gives no quarter; that the Affghans sent spies in the guise of country people, with things to sell, to see what loot the Feringhees had. They report that not only the soldiers, but also the officers, are packed close in small palls, without beds, chairs, tables, or any thing but the clothes on their backs.

April 1st.—A famous hoax went round, that a letter had come from Macgregor, that government were going to ransom us from Mahommed Shah Khan for three lakhs of rupees, and that we were to leave Buddeeabad on Wednesday; that Sultan Jan had been defeated in the Khyber, and that Mahommed Akbar Khan had fled to Cabul.

Letters did actually arrive from Jellalabad subsequently, with very conflicting accounts: Gen. Pollock not expected till the 16th.

A report that Mahommed Akbar had withdrawn all his outposts, and hostilities had ceased; that Dost Mahommed had arrived at the Attock; and that as soon as he entered the country, all prisoners were to be set at large; and our force to quit the country, leaving the Ameer Dost

Mahommed to prosecute his fortunes as best he may.

Sale's letter gives no intelligence of a public nature; but as he proposes getting more shoes made to send to me, it does not look as if he expected us to leave this country soon.

3d.—A report that Macgregor has seized a flock of 200 sheep, twenty head of cattle, and twenty camels that were passing near Jellalabad; that Mahommed Akbar Khan, who it seems cannot have withdrawn his outposts, sent to seize our yaboos when they went out to water, and planted a party for that purpose. Some of our people who went out early, saw them stealing along to their position, and immediately reported the circumstance, when Sale planted an ambush of two companies, one of Europeans and one native. They then sent out the animals as usual, and when the Affghans pounced on their expected prey, they were attacked, and it is said 200 of them were killed.

5th.—I wrote to Sale, but heard that the letter will not go till to-morrow. We are told that three chiefs at Jellalabad are supplying our army with grain, leaving it at the gate at night.

6th.—The Nazir says that a brass six-pounder has been brought in from the Khyber on a camel, and that it has killed two camels bringing it to the

Sirdar's camp; also, that they have brought in thirty Europeans heads. Dost Mahommed Khan has returned from Cabul; whither the Sirdar sent him on business: he reports that there is great commotion in Cabul; and he has brought all Sultan Jan's family back with him for safety, to the Lughman valley. The gun above alluded to, is probably one taken at Ali Musjid; and the Sirdar having brought it to his camp, induces us to think that he has given up the idea of defending the Khyber.

Pottinger gives it as his opinion, that we may probably remain here for six months.

The Nazir tells us that the gun that has arrived has been a month on the road, and has killed six camels; that it is the one taken at Jumroad three months ago, when our people were out foraging; and that Zeman Khan has ordered Shah Shoojah to send a force down from Cabul. What they are going to do, and by whom the troops are to be headed, we know not; but only that the report is that a force has started. The Nazir told Pottinger that the talk of our being ransomed at two lakhs was only a feeler, to see what we would offer: that Mahommed Shah Khan would for that sum allow one gentleman to go to Peshawer to treat with our party there; but that Pottinger would be held answerable for his safe return.

News has just arrived to the Nazir from the Kazanchey, who is with the Sirdar, that all the officers at Ghuznee are killed except eight; that our troops at Khelat-i-Gilzye hold their ground, though they have been attacked several times; that the garrison of Kandahar have made frequent sallies, and scoured the country in every direction for eight or ten miles; and that they have got in a number of sheep and cattle: also, that an army is coming up from Shikarpore.

Further reports assure us that Shah Shoojah left Cabul to proceed to Bégramee, where his tents were pitched; but that he had not got further than the Musjed, where John Hicks's tomb is, in front of the Bala Hissar gate, when he was cut down in his palkee by the son of Zeman Khan, and was immediately cut to pieces.

Three Sirdars are said to have come in to-day; but we know of a truth that the Affghans are burnishing up their arms, and making bullets.

Our force is reported to have arrived at Jellalabad. Our guards are all on the alert. A report that Mahommed Akbar is killed; another that he has fled to Gundamuk.

Our broken towers are manned, and thirteen men added to our guard.

8th. — The first news this morning was, that Mahommed Shah Khan had been here during the night, and that he has removed his family from the valley. It is still reported that Mahommed Akbar Khan is dead. The Sirdar reproached the chiefs for having supplied our garrison with provisions; and the same night, Abdool Guffoor Khan, Abdool Rahim, and Aga Jan, went over to Macgregor with 1000 Affghan cavalry, and told him that the enemy were not prepared; on which a chupao was made on Akbar's camp, with great slaughter. The three chiefs remained as hostages in Jellalabad, whilst their men went with our cavalry to chupao the camp. Akbar's horse was restive; and none of his people waited for him: his own artillery-men turned the guns against him in their flight; and they left their camp standing, their arms, and every thing they possessed; and ran for their lives. Mahommed Shah Khan has escaped; and Mahommed Akbar Khan is said to be within four kos of Buddeeabad.

10th.—We were hurried from daybreak to get ready. Mahommed Shah Khan has taken away all Lady Macnaghten's jewels, to the value of above a lakh of rupees; and her shawls, valued at between 30,000 and 40,000 rupees. He desired to see my boxes; but did not take the trouble of examining them: he, however, knew that I arrived here without any baggage. He sent to inquire if we had any valuables; and, if so, we were to give them up at once.

The Mirza has returned: he, and the Nazir, promise to send a box, which I have no means of carrying, as also our servants, who are unable to go with us, to Jellalabad to Sale: however as they crammed the box into their own godown, I strongly suspect they mean to keep it themselves. My chest of drawers they took possession of with great glee — I left some rubbish in them, and some small bottles, that were useless to me. I hope the Affghans will try their contents as medicine, and find them efficacious: one bottle contained nitric acid, another a strong solution of lunar caustic!

We did not start till past noon, and then did not take the road we expected, leading to Tighree; but an upper one to the right, and were told we were going to Tagow. We had a great number of detentions from the camels that carried the kujavas; the General's broke down; so did Mrs. Sturt's; the General was laid on the ground until another could be brought for him; and Mr. Melville gave his horse to my daughter. Here the Mirza professed to be very kind and attentive: he took a chogah lined with valuable fur, which was particularly prized by Mrs. Sturt, as being her husband's; also his sword; and said he would carry them for her when she was obliged to ride; but he quite forgot to return them, which caused much annoyance to us; and proved that the Mirza, despite his fair speeches, took care not to lose an opportunity of enriching himself at our expence.

We had not proceeded far when we met some horsemen shouting *Kalūs shud,* and we were ordered to turn round: then we heard that our troops had been beat in the Khyber, and had lost ten guns. The next report was, that our troops had penetrated into the Lughman valley; another, that Jellalabad was taken. We went back; and found that the mat houses, and other little comforts we had put up, were mostly demolished; our scraps of setringees taken away, as also our mats, &c.: but the soldiers were very civil to us: one brought back my charpoy, and busied himself in stringing it for me; another brought me a chiragh; and a soldier's wife brought Mrs. Sturt and me each a stool to sit on. These little kindnesses make a deep impression at such times.

We were told not to unpack; and to be ready to start, if requisite, in the night.

A servant who refused to march with us was all activity on our return: he ran here and there, took our horses, and then, best of all, bought some fowls and cooked them for us.

We had been cooped up so long without any exercise, that we were quite ready for and enjoyed our dinner after the ride.

11*th*. — We got an early breakfast; and soon after started again; leaving the soldiers, two European women (Mrs. Wade and Mrs. Burnes), and the child Seymour Stoker, with all the maimed servants, and those that would not go with us. The women and child certainly ought to have accompanied us.

We went to Ali Kund, a rather long march, and found the Sirdar there, seated in his nalkee, and looking very ill. He was particular in bowing to us all, making every demonstration of civility.

Three tents were pitched for us on a pretty and green spot. The valley was beautiful under cultivation; and to us doubly so, from our not having seen a blade of grass for so long a time.

The field pea was in blossom; several sorts of cranesbill, gentian, forget-me-not, campions, &c.

Having taken the precaution to have some fowls roasted over night, we got a good meal; and we design, whenever we march, and can procure them, to do the same.

As we marched through the valley, we saw the effects of the late earthquake: not a fort was entire; very few habitable; and most of them masses of ruins.

Sultan Jan arrived this evening from the Khyber. Truly, the Persian expression of a man's face being blackened is true: he looks very black upon his late defeat in the Khyber; and has returned with 50, all that remain to him of 500 men he took there. I had no idea, before our captivity, that people could become so changed by sunburn; the Europeans looking like the Affghans, and the Affghans as dark as Hindostanees.

12*th*. — Set out at eight A. M., and arrived at our ground at five P. M.; a very long march over a sterile country. We only twice met with water, which was very shallow, and so sandy that our horses would not drink it. We did not see a vestige of a habitation, nor any cultivation.

We left the Adanek Beeduck pass to our left; and travelled up and down a number of very difficult mountain passes. Mahommed Akbar Khan passed us; bowed, and smiled — " He can smile, and smile, and be a villain." I shook hands with Moyenoodeen, who is also arrived from the Khyber. He looks what is vulgarly called down in the mouth. He appeared afraid of acknowledging his acquaintance with me; and stealthily came to inquire if my wound was well. He was with Sale in the Kohistan; and then, and still, professes to be his friend, and the friend of the English in general.

13*th*. — Made a march of about twelve miles:

the country sterile and rocky; the road rather better than yesterday; only one very awkward ascent, when all the ladies got out of their kujavas. I always ride; and have my own saddle: but some of the ladies are obliged to ride gentleman fashion, sitting on their beddings instead of saddles.

The road was mostly up and down hill. We passed two small forts, with patches of cultivation near them, not far from our encamping ground. We found it very hot in our tent. This tent is one division of a common Sipahee's pall. We have taken up our places; and always retain them. Our party consists of Mrs. Trevor and five of her children, and Mrs. Sturt and myself, on one side; on the other Mrs. Boyd and her three children, Lady Macnaghten, Mrs. Mainwaring and child, Capt. and Mrs. Anderson and two children, and Capt. Lawrence. The other tents are similarly crammed: all spread their beddings (which touch each other) upon the ground.

14*th*. — A very tiresome hill on setting out, — the Bādhpush or Windy Back: the ascent rather difficult: the descent could be made good for guns with 100 sappers in a few days. Saw plenty of fruit trees in blossom on the hill; at the foot of which we halted, dismounted, and sat on the ground till all our people got over; and found Mahommed Shah's sons with large bouquets of tulips. I observed the mistletoe, the myrrh, ilex, &c. The rest of the march was along a tolerably good road. We crossed the same stream at least twenty times. Saw some purple iris's. We were detained a long time at the Cabul river; which we crossed on a *jhala* (or raft) supported on inflated skins; and encamped close to the bank, but further down the stream, as the current was very rapid: the river is said to be twenty feet deep at some places. Here we found Mahommed Akbar Khan. Our baggage came up at dusk, as also the tents; but a great deal did not get over, and has to wait for daylight. Several horses swam over; and their efforts, and those of their riders, were a source of great interest to us.

15th April. — We did not leave our encampment until the middle of the day; when we found the sand dreadfully hot. We came only four or five miles to Sehruby; and pitched our tents not far distant from Abdoollah Khan's fort. There were no kujavas to-day, and great grumbling thereat amongst the ladies. A report, which we fervently hope is untrue, that all the hostages left at Cabul are murdered.

I saw plenty of amaryllis in bloom; as also of the Persian iris (the orris of the druggists), which quite scented the air with a perfume resembling that of mingled violets and wall-flowers.

16*th*.—We halted. All manner of reports to-day, — that the King has not been murdered, but is in power with the Dooranees, the Populzyes, and Akukzyes, who are in the ascendant; whilst the Barukzyes are at a discount:—that great commotion exists in Cabul: — that the soldiers, who were left there, are to remain; but the officers are to come and join us at Tézeen to-morrow; whither we are to march, and go by roads impracticable for cattle; all to walk, to Herat: we are to be there in two months, after which we are to be sent to Balkh.

17*th*.— Halted again, probably waiting for the four kujavas that the Sirdar has ordered Mahommed Shah Khan to furnish us with. They say we go to Tezeen to-morrow: the mirza is off in advance, in great haste. Our troops are said to be near; and the Affghans are going to chupao them. The Sirdar has fallen back on the river, to confer with the Chief of Tagow.

This day I was attacked with fever.

18*th*.—Halted. Mahommed Shah Khan is gone off to Cabul; we are to go to the hills above Tézeen, and stay there till all is settled. If only a small force comes up, the Affghans mean to cut them up in the Khoord Cabul; if a large force come, they will succumb at once. I was worse to-day: a pleasant prospect, as we daily expect to march. Our troops are said to be still at Lallpoorah, quieting refractory tribes.

19*th*. — A miserable day, and we marched through heavy rains to Tézeen: we are told that no supplies were to be had where we were. Kodá Buksh Khan's fort, close at hand, is full of loot and plate. The earthquake has brought down part of the fort they have brought us to.

The Sirdar could only get two camels with kujavas; but gave up his own palkee to Lady Macnaghten and me. I was utterly incapable of sitting on horseback: however, as I had to sit backwards, with very little room, nothing to lean against, and to keep a balance against Lady M. and Mrs. Boyd's baby, I benefited but little, except in the grandeur of a royal equipage. My turban and habit were completely saturated by the rain; and I shivered as I went. On arrival at the fort, I was told to go into the room where Mahommed Shah's and the other chief's ladies were. They received us with great kindness; and kept heaping up three large fires for us to dry our clothes by. The court yard was a deep mass of mud; and in the evening Affghans carried us on their backs across it to another apartment, which was nicely covered with *numdas:* our beddings were all regularly sopped through. The whole of the baggage was sent on to the camp, with our servants. A dinner was cooked for us,—a huge dish of rice, with dhye (sour curds) in the centre, and ghee poured over all! This is a favourite Affghan dish, and therefore my bad taste must be arraigned for thinking it not eatable. Fortunately I had a little tea and sugar in a bag, suspended from the crupper of my saddle: they gave us some milk, and I found tea the most refreshing repast. We stretched ourselves on the numdas (coarse felt carpets) in our still wet clothes. In the night I began shivering again; and Capt. Anderson, my nearest bed mate, covered me with a bed cloak, which, strange to say, soon imparted warmth to me. We slept, large and small, thirty-four in a room 15 feet by 12; and we lay on the floor, literally packed together, with a wood fire in the centre, and using pine torches for candles.

20th.—The Sirdar fears if he is taken by us, we shall either hang him or blow him from a gun. Mahommed Shah Khan is in a great fright also. Sultan Jan appears to be our bitterest enemy. The Sirdar says *he alone* could take us through the country: or, if he wished it, he could assemble 5000 men at any point to attack us.

It is said that Mackenzie is to go to Jellalabad on a secret mission. He will not be allowed to take any letters for individuals.

We had rain all day; and our wet chogahs, &c. hanging up, increased the damp. I wrote a few lines in pencil to Sale by a trooper who expected to go with Mackenzie, recommending both this trooper himself (Oomar Khan), and the Rajah Ali Buhadur to him: both have been very useful to us. We had rain all day, and three earthquakes.

Mackenzie did not go after all.

Mrs. Waller increased the community, giving birth to a daughter: she, Mrs. Waller, and Mr. and Mrs. Eyre got a room to themselves and their children, diminishing our number to twenty-nine. A slight earthquake, and a fine night.

21*st*.— A fine sunshiny day: we went out to camp; getting on the first horses we could find: mine was a half-starved beast that could scarcely put one foot before the other. We had scarcely a mile to go. We hear that we are to halt here one day; and then to go to Zenganah, where the snow is four feet deep, and to stay there for four months. Rain in the evening; and very heavy rain at night. The General, who is said to be dying, Pottinger, Mackenzie, Dr. Magrath, the Eyres and Wallers, are left at the fort.

Major Pottinger expostulated with Akbar; and told him that surely he did not make war on women and children, and that it was great cruelty to drive us about the country in the way they are doing; that when the Dost and the ladies of his family (amongst them Akbar's wife, the daughter of Mahommed Shah Khan) went to Hindostan, they travelled with every comfort procurable, and probably many more than they would have experienced in their own country. To this he replied, I will do whatever you wish: but Mahommed Shah Khan is gone to Cabul; the very bread I eat I get from him; and until he returns I cannot do any thing. He however insists that he has a letter from Hindostan, in which it is asserted that his father has twenty sentries over him, and offered to show the letter to Capt. Lawrence; who said he cared not who wrote the letter: it was untrue:—that the Dost has a guard: but so far from being a close prisoner, he being fond of hawking, &c., goes out when and where he pleases, with an escort of horse, which would be given in compliment to his station, as in the case of the royal families of Delhi, &c.; and that any restraint the women are placed under, is at the sole desire of the Dost himself.

22*nd*. We were roused before daylight with orders to march immediately; and as we had fully expected to halt for another day or two, all was confusion.

I was still too weak to ride; and Mrs. Boyd kindly gave me her place in the kujava, I carrying her baby. It was my first attempt, and the conveyance was a particularly small one of the kind; for when the resai was put in to sit on, there was not one foot and a half square; and I found (being rather a tall person) the greatest difficulty in doubling up my long legs into the prescribed compass.

On inquiry, I found that our departure was occasioned by the arrival of a letter from Cabul; stating that Futteh Jung, son of the deceased Shah Shoojah, was coming with 400 horse to carry us off, as a card to play in his own favour.

Zeman Shah Khan, acting-King in Cabul, also demands us. Akbar wants to keep us: but both he and we are in the hands of Mahommed Shah Khan; who says he never took place or present from us; that he hated us always; and will be our enemy to the last.

We came to-day about twelve miles up the bed of a deep ravine, crossing the stream at least fifty times. From our last encampment we could see Kodah Buksh Khan's fort, looking very pretty, surrounded with fine trees in blossom.

On first starting, we passed on our right a large mountain-slip, caused by the earthquake near to a cave, where there are a great number of bodies. The hills were very precipitous on our left, and high on both sides. We also passed a cave at some small distance, in front of which were some dead bodies and many bones strewed about: and, from the blood close to its entrance, there is every reason to believe that the inhabitants were supporting nature by devouring each other. I saw three poor wretches crawling on hands and knees just within the cave: but all we had to bestow upon them was pity, not unmingled with horror at the evidences of cannibalism but too apparent. These miserable creatures called to us for that relief which we had it not in our power to afford; and we can only hope that their sufferings were speedily terminated by death.

No guns excepting those of the mountain train could travel this road; and cavalry and infantry would be greatly annoyed from the heights.

We did not go direct up the Tézeen valley; but took the right hand valley, which leads to the Jubhar Khail country, considered as the strongest of the Ghilzye mountain fastnesses. We passed an old Ghilzye fort on an eminence on our right; also a small colony of charcoal makers, resident in mud huts, and encamped at a second place of the same kind. Ice six inches thick in places close to the road; and plenty of snow from six to eight inches deep on the sides of it.

23rd. Being still very weak, I am glad to hear we are likely to halt here eight days. Khojeh

Mahommed Khan seems very anxious regarding some terms being made with the Feringhees: he *bahadurs* notwithstanding; and says he can bring two lakhs of fighting men against us.

The Ghazeeas are getting discontented; and complain that they have had no food for four days.

The Sirdar has ordered our horses back to Tézeen: he says he cannot feed them here.

24*th.* The General died last night, and his remains are to be sent to Jellalabad. Mackenzie was sent there on a secret mission just afterwards. The General's death was hastened by a rumour of a Chupao from Cabul the very day we left Tézeen. At mid-day all were put on horseback, and sent off to a fort near at hand. In the general hurry to save themselves, Mrs. Waller, with her two children, seemed to be quite forgotten. Mr. Waller went to Major Pottinger, who was mounted on his horse, and who said all must do the best they could for themselves; but that no doubt accommodation would be given. On this Mr. Waller, who cannot speak Persian, applied to Capt. Mackenzie; who went to Akbar Khan, and represented to him how shocking a thing it was to leave a lady and two children to have their throats cut. An old kujava was found, and strung; and some Affghans carried it on a pole. Three wives of one of the chiefs were also left in a great fright; but they procured some conveyance also. Pottinger was hurried off in such haste that he could not remonstrate.

Mahommed Shah Khan says he will not give us any thing besides ottah. I suppose he keeps all the good things for the Affghan ladies; some of whom inhabit two mud huts on the hill, and the others are lodged in black tents more fragile than our own. Mahommed Rufeek, our present keeper and purveyor, has purchased twelve sheep on his own account for us; and Mahommed Akbar Khan has sent twelve camels to Cabul to bring rice and ghee. We are also busy making chebootras: we hang up our resais and blankets for roof and walls, and find they make very comfortable places to sit in all day.

25th. — A report that Macgregor is to exchange us against an equal number of Affghan ladies and children at Loodianah; and that we are to be released in a few days.

26th. — A report to-day that the Jellalabad army are moving upwards and the Cabul one downwards. The Affghans say that their force consists of 11,000 men.

27th. — The Sirdar and Major Pottinger paid us a visit. The former tells us we are not to be angry; that nothing is procurable here; that he has sent to Cabul for every thing for us. He brought some native shoes and cloth for distribution. Miller and Moore, the two soldiers who attended on the General, have been liberated: but Akbar says that it is not prudent to let them go at present, as the roads are unsafe!

28th.—We have converted our chebootras into arbours made of juniper. We were driven from ours to-day before dinner by a shower of rain. At night we had thunder, hail, and showers of rain, that came on in gusts.

It is said that the Sirdar has intercepted a letter from Conolly to Macgregor regarding some treaty with Amenoollah Khan for 3 lakhs : and that Kohundif Khan (the Dost's brother), with 8000 Persians, is moving on Kandahar. If this is true, it involves a quarrel with Persia.

A number of the Sirdar's men are said to have gone off to-day; having struck for arrears of pay. The Sirdar offered them 5 rupees each, but they demanded 10. A relief guard of seven men has arrived with some petty chief.

We have just heard that Miller was disguised as an Affghan to lead the camel that conveyed the General's body. Moore looked too English to attempt it. Near Jugdaluk, the party of ten horsemen were attacked, and the box, which was supposed to contain treasure, broken open. We at first heard that they had mutilated the poor old man's body; but only a few stones were thrown, one of which struck the head.

Miller was beaten a good deal, and wounded with a knife; but saved his life by saying he was a Mussulman : he had to return. The body was sent on; but I believe there is as yet no authentic account of its arrival at Jellalabad.

Mahommed Shah Khan arrived at night.

30*th April.* — A messenger came in from Amenoollah Khan. The government have refused to pay the 14½ lakhs; and the Affghans say that Pottinger and Lawrence are answerable for it. Is not Akbar more answerable for the non-fulfilment of the treaty? he who went to the Durbar, booted, (on the 7th of January,) ready to start after our army for the avowed purpose of its annihilation?

The Rajah has come in; he goes off to Cabul again to-morrow. Goolam Moyen oo deen also came to see us: he goes with the Sirdar to Tézeen to-day.

All accounts seem to agree in this: that although the Affghans are raising troops in Cabul, yet they seem to be as likely to fight against each other as against us.

Our soldiers who were left at Cabul, have been sent to Logur (Amenoollah's country). The hostages are placed in the hands of the son of the high priest, Bucha-i Meer Wyse.

It is reported that the Dost has written to Akbar Khan to say, that, if there is any chance of regaining the throne, he was to fight for it; but if not, not to drive us women and children about the country; as it was against his interest that we should be ill treated. Perhaps he pities the wives of all these Ghilzye chiefs, who go wherever we do: they however have the best and largest kujavas, and plenty of them; whilst with us, many ladies very unfit to ride, are forced to do so, and even without side or any saddles; for myself, I would rather walk than be again packed into a kujava.

1*st May.*—Futteh Jung, Amenoollah, and the Populzyes are in the Bala Hissar. The new king, Zeman Shah Khan, and Osman Khan, with the Barukzyes, are in the city. They have sixteen guns; and want the former party to join them; but they refuse to do so, saying that the others inveigled Shah Shoojah out, and killed him.

Neither party will have any thing to do with Akbar; who, they say, plays a double part, and killed all our army. Mahommed Shah Khan wants to get Akbar to Cabul: but he refuses to go, from dread of assassination.

He (Akbar) wishes to be made a consequential chief of some part of the country; and would probably give us up, had he the power: but Mahommed Shah Khan is very powerful, and averse to the project.

2nd. — All Cabul is in an uproar, the people fighting amongst themselves. Khojeh Mahommed took some of the officers out shooting: whilst on the hills, they heard the report of guns; and were told that the firing was at Cabul; about thirty miles off in a direct line.

In a conference with Pottinger, Troup, and many other English and Affghans, — amongst the latter Mahommed Shah Khan, — Mahommed Akbar Khan became greatly excited. He said, that on the religious cry being raised, he killed the Envoy, he destroyed our army; and now that he has drawn down the vengeance of the British upon him, the rest are deserting him: that he has kept his feelings pent up within his own breast, until they have preyed upon his vitals; and that, were he in power now, he would exterminate every one of the recreant Mussulmans who have deserted him, and left him to obloquy.

A cossid has arrived from Cabul; where there has been a fight, in which Zeman Shah Khan has been victorious. One of Amenoollah's sons is killed; and Hamza Khan is wounded: but Futteh Jung and Amenoollah are still in possession of the Bala Hissar.

3rd.—Amenoollah Khan has been worsted. The

Sirdar has sent troops, under his cousin Shamshudeen, to lay waste the Logur country, destroy the forts, and capture the women: for all which Akbar promises a reward of 30,000 rupees.

It is now reported that we are to go in three or four days to Ghuznee, where the Sirdar's cousin Shumshudeen commands. I heard from Sale. The Wallers and Eyres arrived from Tézeen.

4*th*. — The Sirdar is gone or going to Cabul.

Capt. Troup is just summoned to join him and Pottinger: Magrath remains at Tézeen; and Mackenzie, they say, is gone back to Jellalabad again.

Another account states that Amenoollah has fled to the Logur country, and that Futteh Jung holds the Bala Hissar. Further accounts state that Amenoollah, although defeated, got safe into the Bala Hissar. 200 horsemen have been sent from Cabul to the Sirdar: Zeman Shah Khan invites him to assume the throne. He was sleeping when they arrived; but the prospect of a crown soon chased his slumbers; and he was quickly on horseback with Pottinger, leaving orders for Troup, on his arrival, to follow. Mackenzie was not to go to Jellalabad; but to wait half way for further orders from the Sirdar.

The Sirdar has been urgent (but ineffectually of course) with Mr. Eyre to go to Cabul to lay his guns for him. We hear that the hostages are all again with Zeman Shah Khan.

7th. — I have before adverted to Mackenzie's secret mission to Jellalabad. It was first, to ascertain what terms our party would propose: the reply was an offer of two lakhs of rupees for all the prisoners, and that the sooner we were given up to our own people the greater would be the friendship of our government; that, in consequence of the protection afforded us by Dost Mahommed Khan, and Mahommed Shah Khan, their families and possessions would not be attacked: but that the grand question of peace or war, and the settlement of the country, must depend upon replies to be received from the Governor-General. The Sirdar has sent in his rejoinder by Mackenzie; saying, he does not want money; nothing but the friendship of our nation; and that if the ladies and children go, he cannot part with the gentlemen yet.

Gen. Pollock has issued a proclamation, that whoever remains quiet will be unmolested.

Threats are held out that if our troops move up higher than Gundamuk, we shall also be taken 20 miles further up into the hills. To this there are two objections: we are now above the Tézeen valley, in the Jubhar Khail country; these people declare we shall not go further, or if we do they will themselves take us to our army, for they do not want to bring down upon themselves the vengeance of our nation; secondly, we have no carriage: there is little doubt, that Mahommed Shah Khan would care little for our being obliged to leave behind our clothes and the few comforts we have, but we cannot be expected to walk; and the Sirdar or some of the chiefs have taken away to Cabul both our riding horses and baggage ponies.

I consider myself fortunate in having had my horse selected to carry Capt. Mackenzie to Jellalabad: it arrived there lame, and was left with Sale. We have this day seen the general order with Col. Palmer's capitulation at Ghuznee; and dreadful was the tale that shortly followed it. On the faith of the orders received, and the promises of the treaty with the chiefs, these devoted troops left Ghuznee, under the charge of Shumshudeen (the Sirdar's cousin). Treachery seems to be inherent in the blood of this family.

A Ghazeea shot an officer, another shot the Ghazeea; a fight ensued; the whole of our troops were cut up; exertions were made to save the officers, but every Sipahee fell. Seven of the officers are said to be alive, and poor Mrs. Lumsden. It is exactly the counterpart of what occurred with the Cabul force.

Regarding our climate.—The snow has melted on the hills immediately in our front and rear; but the tops of those within a moderate v k (were we permitted to go out of the bounds assigned to us for exercise) are still covered with it.

This morning, when we were dressing, and long after sunrise, the Bheestee took his mushk to the stream, not 50 yards from our tents, and filled it: on his return the water was frozen so hard he could not pour it out; and we had to thaw it by the fire.

8*th*.—A very gloomy day, and cold: we kept up a good fire in the bower. A little snow fell. Serj. Deane's wife, a Persian woman, has been taken by force and married to a younger brother of Mahommed Shah Khan. Whenever this man enters her presence, she salutes him with her slipper. It is only within a few days that she has been told of Deane's death: she appears to have been sincerely attached to him; and is represented as a very pretty young woman.

The man who took the General's body to Jellalabad has returned. He seems highly pleased with the present he has received of 200 rupees: and it appears to have had a good effect; for he reports in glowing terms on the grand turn-out for the funeral, the salvoes fired, &c. on the occasion; and the magnificent appearance of our troops.

10*th*.—Capt. Anderson's little girl was restored, to the great joy of her parents.

Parties run high at Cabul: Zeman Shah Khan says he will be King, Akbar ditto, Jubhar Khan the same, and Amenoollah has a similar fancy, as also Mahommed Shah Khan, and Futteh Jung the Shahzada.

The troops go out daily to fight; Amenoollah's to Ben-i-shehr, and Zeman Shah Khan's to Siah Sung; they fight a little, and then retreat to their own positions. Zeman Shah Khan has been driven out of his house, and Amenoollah out of his; but have part of the town in their favour.

The citizens are ruined by the perfect stagnation of trade; and would probably side with us were we to show in force. Now is the time to strike the blow, but I much dread dilly-dallying just because a handful of us are in Akbar's power. What are *our* lives when compared with the honour of our country? Not that I am at all inclined to have my throat cut: on the contrary, I hope that I shall live to see the British flag once more triumphant in Affghanistan; and then I have no objection to the Ameer Dost Mahommed Khan being reinstated: only let us first show them that we can conquer them, and humble their treacherous chiefs in the dust.

There have been a number of reports to-day, which I believe to have no foundation in truth: amongst others, that the Ghilzye ladies have been packing up all night; and are going to give us the slip and leave us, in consequence of hearing that our force is coming up in four divisions; one of which arrived at Tézeen at four this morning, and looted the place: and that we are to be sent forty kos higher up into the hills. This is, however, contradicted, as some persons who were sent out yesterday to explore have returned, and say that the snow is two feet deep and impracticable.

A letter arrived from the Sirdar; stating that whenever it might be requisite for us to move, he would send us camels, ponies, and all the carriage we require; and that we are positively not to move without his especial order.

11*th*.—Futteh Jung wrote to his brother Timor at Kandahar to come and assist him: Timor sent him 3000 Juzailchees; and assured him that he was himself coming up with the British army.

Major Pottinger writes that there is no present chance of our liberation.

Mahommed Akbar Khan professes that he does not want money from us; but he laughs at our offer of two lakhs for the whole party; and has sent back to say he wishes for eight. It has been recommended that we should offer him five; but the general opinion is that we shall remain in captivity till all is settled.

13*th*.—The Akhonzada says, that, after we left Buddeeabad, all the natives were turned out, and told they might make the best of their way to Jellalabad; being first stripped of their clothes and all that they possessed. Those who had lost their feet of course could not attempt it; and the greater part of the rest, we are told, have been taken as slaves.

We have a slave merchant here now. We learn that men sell for forty-six rupees, and women for twenty-two, each: they are sent off to Khoolloom. 400 Hindostanees have been entrapped at Cabul, under an assurance of safe conduct to Jellalabad.

14*th*.—People have come in from the Lughman valley, who report that the wheat and barley there are ripe, and also the mulberries. Here the crops have not attained the height of six inches.

The booming of heavy guns heard: on which the guard here said the Kulma; hoping that it was something in the Sirdar's favour.

It is reported that Futteh Jung is King, the Sirdar Wuzeer, and Zeman Khan Sirdar-i-Sirdaran. About thirty shots were heard in the night. .

15*th*.—More of Mahommed Rufeek's people have come in from Cabul: they say that Mahommed Akbar Khan is proclaimed King, until his father's return; that he resides at present in the Ben-i-shehr; and that Amenoollah has free ingress and egress to and from him, for the purpose of meeting with Futteh Jung. The Sirdar has sent for all our horses, ponies, &c. The Naib Shureef has sent Mrs. Sturt and me tea and sugar: — a kind attention and great comfort.

Akbar says he will fight our army. This is expressed in a letter written to Suballan Khan, the captain of our guard. Dost Mahommed Khan asserts that it is Major Pottinger who retards our release: but he is as much a prisoner as ourselves.

16*th*.— I kept the anniversary of my marriage by dining with the ladies of Mahommed Shah Khan's family; who told us that Futteh Jung was King, Mahommed Akbar Khan Wuzeer, and Mahommed Shah Khan the Sirdar-i-Sirdaran. It was an extremely stupid visit. We had two female servants to interpret for us. Three of Mahommed Shah Khan's wives and some of Dost Mahommed's, with the mother of the chiefs, and two of their unmarried sisters, were present. They were, generally speaking, inclined to *embonpoint*, largely formed, and coarsely featured; their dress inelegant, and of the coarsest materials. The favourite wife, and the best dressed, was attired in a common Cabul silk, with a coarse piece of chintz inserted behind, evidently for economy's sake. The dress, which covers the whole person, nearly resembles a common night-dress; and has tacked on to it coins, or other pieces of silver or gold, such as crescents, &c., all over the sleeves, the front and sides, from the shoulders to the feet. A breast-plate is worn, commencing at the throat, of coins strung together: this descends far below the waist; and when they sit down, it hangs in festoons on the lap. Only the favourite wore gold coins; those of the other ladies being of silver. They had nothing in the way of jewels, properly so called. About seven common-sized pearls surrounding an emerald full of flaws, the whole set as a nose ornament, was the handsomest thing I saw in the trinket way. Some of them had very inferior ear-rings of gold and silver. They wear their hair in innumerable small plaits hanging down: these are arranged once a week after taking the bath; and the tresses are then well stiffened with gum. The unmarried women bend their hair in a flat braid across the forehead touching the eyebrows; which gives them a very heavy look. These said eyebrows, whilst they are maidens, remain as nature formed them: but when they marry, the hair of the centre is carefully picked out; and the arch, thus most unnaturally raised, is painted. The Cabul women are much addicted to the use of both white and red paint; and they colour not only the nails, as in Hindostan, but the whole hand up to the wrist, which looks as though it had been plunged in blood, and to our ideas is very disgusting. A particular plant is often used for this purpose.

The upper part of the leaf sparkles, and resembles the ice plant; but the lower side is red, and on being pressed gives a fine dye. A chuddah is thrown over the head and shoulders in the house, as in Hindostan; and when they go out they wear the bourka, ru-i-bund, and legwraps: high-heeled iron-shod slippers complete the costume. After a time an extremely dirty cloth was spread over the numdas in front of us, and dishes of pillau, dhye or sour curd, and férnéz or sweet curd, were placed before us. Those who had not taken a spoon with them, ate with their fingers, Affghan fashion; —an accomplishment in which I am by no means *au fait*. We drank water out of a tea-pot. A dinner was given to the gentlemen by Abdoollah Khan at his tents about two miles off, nearer the snow.

In the evening Capt. Mackenzie arrived; and I received a letter from Sale.

There seems to be no present prospect of release. We hear that the force under Gen. Nott has been reinforced by Brig. England; who had nevertheless been beaten back in the first instance: —that Gen. Nott was to march towards Cabul as yesterday (the 15th); and that Gen. Pollock was still awaiting orders from Lord Ellenborough; but that whether they arrive or not, we must now wait until Nott's force gets near to Cabul to make a simultaneous attack. Now as Akbar only boasts of

12,000 men against us, and as we have fully that number at Jellalabad, with 18-pounders, Pollock's force would easily capture Cabul in the present position of affairs. A short time ago it would have been still easier, as there was then more division among the Affghan troops.

A letter from Mahommed Akbar Khan to Sultan Khan has been intercepted; in which he acknowledges, that for every rupee he can muster, the Shahzada (Futteh Jung) can produce a gold mohur.

An European and some natives were murdered near our camp at Jellalabad: and, vigorous measures not being taken, the offence was repeated; and a duffodar of Tait's horse fell a victim to the Affghans. On the murderer taking refuge in a village, Tait immediately surrounded it with his men; and then reported the circumstance to Gen. Pollock; who, after consulting with Capt. Macgregor, sent to tell the people of the village that if they did not, within a specified time, give up the malefactor to be hanged by us, he would burn the village, and put every living being in it to death. The time had not expired when this news came. Cruel as an action of this kind may appear, it is probably the best method of striking terror into these savages, and perhaps of eventually preventing bloodshed.

Capt. Mackenzie has brought me intelligence of

Sale's having broken three of his ribs, from his horse falling with him; and that he has suffered also from inflammation in consequence of the accident; but that he is fast recovering, if not, as he says he is, quite well and fit for work again.

17*th*. — I heard this morning that part of my letters regarding the siege had arrived in England, and been laid before the Court of Directors.

20*th*. — Lady Macnaghten and a part of the ladies breakfasted with Dost Mahommed Khan and his ladies. They were told that, if the Sirdar gains the Bala Hissar, we shall all go there; if not, we go to Jellalabad.

One report states, that the Sirdar, who is resident at Ben-i-shehr, was to meet Futteh Jung on amicable terms; but that the latter refused to go outside the Bala Hissar until Mahommed Shah Khan and Sultan Jan were given up to him as hostages, which was done: but when Futteh Jung got as far as the Musjid, finding Akbar at the head of 3,000 men, fearing treachery, he retreated, shut the gates, and fired on Akbar's party. Another account states, that when the gates were opened for Futteh Jung to go out, Amenoollah released the hostages, and then went over to the Sirdar himself. Mackenzie is supposed to be at Tézeen to-day; and will be here either to-morrow or in three days. It is worthy of remark, that during Lady Macnaghten's visit to the ladies this morning, Dost Mahommed Khan was present the whole time; which was decidedly, according to Affghan custom, an insult; as the men never are present when their wives receive company.

A Kandaharee female servant of these ladies told them in Hindostanee not to believe a word that Dost Mahommed said to them; as his intelligence was all false and was intended to mislead them.

A storm of thunder and rain at dinner-time: in the evening we ascended the hill, about 150 feet; and then found the view bounded by another: so we fatigued ourselves to no purpose. A fire beacon lighted on the hill at night.

21*st*.—Lady Macnaghten and two other ladies breakfasted with Khojeh Mahommed Khan's family; and on this occasion two men were present. The rest of us were not invited.

Khojeh Mahommed sighed much and seemed out of spirits. According to the statement of their servants, the ladies have not had food cooked for them for two days in consequence of their grief. In these parties they do not eat with the Kaffirs; but are profuse of their expressions of good will; and desire us to ask them for any thing we require.

Their professions were put to the test; at least those of Dost Mahommed himself: a gentleman asked for a chillum, and was told to go to the devil (Goom Shud).

THE CAPTIVITY. 351

I received two notes from Sale dated the 15th; informing me that he had received a highly gratifying letter from Lord Ellenborough, and another from Sir Jasper Nicholls, regarding the holding of Jellalabad, the chupao on Akbar's camp, &c.; and stating that the 35th were to be made light infantry; the Company's troops to have medals, and to bear " Jellalabad " and a mural crown on their colours: also that Lord Ellenborough would request Her Majesty's permission that the 13th should be similarly honoured.

Chintz, sugar candy, tea, and cheese, distributed amongst the ladies; they were sent to us by our friends at Jellalabad: also Shalu (Turkey red cotton cloth) and jean, with boots and shoes for the gentlemen. We also received the March overland mail. I heard a droll anecdote of Akbar when he went off to Cabul from Tézeen. His followers asked him what tent they should take for him: his reply was given with great good humour (he believed himself on the point of mounting a throne);—" The ladies and people above have got all our tents here; but you may send my salaam to Gen. Sale, and ask him to lend me one of those he took from me."

22nd.—The first thing we heard this morning was, that ponies had arrived and that we are going to Cabul. They afterwards told us that we are going to Shéwakee, a fort near the Pillar. The officers went to Dost Mahommed and informed him that only thirty-three ponies had arrived, and no camels; and that it was impossible we could move without more means of transport: so the order to march at mid-day was rescinded; and we have been promised animals to start with early to-morrow morning. We are to go to Khoord Cabul, seventeen miles, as our first march.

23*rd.* — Mules arrived for three kujavas; but no camels, as we take a road that is bad for these animals.

Started at a little before 10 A. M., and got to the fort we formerly went to at Khoord Cabul, at 6 P. M. We travelled fully twenty-two miles, following the road to Tézeen, by which we came to Zanduh, for some time, and then turning to the left. Except in a few places the road was tolerable. We crossed a highly cultivated valley studded with forts; a perfect oasis in our barren mountain track. The yellow briar-rose is in bloom, and asphodels of three different colours, yellow, pink, and a greenish brown, a pretty description of borage, and a plant resembling sage with a red flower; and blue sage in blossom was found amongst the wells and stones. The climate here was much warmer than at Zanduh. We did not strike into the regular road till we arrived at the Huft Kotul; and here we came upon a sad scene of decaying bodies, amongst which poor Major Ewart's was still recognisable.

There is a fort opposite to the point where the short road turns back to Seh Baba; and another at Thana Tariffa, which is the entrance to the Thungee on the Jellalabad side. This was also dreadful to go through; both to the sight and smell equally offensive.

Immediately after emerging from the pass, we took a short cut to the left of the regular road, which brought us to the fort. In its immediate vicinity there was rich cultivation; but a great deal of land formerly tilled lies fallow this year.

24*th*.—We left the fort at about the same time as yesterday: our march was eighteen or nineteen miles over hill and dale, with a rich valley but scantily cultivated on our left. We had a difficult ascent over a rocky hill; after which we passed a tope which has no appearance of having been opened. There is a fine tank nearly opposite to it, shaded by trees, and containing small fish: it is supplied with beautifully clear water from the Karez, near it; from which, I suppose, it takes its name of Káreza. We then pursued our way over a plain, covered with stones, till we ascended a difficult rocky hill, which was surmounted by the famous Pillar generally ascribed to Alexander the Great. It is evidently not of Affghan workmanship; and is now out of the perpendicular, leaning back, as if it shrank from Cabul. The outer casing is quite gone; and it is not therefore wonderful that no inscription exists: and the greater part of the square base it rested on has also mouldered away. From this spot there is a magnificent view. Immediately below us was a richly cultivated country studded with forts and fruit trees, the Logur river, beyond it the Siah Sung, and a distant view of Cabul, and then ranges of hills, the whole bounded by the mountains of Kohistan and the Hindo Koosh, covered with perperpetual snow. The descent on the Cabul side is rather more difficult in parts; particularly when you have not an acquaintance of long standing with your horse; which was my case, having hired for the day a mere baggage poney, for the large sum of two rupees six anas. The creature was evidently not used to scrambling; and did not like it. Whenever he came to a difficult place, he jumped down with his two fore feet; and then considered whether he should bring the hinder ones after them; and in this way jumped up on rocks, where kids would joy to disport, but where he shook with fear. However, riding was less trouble than walking on such a road; and I got safely through. We passed another tope which had been opened, and a succession of forts; and at length arrived at Noor Mahommed, the Meer Akor's Fort: here we were not expected; no notice having been given. The truth is, that the Sirdar ordered us to be sent to a fort of Mahommed Shah Khan's, two miles from this one; but Mahommed is to bring his family hither; and was determined to keep his own fort for them. We were first told that two open stables or cowsheds, down a narrow gulley in the outer square, were all the accommodation they had to give us.

As no one would fight for the ladies, I determined to *be Yaghi* myself; and I went with Mr. Melville to Dost Mahommed Khan and Mahommed Rufeek. At length our bower party got a small room over the gateway of the inner fort; with a promise of better quarters for all to-morrow.

The reason given for our sudden flitting from Zanduh is an expected chupao from the two chiefs, Azaid Khan, and Aziz Khan; who offered, if Macgregor would furnish the cash, to raise 2000 men, and carry us off to our friends.

There was firing of guns all day long; and at night very sharp firing, without much intermission. Being in pain from the arm that was wounded, and in great anxiety for the result (having heard from the Affghans here that Akbar meant to surprise and take the Bala Hissar), I never closed my eyes until after daybreak; when we heard the muezzin call to prayers.

25th.—The tables were turned last night; for a sally was made from the Bala Hissar; and Mahommed Akbar Khan was, they say, nearly caught. He escaped to a fort near the Shah's camp, behind Siah Sung.

The females were removed from this fort, and we all got excellent quarters. In addition to the two rooms apportioned to our party, we have permission to sit, in the daytime, in a room in a bourj, a small octagon with oorsees or open-work lattices. There are two flights of steep steps to mount to it from our apartments, which are upstairs; but the view from it is so refreshing, looking over all the forts and highly cultivated grounds; it has the advantage of being always cool; and which compensates for the trouble in getting there.

The Sirdar says he will not remain here when our force comes up, but retire to the Kohistan, and allow the English to take Cabul: after which he will come forward with an offer to go to Hindostan, and take his father's place, if they will permit the Ameer Dost Mahommed Khan to return and rule in this country.

26th. — We heard a few guns early in the morning. This day they say the Sirdar is to have a friendly conference with Futteh Jung; but it is to be hoped that the latter will not put himself into the power of his treacherous enemy.

Khan Shireen Khan, the head of the Kuzzilbashes, keeps neuter. Zeman Shah Khan seems to be but a lukewarm friend of the Sirdar.

The gentlemen of Cabul are all disgusted at the treachery that took place, ending in the murder of Shah Shoojah.

The shopkeepers and merchants wish for us back; as the circulation of rupees is much less than in our time: and the cultivators would fain leave the army and look after their crops.

Gen. Pollock offers to exchange the captive ladies and children, against Akbar's family of four wives with their children. One of the former is a daughter of Mahommed Shah Khan; and another is a sister of Sirballan Khan's. Capt. Troup came to see us, and brought us a message from the Sirdar, desiring we would all write to him, and state whatever we required, that he might send it to us.

27th. — Capt. Troup returned to the Sirdar, and took our notes and lists with him; also a letter for Sale, though he doubts its being sent immediately. This day was fixed for a conference between Akbar and Futteh Jung: Akbar required him to vacate the Bala Hissar; and says he may go into the strongest fort in the neighbourhood, and keep all his guns; giving up his army, wherewith Akbar is to go down and fight the British force. No firing heard to-day; but we hope that Futteh Jung will manage to hold out until our force comes to his assistance.

28th.—The advance of our army has arrived at Gundamuk; and the rest are following, purchasing up carriage at any expense.

The Kandahar force have been attacked by the Affghans; who have been signally defeated; which has struck such terror into them, that they are flying in all directions: this is their own account.

29th.—Sujat Dowlut, the son of Zeman Shah Khan, and the murderer of Shah Shoojah, came to the fort to visit Ali Mohammed Khan. To his father's honour be it said that he refused to see him for some time after the murder. It is reported that we leave this place in six days for — no one knows where.

30th.—There was firing late in the evening from the Bala Hissar and the city. A man of some respectability, with three or four followers, came to see Capt. Johnson, and bring him some things:

they were all taken away by the Affghans; and the people carried off prisoners to Akbar.

The Kuzzilbashes have openly declared in favour of Futteh Jung. They are throwing provisions into the Bala Hissar; and strengthening the works.

Our troops have been some days at Gundamuk. There are orders that the officers are not to go out of the fort, as they did before, to bathe. We hope we shall not be interdicted walking in the garden, as we always have guards with us there; and every night we are locked into the square; and the servants cannot go outside the gate for any purpose without a guard.

1st *June.* — The Naïb Shureef is obliged to hide for safety. Mahommed Rufeek is sent away; and Ali Mohammed Khan has now sole charge of us.

2d. — It is true that our troops left Kandahar on the 16th of last month. General Nott's force has given the Affghans a fourth beating at Khelat-i-Gilzie; and killed 2000 men. Gen. Pollock's division is expected here on the 15th.

Sharp firing all day; particularly in the afternoon, evening, and all night.

3d. — The servants have a report that whenever we leave this place, Futteh Jung means to chupao us; and that twenty men are always on the watch, mounted, to carry the intelligence of our removal to him.

4th.—Capt. Troup came to us; and brought me two parcels from Sale; one of which was for distribution amongst the ladies. Also letters enclosing copies of Lord Ellenborough's and Sir Jasper Nicholls' letters to him. Their contents were so gratifying that I shook off all my feverish feelings and concomitant weakness; and in the gladness of my heart felt quite well again.

Troup seems to think that the Sirdar will succeed in getting possession of the Bala Hissar. He assures Futteh Jung that he has a mine all ready to spring; but will not have recourse to it till the last moment. Now this is an evident *ruse;* for if he had the means he would take the Bala Hissar at once: and we have heard that he has mined in three places to the extent of twelve hauts; but has each time come to solid rock, on which the miners can make no impression. The cossid, who brought our letters, brought one also for the Sirdar; and another for Futteh Jung from Macgregor: on the receipt of the latter, Futteh Jung fired a royal salute and made a sally.

The Sirdar sent us some coarse cloth, soap, an Affghan chillumchee, and some tallow candles: others received sundry donations of the like kind.

6th.—The Sirdar is said to have possession of the Bala Hissar; and to occupy the gate nearest to us: while the Kuzzilbashes hold the Chandowlee gate; and Mahommed Shah another. Futteh Jung is said to have given up two lakhs of rupees to Akbar.

The tale of the mine was true; but Futteh Jung had filled it with water.

Mahommed Shah Khan and Sultan Jan have been daily for three days at the Bala Hissar, unattended; in conference with the Shahzada, who gave them khelluts, &c. He then asked Mahommed Akbar Khan to meet him in friendly conference in the gateway, each to have only five followers: but the Sirdar refused to go further than John Hicks' tomb, fearing treachery. He had previously warned Mahommed Shah not to trust Futteh Jung; who might easily have secured the two others each of these days: but we suspect his aim was to lull them into security, to enable him to seize the Sirdar.

Here he has shown bad policy: for though Akbar is the superior in rank, Mahommed Shah has the troops, and what money they can raise at command. Sultan Jan is the fighting arm of the trio, under the latter; whilst Akbar sits in durbar, laughs, talks, and squeezes all who are suspected of having money. He has carefully kept all our notes to him, asking for or thanking him for things received: no doubt to produce at the last; as a further proof of his kindness to his captives. Dr. Grant is said to be alive and safe with some Bunneah; who of course keeps him secreted from the chiefs, that he and not they may have a reward: but we heard so positively that he was killed, near the lake beyond Behmaru, that our hopes are but faint.

Much firing in the evening and night.

7th.—We hear that last night there was a sortie from the Bala Hissar; and an attack made on two guns of Mahommed Akbar's. They did not succeed in capturing them; but took some ammunition and camels. An attempt was made to carry off the camels belonging to this fort, which were out grazing; but six horsemen went from hence and rescued them.

Akbar says he does not spring his mine because it will damage the walls of the Bala Hissar, and make it easier for the English to enter the place; and that even were the gates open, he doubts the courage of his troops to enter them.

Amenoollah Khan has been for some time soliciting permission to leave the Sirdar, to go to Loghur on important affairs of his own: this has induced the Sirdar to seize him, which is now supposed to be the cause of all the firing we heard last night. Whether this will prove for our advantage or not, remains to be proved.

This chief is said to have eighteen lakhs of rupees; which Mahommed Akbar Khan will probably endeavour to squeeze out of him: however, he is not likely to have it here. If his treasure is secure at Loghur, and his sons rise in his favour (as he can bring 10,000 men into the field), a very powerful diversion may be formed, whether they join us or Futteh Jung: if, on the contrary, Akbar procures even one lakh of ready cash, he can do much mischief; by raising troops even for a few weeks to annoy our force. The celerity with which troops are raised is quite astonishing to us; who are accustomed to see recruits drilled for a length of time. Here, every man is born a soldier; every child has his knife, — that weapon which has proved so destructive in the hands of a hostile peasantry, incited against us by the moollahs, who threaten eternal perdition to all who do not join in the cause of the Ghazeeas; whilst heaven, filled with Houris, is the recompence for every man who falls in a religious war. With them, the only expense attending the soldier consists in his pay, which is scanty; his horse, if he have one, is his own; and every Affghan is armed completely with some three or four of these knives, of different sizes — from that as long as a sword to a small dagger — pistols, and a juzail; which latter predominates over the matchlock: they carry much farther than our muskets; so that when our men are beyond range to hit them, they pour a destroying fire on us. Regarding these same muskets being better than matchlocks; those who had only the latter may have taken them of late in exchange; but, generally speaking, the only useful part to the Affghans are the locks; which they tear off, and leave the rest.

Capt. Troup did not return to the Sirdar till this morning. The man, who went with him, has returned; and states that the Sirdar has blown up the bastion of the Bala Hissar which is nearest to the Shōr Bazar. There is, however, some discrepancy in his account; as he states that he saw the Sirdar's men parading about on the tops of the very bastion that has been destroyed: he also added, that they were busily employed in throwing out the dead bodies.

It is a great pity that Gen. Pollock's force does not move up. Futteh Jung pays the Hindostanees in the Bala Hissar a rupee a day to keep watch at the gates; being afraid to trust the Affghans.

Mahommed Akbar's guns are worked by three Chuprassies, two Buglers, and a few other of our runaways.

It is said that whenever we leave this place, there will be great opposition made to our removal; and that various parties will endeavour to get us into their power.

3 p. m.—Further accounts have just been brought in; stating that yesterday's fight, at the Bala Hissar, was commenced by Sultan Jan. When he got tired, Mahommed Shah Khan took his place; and when he too was fatigued, the Sirdar assumed command in person. When he brought his gun to bear on the mine at the bourj, Futteh Jung ran another gun opposite; and blew the Sirdar's gun away!—a novel method of firing a train; nevertheless it seems the mine was fired; and, by some bungling, Akbar blew up 300 of his own men. But Futteh Jung gave in, and the Sirdar is supposed to have the Bala Hissar. We only obtain such information as the Khan and his guard are pleased to communicate; excepting those of our party who perchance overhear them speaking amongst themselves; when, however, they generally use Pushtoo, to prevent our understanding them. Four Coolies have arrived with two tin boxes and two baskets from Tézeen. They are supposed to have come from Jellalabad; as all were quickly huddled into a room and locked up; and a man despatched to the Sirdar to know his pleasure concerning them.

The packets have been distributed; mostly medicine for Dr. Magrath.

There were letters and newspapers; but those have been sent to the Sirdar.

In the garden in the evening we heard that the Sirdar had sent his salaam, that he was master of the Bala Hissar; but just as we entered the gate we heard that, so far from that being the case, he had only taken the bourj above. Now that same bourj above completely commands the fort. However Akbar has no guns in it; though by manual labour he could easily drag them up. The mountain train guns go up on mules well; and I have seen them myself practising over that very hill.

There is another report that Gool Mahommed is to chupao us in four days. We heard the report of some juzails between nine and ten p. m.

8th. — The servants declare, that above forty guns were fired last night between eleven and twelve; but some of the officers, who were awake, did not hear them any more than I did. On the same authority we have a rumour of Futteh Jung's having taken two of the Sirdar's tents and some ammunition; and of his having killed forty of his Ghazeeas.

They say that the Sirdar sent Zeman Shah

Khan to treat with Futteh Jung; and to propose that the latter should remain king; making Akbar his wuzeer; and that he should make over all the guns and troops to him, to go and fight the English with. Futteh Jung has placed Zeman Shah Khan in confinement, until he gets a reply to his message to the Sirdar, in which he accedes to his request; on condition that he previously places all the captives in his hands.

9*th.* — Capt. Mackenzie arrived; and brought some newspapers and letters, — those which we have been expecting back from the Sirdar: and we strongly suspect that he has kept many. Mackenzie assures us that Futteh Jung has surrendered the Bala Hissar to Akbar Khan; who has demanded all his treasure, as the first step he takes.

There seems to have been no military necessity for the surrender. One bourj had been mined; but traverses might have been thrown up to render the place perfectly secure from any Affghan attack. It is probable that the Arabs were intimidated by the effect of the mine; *that* being a species of warfare they particularly dread. Futteh Jung had held out for a month — the time, it is said, he had promised to do so; and Pollock's force not moving to his succour, he probably became disheartened. He now has not only lost his treasure; but it is likely he may lose his life also: for he never can feel safe whilst in the power of Akbar and Mahommed Shah. The latter resides in the Bala Hissar; the former in the Shōr Bazar. Both Mahommed Shah and Sultan Jan were wounded in the explosion of the bourj, by stones falling on their heads.

Pollock's force is suffering from sickness; occasioned by the great heat of Jellalabad.

Col. Parsons' arrangements only extend to camels and carriage cattle as far as Peshawer. Capt. Mackeson, with great difficulty, prevailed on them to go as far as Jellalabad; but no further: and immense exertions have been made to enable the force to leave that place. The arrangements are, we hear, nearly completed: but now that Akbar has money (18 lakhs, it is said) at his command, he may raise troops to harass ours.

Gen. Nott is said still to be encamped on this side of Khelat-i-Gilzie. A week or ten days ago, one brigade might have taken Cabul without opposition.

The Affghans are very jealous of any people coming to us; lest we should obtain information. A young man of great respectability, who came to bring some things for Capt. Johnson a few days since, has been fined 6000 rupees; and in addition to that has been tortured, and had all his nails torn out.

10*th.*—A slight earthquake in the morning; and four shocks during the night.

11*th.*—Our guard is increased by thirty men.

The fruit in the garden is sold to a Khoord; who says, if we will pay him a few rupees, we may eat any we like: but the grapes are sour, and will not be ripe for these six weeks at least. The sour plums make preserves.

It appears very uncertain what power Akbar really possesses. The Kuzzilbashes occupy the gate which commands their quarter. Mahommed Shah Khan has one. Futteh Jung is still king, and lives in the interior of the Bala Hissar. Akbar still inhabits a house in the Shōr Bazar.

12*th.*—A Hindostanee was severely beaten at the gate; being suspected of bringing in news.

13*th.*—A Peshawer-i-Suwar was beaten, and had his horse taken from him, for attempting to come here: if he had any letters, they were not discovered.

Various reports to-day: some, that our troops are at Gundamuk; and others that the forces both at Jellalabad and at Kandahar, &c. are all retreating to the provinces, and leaving us to enjoy the gentle mercies of our captors.

14*th.*—Ali Mahommed Khan says that we shall not leave this fort: that even if Akbar meditated our removal, the various tribes, by whom we are surrounded, would look to their own interests; and interfere to get us into their own hands. This agrees with what Dost Mahommed Khan told us at Zanduh; that the Sirdar had been peremptory in ordering our removal to Cabul; but that he had, in so doing, committed a great mistake; as he would probably find out in three or four days after our arrival at the capital; and when it would be too late to rectify his error.

15th.—In consequence of having yesterday given a rupee to the Khoordish Baghwan; he had this evening two dallies of the finest mulberries the garden produced (the Bédanas) ready for us; nicely cooled by the rill of the stream, and covered with a shower of roses. We filled our basket; and sat and ate the fruit under the vines; and look forward to delicious sherbet from the flowers to-morrow.

6th.—Towards morning we were awakened by such a noise, that we could not possibly imagine it to be less than a chupao! on inquiry it proved to be a row between an ayah and a bearer.

The *on-dit* of to-day is, that 4000 Sikhs are to hold Jellalabad, whilst our troops come up to Cabul. The Affghans say that eight of our regiments are at Gundamuk. On the arrival of the force it is expected by the Affghans that Akbar and Mahommed Shah will flee; but that very few of their followers will accompany them. They will take us with them; either to Mecca or Room! By the latter they mean Constantinople.

They tell us that Futteh Jung is a prisoner.

Late in the evening news arrived that Kamran (who, by-the-bye, we heard was put to death by his minister, Yai Mahommed, some time since) is coming with an army from Herat; to form a coalition with Futteh Jung, Akbar, the Ghilzyes, and all the Affghan chiefs. They are to go down and fight our force: if they are successful, we are to remain as we are; if not, to be sent via Charekar to Turkistan.

A report prevalent amongst the Affghans that our force has marched from Jellalabad; and that we consequently shall soon be removed from hence.

The Prince Futteh Jung is still in confinement. Mahommed Akbar Khan, Mahommed Shah Khan, and the Ghilzye chiefs, are bent on having him put to death. Zeman Shah Khan, and the more moderate party, oppose it: not from affection for us or him, but as a measure of better policy. The Ghazeeas, however, are determined to steep the chiefs as deeply in blood as they can, to prevent the possibility of their making any terms with us. They say the captives shall not be taken away from Cabul; and that if the Sirdar or any of the Ghilzye chiefs attempt to fly, they will put them to death.

Zeman Khan wishes the Sirdar to send him to Jellalabad to treat; taking the captives with him. This Akbar will not hear of: and they have had a quarrel, ending in a fight. The sound of cannon has been heard; also vollies of musketry. A grand battle is to come off on Sunday.

18*th.*—Waterloo day.—It seems that we are to be sent viâ the Kohistan to Bokhara. Mackenzie writes, that we are to be prepared for a sudden move.

19*th.* — A letter is said to have arrived from Gen. Pollock to Akbar; who, with Futteh Jung and all the chiefs, is going in four days to Jellalabad to salaam. The Ameer is on his way up to resume the throne.

21*st.* — Henry's birthday; celebrated by a great battle in Cabul; in which Akbar has been victorious; though he has lost from sixty to eighty men.

Zeman Shah Khan is said to have been made prisoner, with both his sons.

Another report states, they have all three escaped: also, that Zeman was surrounded in a fort, but contrived to get away from it. He had eighteen guns out; and the Sirdar had as many:

the latter is going down to Jellalabad, to give battle to the English force there.

22d.— Various reports to-day: — That Zeman Khan lost fifteen guns yesterday, and all his treasure: — that to-morrow there will be a great fight between the Sirdar and Khan Shireen Khan.

Later accounts in the evening state that Khan Shireen has made his salaam; and that we are to go to the Bala Hissar. Plenty of firing heard by us: said by some to be fighting; by others to be salutes in honour of Futteh Jung being *declared* king.

23d.— The Dost is not to come up until after the rains. No chance of our removal at present.

25th.— Mackenzie and Troup arrived.

Colonel Palmer is said to have been tortured at Ghuznee. Mohun Lull has been seized, and tortured. Humza Khan has been imprisoned by the Sirdar. Ali Bega, Naïb Shureef, and Jan Fishan Khan have fled: the latter's two sons have been murdered. Osman Khan (the late wuzeer) has been seized by Akbar. Nott is said to have returned to Kandahar; after putting to death all his Affghan captives, and blowing up Kelat-i-Ghilzie. This seems (if true) to be a strange proceeding, if we are to retain the country; as the fortress was but just completed; and was considered an indispensable site for a granary and depôt of troops. Major Rawlinson's opinion is, that our troops will all be withdrawn in the autumn: but this does not square with the order, received by Ali Bega from Dallas, to lay in all the provisions he can possibly store in Cabul.

Ali Mahommed tells us that the Khyberries have risen; and that we have sent two regiments and two guns against them: but there is an inkling that more guns have arrived at Jellalabad; and therefore we might have sent a force to protect them on their way up. They say, also, that Pollock has actually moved up as far as Gundamuk; and there is a report that our men at Buddeeabad have been set at liberty by our troops; who blew up the fort, and also that at Tighree.

26th. — A report that 10,000 Sikhs have come up from Peshawer; that they are in the Lughman valley; have destroyed Tighree; and, fearing a chupao on Buddeeabad, all the prisoners there were brought away: they were fed on bread and water only after we left them. The day after our departure, Mrs. Wade (wife of a sergeant) changed her attire, threw off the European dress, and adopted the costume of the Mussulmans; and, professing to have changed her creed also, consorted with the Nazir of our inveterate enemy, Mahommed Shah Khan; and gave information of some plans laid by the men for their escape; which nearly caused them all to have their throats cut. Having reported to her Affghan paramour the manner in which her husband had secreted some gold mohurs in his jorabs, he was of course plundered of them. The Hindostanees were stripped of every article of clothing they possessed; and had even the rags taken off their sores, to ascertain there was no money concealed: they were then turned out. Some got to Jellalabad; through the kindness of a Hindu Bunneah, who sent them down on a jhala; others have been made slaves. Of the unfortunate servants, Mrs. Sturt and I left behind us, we have no tidings.

The Europeans found it dreadfully hot at Buddeeabad; and most of them were attacked by fever: their only remedy being bleeding with a penknife; in which Mr. Blewitt was very successful. One man (Sergt. Reynolds), who was left there with a broken arm, died of lockjaw.

Sergt. Fare brought with him the colour of the 44th which has been before mentioned. A few days after Capt. Souter's arrival at Buddeeabad, Brig. Shelton expressed a wish that the colour should be given to his servant (Moore, of the 44th); for the purpose of sewing it in a piece of cloth; and to keep it in his possession. Previous to our quitting Buddeeabad, the Brigadier suggested that the colour should be left with Sergt. Fare; who, with the party that was left at the fort, would, it was expected, be released before those who proceeded to Cabul. Sergt. Fare kept the colour concealed by wrapping it round him; and when he joined us here (at Shewakee) he made it over to Gen. Shelton; who retains it in his possession.

Of so incorrect a personage as Mrs. Wade I shall only further say, that she is at Mahommed Shah Khan's fort with her Affghan lover; and has taken with her young Stoker. As he is the son of a man in Sale's regiment, I am doing all I can to get the Sirdar (through Capt. Troup's entreaty) to have him brought here; and again placed under Mrs. Burnes's care. She and her infant are looking very miserable, as are most of the men.

Col. Stoddart and Capt. Arthur Conolly are prisoners at Bokhara. The latter had been enthusiastically employed in endeavouring to effect the release of the slaves in Kokan. The king of Bokhara conquered the chief of that country; and placed Conolly in confinement at Bokhara. He and his fellow-prisoner, by the last accounts, had been 126 days confined in a dungeon underground, without light: they had never changed their clothes, nor washed; and their food was let down to them once in four or five days. A native, who had compassion on them, received a message through the person who took their food to them; and through him Conolly has communicated with his family here; who, alas! are now powerless to assist him.

We ate the first really ripe apricots (*zerdaloos*) and cherries (*gulas*) brought in from the city: but the produce of the Kohistan, the aloo baloo, or sour wild cherry, in the garden, is now pretty ripe; and the apricots and some of the green plums are ripening. The peach of this garden is very inferior to what I used to purchase last year. The best apricot in it is the white one; it is called kysee; and has a flavour of rose-water.

The red plum is not permitted to ripen properly: it has some flavour; and is called turnasook. The green plum looks something like a greengage; but has no flavour except that of *eau sucrée*.

It is said, on the authority of Sergt. Wade, — who was informed by his wife, who professed to have her information from Mahommed Shah Khan's family, — that we are all going to be sent to Bokhara. There is also a report, not however traceable to any foundation, that Pollock's force is not to move upwards until the middle of August.

28*th*. — An earthquake about 11 A. M., and another about 9 P. M.; sufficient both times to make the roof creak.

We have heard from undoubted authority that Mahommed Akbar Khan said in the durbar, before he left Cabul to follow our troops in January, that it was his intention to go and *kuttle kurra*, or cut the throats of all our force; *and, after that, let* THEM *beware,*—meaning the chiefs. He seems to be now verifying his promise; and is, by all accounts, squeezing as much wealth as he can out of all those who are in his power; and disgusting every one of them.

29*th.*—Jan Fishan Khan has escaped to Jellalabad. Khan Shireen Khan, and many of those friendly to the English, have retired into the hills.

30*th.*—Troup left us; taking part of my journal, and plenty of letters; as it is said he is to be sent to Jellalabad. Mackenzie is ill with fever; and unable to go with him.

July 1*st.*—The Sirdar has promised that Stoker shall be sent back to us; but he has not yet arrived.

3*rd.*—Troup arrived; and brought us a comb and two caps from Mahommed Rufeek. The Sirdar still talks of sending him to Jellalabad; but says he must wait four or five days, as he, the Sirdar, is busy collecting his revenue. The hostages

THE CAPTIVITY. 379

are all coming here to-morrow or next day. I fear their arrival will crowd us very much; and at present we have Mackenzie, Waller, and Melville laid up with fever.

Timor Shah says that if the English will support him on his father's throne, well and good; if not, that he will prefer going to Loodianah, on a pension.

A man has just come in, and reports that our troops are in the Lughman valley. We conclude they are foraging parties, collecting grain.

4*th*.—The Cabullees say they will cut Akbar in pieces, before they will permit us to be taken away. The hostages are sold to Akbar for 400 gold mohurs.

Sultan Khan, said to be made Sirdar-i-Sirdaran.

5*th*.—The Wuzeer Akbar Khan went to reside in the Bala Hissar. Troup, who left us, had to follow him there with Pottinger.

6*th*. — All the hostages are to come here; except Conolly, who is to remain with the Wuzeer in the Bala Hissar. There are reports that our troops have left Kandahar; having received a number of camels from Sindh. When the cossid started, they had made three marches hitherwards. As a cossid takes eight or ten days to come, they must have left Kandahar about the 26th or 28th. They have twenty-two marches thence to Cabul; which, with the detention at Ghuznee, and on the road, if they have any fighting, will retard the arrival of the force until from the 25th instant to the 1st of August.

Akbar has ordered the ditch round the Bala Hissar to be cleaned out; and proposes sending 6000 men, under Mahommed Shah Khan, to occupy the passes between this place and Jellalabad. But his grand battle is to take place here, on the plain in front of the Bala Hissar. Akbar has ordered every one to be fined who addresses him, or speaks of him, otherwise than as the wuzeer. Mrs. Burnes' child died; and was buried under the hill: the service was performed by Mr. Eyre.

7*th.*— The news we heard yesterday is confirmed by Troup and Conolly; with this addition from the Khan, that Timor Shah is proclaimed King of Kandahar. Col. Palmer is said to have died at Ghuznee. When Mahommed Akbar Khan went to the durbar the day we left Cabul, prepared for his journey, and publicly declared that it was his intention to *kuttle kurra* all the English, Zeman Shah Khan sent to Conolly, who wrote off to Major Pottinger, to put him on his guard. This letter arrived at Bhoodkhak while Pottinger and Akbar were in conference: the treating went on notwithstanding, and the result was the hostages being given. At this time, the people at Cabul all supposed that, as Akbar had only about 300 men with him, we should make him prisoner.

When Shah Shoojah was killed, a letter was found on him from Capt. Macgregor, dated in April; telling him to hold out fifteen days longer, and he should have assistance.

The Nawaub Zeman Shah Khan has spent two lakhs in raising men on our side; and in feeding troops to act against Akbar. He has still 1000 men; but now wants money. He also fed hundreds of wretched Hindostanees, who were starving in Cabul; great numbers of whom were seized, sold for one and two rupees each, and sent to Turkistan. Zeman Shah Khan did every thing in his power to put a stop to this.

8*th.* — Mishdeen, in the Ahmedzye country, S. E. of Tezeen, belongs to Sultan Khan. This is the place we are likely to go to, if we are removed from hence. When little Tootsey (Capt. Anderson's child) was carried off in the Khoord Cabul pass, she was taken direct to Cabul: and the Khan rode up and down the streets with her; offering her for sale for 4000 rupees. After some negotiation regarding the price, Conolly purchased the child; who was in the hands of Amenoollah Khan. A plot was laid to take Conolly's life, and that of the other hostages; but Taj Mahommed Khan gave them timely warning not to attend the King, should they be sent for. The restoration of the child was a good pretext: and Amenoollah tried to persuade them to go and thank the king for his kindness; when, as soon as they reached the door, they were to have been assassinated. They made some excuse of ill health; and escaped. Nothing could exceed the kindness of Zeman Shah Khan, both to the hostages and the little girl; who became much attached to her new friends. Taj Mahommed Khan, Khan Shireen Khan, the Naïb Shureef, and many others, did all they could, consistently with the safety of both parties, to make them comfortable.

9th.— Two men have come in; who repeat the old story of ten days since;— that there has been a great battle at Peshbolak; where every man, woman, and child was killed; that at Ali Baghan the men were all killed, but the women and children spared; and that the slaughter of the Affghans has been great. By the account of another cossid, who came in yesterday in twelve days from Kandahar, Nott's force ought to-day to be at Mookkoor.

11th.— The Wuzeer is to be married to one of Amenoollah Khan's daughters.

Our fever cases to-day consist of Mackenzie, Waller, Freddy Eyre, Mrs. Waller, Magrath, two ayahs, one or two Hindostanee servants, and several soldiers.

An earthquake at night.

Major Pottinger arrived. Troup went to Jellalabad the night before last. There is a report that we are building a fort at Jugdaluk: also that 70,000 men are collecting at Ferozepore; 25,000 of these are to form a corps of observation there; 15,000 are now at Kandahar; and 20,000 at Jellalabad; and 10,000 are coming from England. These are independent of Gen. Brookes's force in Sindh.

13*th*.—The Wuzeer had all the kujavas ready to move us in two days; but the Cabullees would not let him.

Yai Mahommed, who is supreme at Kandahar, having, it is said, Shah Kamran in *hyde*, has invited Akbar to go to him at Herat: but he, good man, has other views; such as friendship and alliance with the Feringhees. He *only* asks to be acknowledged King of Affghanistan; and to have a subsidiary force with which to conquer Bokhara.

14*th*. — Shumshudeen Khan refuses to give up the Ghuznee prisoners. Only Lumsden and his wife are killed. Col. Palmer is said to have died of a fever; but whether brought on by the torture said to have been inflicted on him, or not, is not known.

Four of our regiments are at Gundamuk; erecting a fort.

Mrs. Trevor gave birth to another girl, to add to the list of captives.

Two earthquakes to-day.

15th. — Mr. Campbell, assistant surgeon of the 54th, who was left at Cabul with the sick of the various regiments, came here a few days since to consult regarding Capt. Mackenzie's case. It is now decided that he remains here; as the men at Cabul are very healthy, and we have got what seems very like a gaol fever amongst us.

16th. — Conolly and Airey came to pay us a visit. A letter has been received by the former from Gen. Pollock; who offers to exchange all the Affghan prisoners in Hindostan against the captives that are in this country. He writes, that if Conolly thinks his going to Jellalabad will facilitate arrangements, he is to go thither, accompanied by all those who appear to have been foremost in civility to us, — Khan Shireen Khan, Mahommed Shah Khan, &c. (How our friends and enemies are here mixed up; for the latter chief is our most inveterate foe!) He tells him also of the force now in the country, and of that expected from Hindostan and England; the army of observation to be commanded by Sir Jasper Nicholls: and states that if we are driven to extremities against the Affghans, their punishment will be fearful.

Also, that if Akbar wishes to make friends with us, he ought to give up all our guns. As far as I can understand, the captives on both sides are to be placed in the hands of the Sikhs.

18th.—The Wuzeer, Mahommed Akbar Khan, and the Sirdar-i-Sirdaran, Sultan Jan, Mahommed Shah Khan, &c., paid a visit here; and sat in the garden, which was quickly despoiled of all the fruits: no doubt greatly to the Khoord's disgust; although some small sum was given to him as a recompence.

We received letters and papers from Jellalabad which must have been lying with Akbar for above a month.

Lady Macnaghten has had a part of her jewels restored to her; but in a sadly broken condition. They *talk* of giving back the rest.

19th.—Half rations issued to us, and no meat. This is to repay Ali Mahommed for the expense of feasting the great people yesterday, I suppose: though he saved all the expense he could; sending to one person for tea, to another for sugar; and saying it was for the Wuzeer, who sent his salaam for it. I believe Akbar pays high prices that he may have plenty of the best of every thing; and is of course cheated by his purveyors: but he would never send to us to supply his wants.

20th.—Ali Mahommed Khan reports that 1000

men are gone to defend the passes: he also hints that we shall be released soon.

22d.—Dost Mahommed Khan came. He says we shall be kalôss in twenty days; that there is to be an exchange of prisoners; and that the guns are to be given up.

23d.—Commemoration of the capture of Ghuznee; over which, in its recaptured state, we groan in spirit. An earthquake at night.

24th.— At two P.M. Mrs. Sturt presented me with a grand-daughter;—another female captive. Capt. Troup and Hadje Bukhtian are accepted by Pollock; who will have nothing to do with Major Pottinger. It seems all the Politicals are set aside. The terms are, that Akbar gives up the guns and all British subjects attached to the camp, in exchange for the ex-Ameer and all the Affghan prisoners. A truce agreed to for a month: the agents to remain at Jellalabad, until Gen. Pollock hears from Lord Ellenborough whether he will enter into an alliance.

26th.— They now require that all Shah Shoojah's family be given up to Akbar; to be dealt with as best pleases him and Mahommed Shah Khan. A report that our force is coming up.

27th.—Troup arrived from Jellalabad. Akbar has deceived us: there is no armistice; no collection of revenue by him where our troops are.

On the contrary, we have taken supplies to the extent of six months' provisions, without payment, in the neighbourhood of Jellalabad.

Nothing had been decided on which tends towards our release.

28*th.*—Troup, who purchased a quantity of things of all kinds for us at Jellalabad, *opened his shop;* and I procured arrow root, cotton gloves, reels of cotton, tape, soap, jalap, and cream of tartar.

Troup left us in the evening, and went to the Wuzeer. He expects to be sent to Jellalabad; and I gave him more of my Journal, to take to Sale.

30*th.* — At two this morning Troup and Lawrence left us for Jellalabad. We hear that orders have been sent to the Kandahar force to move up; and that there has been some fighting, and a great many Affghans killed. On inquiry being made, the Affghans told the following tale:— That one regiment was out beyond Lughman, foraging; that in the night the people rose, and our troops retired; on which we sent 12,000 men! with a park of artillery! against which, of course, the Affghans could not stand. There has been probably some trifling skirmish. The Kandahar troops are ordered up; and the Wuzeer told Lawrence (who says he never saw him appear so angry before) that if our troops advance, he should take us all to Bameean, and make a present of us to the chiefs of that place; so that our prospects appear gloomier than ever. I cannot understand the motive of moving up the troops both ways. Nott is to go to Ghuznee to receive the prisoners: not to fight, but only to defend himself if attacked; and then to come here and join Pollock: and, having received us, all are to walk back hand in hand. We are not to attack Cabul, &c., but to evacuate the country; with Akbar, the Ghilzyes, the Barukzyes, and all the other *Zyes* hanging on our flanks and rear: and if they can but get us to procrastinate, so as to give them the advantage of their faithful ally *the snow*, the Affghans will have the satisfaction of destroying another and still larger army this year.

31*st*. — Had Skinner lived, he would have thrown more light than any other person upon the late events; as he was the bearer of the messages, more especially of the one sent on the night before the Envoy's death. It is as nearly certain as such an event can be, that poor Skinner, who was evidently a dupe to Akbar Khan, was put to death by his orders. At Jugdaluk, after the General, the Brigadier, and Johnson were in the Sirdar's power, Major Thain went to the other officers and said, " I fear there is treachery:

poor Skinner has been shot; and had the object of the Affghan only been to kill a Feringhee, he would not have passed *me* to shoot *him*." There can be little doubt, that the Sirdar was anxious to put out of the way one who could give such fearful evidence against him. Trevor was also much in the Envoy's confidence; and he also became a victim. I have, however, heard that Skinner was not in reality the dupe he appeared to be: and that he had expressed to the Envoy his conviction that the Sirdar was not trustworthy. Yet, if so, it is strange he should have placed the faith he did in him during the retreat; and have advised our going over to him;—unless indeed he saw further into Akbar's policy than others; and believed that we should be treated with honour and kept by him as a *dernier ressort*. What will now be our fate seems very uncertain: but I still think he will not cut our throats;—not out of love to us, but because the other chiefs would resent it; as, having possession of us, they could at least obtain a handsome sum as our ransom.

The last time Troup came from Jellalabad, three ponies were sent from thence loaded with different articles for us: but money was put in one of the boxes; and this was known to the Affghans in charge; and ponies and all disappeared. I have lost my letters from England and the provinces, and from Sale; and also newspapers and medicine; the latter invaluable; as we are very sickly, and have scarcely any. A part of the things coming were clothes for the captives, sent, by subscription, from the provinces. But the medicine is our greatest loss; as this gaol fever seems to be going though all the party, ladies, children, officers, men, and servants, both male and female. I think it arises in great measure from malaria. This valley is full of rice cultivation; which is all under water in a stagnant state: and we are also devoured by musquetoes, which breed there.

At first we hoped that though the money, probably not more than 300 or 400 rupees, would be abstracted from the boxes, we should recover the parcels: but now we have give up that hope.

A letter has been received by Ahmed Khan; stating that every fort from Tighree to Buddeeabad has been sacked by the force that have entered the Lughman valley: some say they are a part of a foraging party of ours; others conjecture that they are our Sikh allies.

Should the Wuzeer attempt to remove us to Bameean, Goolam Mahommed, the father of Taj Mahommed, as also the latter, the high priest of Cabul, and Khan Shireen Khan, have determined to prevent it: but Khan Shireen Khan is the very man who had charge of the hostages some time since; and assured them nothing should induce him to give them up: — yet he did so the very next day, on the Sirdar sending him 4000 rupees. So, much dependence cannot be placed on *him*.

The Kuzzilbashes ever side with the strongest party; and therefore, if our troops come up, it is likely that Khan Shireen Khan may keep his word. He has many friends in the Huzara country, through which we must pass; and he may direct them to seize us. In that case we shall probably, during the conflict with our guards, lose the few comforts of clothing, &c. which we now possess.

A kafila is going down to Jellalabad; and at the same time Akbar sends 2000 men towards that place to line the passes. He sent 3000 some time since; but their commander did not proceed further than Bhoodkhak; whence he wrote to the Wuzeer, that his force was too weak to cope with Pollock's.

August 2*nd.* — Reports that all the forts from Tighree to Buddeeabad are destroyed.

3*rd.* — An earthquake.

4*th.* — Three more fever cases; and Conolly very ill. We hear that immediately on Troup's arrival at Jellalabad, all our outposts were withdrawn.

Zeman Shah Khan's party is increasing again: and it is thought, if our troops come up, that the owner of the fort may side with us; and give us arms to resist being taken away.

6th.— Mohun Lull says, that letters have passed through his hands from several chiefs to Gen. Pollock; stating, that if he will forbear from injuring the city of Cabul, and respect their lives and possessions, they will engage that we shall not be taken from Cabul. Amongst these chiefs are, the high priest, Zeman Shah Khan, Khan Shireen Khan, and Goolam Mahommed Khan (father of Taj Mahommed): the latter is in hopes, should we obtain the ascendency, that he may obtain office, as of old; his family being the hereditary Wuzeers.

7th.— John Conolly died, at thirty-two minutes past noon. The Wuzeer has sent a Khan to order his coffin; and offers to send the body to Jellalabad.

8th.— Ahmed Khan informs us, that the baggage, of the army at Kandahar, has been sent out eight miles on the road towards the provinces; and that our eighteen-pounders at Kandahar have been destroyed. Some days since we had a report that the force there, consisting, as the Affghans say, of 8000 men, have been exterminated, with every man, woman, and child thereunto appertaining; and Kandahar taken and burnt.

Three regiments have been sent from Kandahar to reinforce Quetta; and the story concerning the baggage is probably true; and Gen. Nott has taken advantage of this force to send down all superfluous baggage, and also the sick; preparatory to a move upwards.

8*th.* — Camels have come; but none of them are strong enough to carry the coffin; and they say they will send mules at mid-day to carry it.

9*th.* — Major Pottinger arrived.

The Wuzeer refuses to allow Conolly's body to go to Jellalabad until Troup returns; and then, if all is not peace, he says he will not allow him to go, alive or dead.

There is a report to-day amongst the Affghans, that Pollock has written to say, that if it is attempted to remove any one of us from Cabul, he will lay the city in ashes.

We hear that the Kandahar force is coming up; and it is expected that the one from Jellalabad will do the same.

The Sappers and Miners have long been at Charbagh; and they generally precede the army.

Conolly was buried at sunset in the garden of the fort.

Hadje Bukhtian writes to his brother Ahmed Khan, that Gen. Pollock has written to say it is all one to him whether it is a day or a month; but that immediately on the arrival of the prisoners he will return to the provinces.

The servants have a report that we are forthwith to be taken away, to, or towards, Bokhara. For two days there have been eight camels here, with their surwans ready; which looks as if the Wuzeer meditated our removal, in case of the force coming up; or to send us to our friends, should the negotiation prove unsuccessful.

We heard to-day that the Sappers had advanced as far as Gundamuk.

10th. — Troup and Lawrence arrived. I received letters, &c. from Sale. No present hope of release: nor fear of a move, I trust. Nothing appears to have been done beyond *talk*. Pollock, has threatened, if we are not sent down in eight days, to come up and destroy Cabul: but Akbar knows, as well as he does himself, that Pollock has no carriage. The 1st brigade are gone to Jellalabad. Sale writes me, that, in addition to it, he has with him the 3d dragoons and a troop of horse artillery: but it does not appear that they are coming up further. Indeed, without more troops to back them, or rather to flank them, they cannot come through the passes. They might do it well with three brigades, having one on each flank keeping the heights and adjacent country.

A durbar held by Mahommed Akbar, Mahommed Shah, &c. to consult on the steps to be taken regarding Futteh Jung, Amenoollah, the Meerwyse, Zeman Shah, &c. who all wrote advising the immediate advance of our troops. A letter from Futteh Jung to Gen. Pollock, to that effect, had been intercepted: but, until Troup's return, it was not safe to make any stir in the affair.

11*th*. — There was a report last night, that two Europeans (officers) had been taken prisoners in Cabul; having come from Kandahar, disguised as natives of the country, with thirty followers: and that they had been purchasing up all the gunpowder.

To-day it is said, the same persons are now with the hostages; and that they are either adventurous persons, who have come up from Nott's brigade, for some purpose, as yet unknown; or that they are part of the Ghuznee prisoners, attempting to escape.

Late in the evening we heard that the above tale has arisen out of the arrival of an Arab Hadje. He calls himself a soldier of fortune; and offered his services to Gen. Pollock; who declined them. He is suspected of being a spy; and has just come from Hindostan.

The deliberations in the durbar have ended in Futteh Jung's being placed in confinement.

12th. — All the hostages have come over to our fort; and there is a talk of our being all sent away, — some say to Soorkhab, four marches off, on the confines of the Loghur country; others say to the Kohistan, or Bamecan.

We know that Sale's brigade, the 3d dragoons, and a troop of horse artillery, were to leave Jellalabad for Futteabad on the 6th; which would bring them only fifteen miles nearer to us. The women are being sent out of the city; and we have packed up our little all, to be ready whenever the *hookm* arrives: we have moreover purchased two ponies.

13th. — The republic has only endured a day. Zeman Shah Khan is again Shah Zeman Shah. We heard guns, probably in honour of the event. This is news to mark my birth-day; which is not likely to be spent much as a *jour de fête* by a prisoner.

I fear Zeman is too much in the hands of Akbar and Mahommed Shah for him to do us any good; although he is, and ever has been, well disposed towards us: he acted with the greatest kindness to the English left with him; and when he had no longer power to protect them, and they were forcibly taken from his house to that of the Bucha Meerwyse or high priest of Cabul, he took off his turban, placed it at his feet, and protested against the measure: and finally sent his eldest son with them; that, in case evil befel them, his family should not shrink from sharing in it. The priest's professions were great; but he ended in giving the hostages up to Akbar for the value of 4000 rupees. As they were sold for that sum, we tell them they are Akbar's slaves.

There is now an idea,—whether only the fertile emanations of prisoners' brains or not, time must unfold,—but an opinion prevails, that Akbar is so ungallant as to be heartily tired of dragging the women and children about the country at his heels; and that, if any flight is designed, it will be that of himself and four hostages; Pottinger, Lawrence, and Troup, to be decidedly three of them: we are not so certain of the fourth; but at present we have selected either Gen. Shelton or Capt. Johnson.

15th. — The news of to-day is, that Nott's force has left Kandahar; taking Timor Shah with them. They are said to have taken the route leading to Dera Ismaël Khan; but it is thought possible they may, about ninety miles from Kandahar, at *Gulnarye*, strike to the north, and pursue that road to Ghuznee; which would be far preferable to crossing the mountains by the Gholary pass, near the river, and that they will thence cross over to the left again to the Abistadeh lake, and fall into the regular road to Ghuznee at Mookkoor. This is a wild and roundabout tract of country; which is probably not feasible with guns. Akbar says, that 5000 men have been sent to oppose them. He also says, that our force at Jellalabad is *in statu quo;* but that if it moves up, we shall be sent off at half an hour's notice, to a fine climate, with plenty of ice; which we conclude to be Bameean.

16*th.* — Futteh Jung has made his escape.

Our troops are reported to have made sixteen marches from Kandahar. Akbar ordered 5000 men to go and meet them; but it is said, he has mustered 400 only.

17*th.* — Mrs. Smith (Mrs. Trevor's servant) died of fever and water on the chest.

19*th.* — We hear that the men, who went towards Kandahar, have been beaten; and that more are to be sent.

Futteh Jung escaped through a hole made in the roof; from whence he let himself down by a rope. The Wuzeer says he is gone to Tagow; but the general opinion is that he is gone to Jellalabad. Troup went to see the Wuzeer to-day; who told him, he purposes sending for him and Pottinger, to stay with him in the Bala Hissar.

A thunder-storm at night, with heavy rain; the lightning vivid; but it was all over in an hour.

This storm was immediately preceded by an earthquake, between 10 and 11 o'clock.

Akbar has written to Lord Ellenborough to say he will only treat with him; and that he will not have have any thing to do with Gen. Pollock; who is " a fool!" This is complimentary.

20*th*.—We heard a great deal of firing in the evening.

Futteh Jung is said to have been taken on the road to Jellalabad: but Abib Khan declares it is not true. They also say that there has been a fight at Gundamuk; that our troops have arrived there; and that the Affghans have lost several men in their defeat; that one of the fugitives has just arrived; and that Akbar will send 5000 more men there. They also say, that the Kandahar force is within two marches of Ghuznee. Three horses are kept ready saddled to start with messengers at a moment's notice, night or day; and the Khan says, he thinks we shall not be here more than three days longer.

21*st*.—The late newspapers have not a little amused me. They show that the editors catch at every expression, used in any letters they have read; or on any comments they hear on news from Affghanistan. A regular controversy has arisen between one, who asserts that Lady Sale in her letters evinces a strong prepossession in favour of

Mahommed Akbar Khan, and another, who thinks Lady Sale wrote, as she did, because she was a prisoner: to which the first rejoins, that he does not think Lady S. would, under any circumstances, write that which was false. *There* he is right: but I would not have written on the subject at all, unless I wrote as I thought: if people misunderstand, it is their fault and not mine. Again, they say it were better I had never written at all. Perhaps so: but it seems that details were wanting; my letters to Sale gave those; and he thought them of sufficient consequence to send them to the Governor-General and the Commander-in-Chief. They were afterwards sent to England by the former; and, if the papers tell truth, excited some attention in the highest circles. As to my "great prepossession" in favour of Akbar, my greatest wish is, that Gen. Nott's force should march up to Ghuznee; release the prisoners there; and then that a simultaneous movement should take place of Nott's and Pollock's forces upon Cabul. Once again in power, here, I would place Akbar, Mahommed Shah, and Sultan Jan *hors de combat;* befriend those who befriended us, and let the Affghans have the Ameer Dost Mahommed Khan back, if they like. He and his family are only an expense to us in India; we can restore them, and make friends with him. Let us first show the Affghans that we can both conquer them, and revenge the foul murder of our troops; but do not let us dishonour the British name by sneaking out of the country, like whipped Pariah dogs. Affghanistan will become a byword amongst the nations. Had we retreated, as poor Sturt proposed, without baggage, with celerity (forced marches to get through the snow), and had the men stood by us (a doubtful point, — they were so worn out and dispirited), we might have figured in history; and have cut out Xenophon's account of the retreat of the 10,000.

As to the justice of dethroning the Ameer Dost Mahommed, and setting up Shah Shoojah, I have nothing to say regarding it: nor regarding our policy in attempting to keep possession of a country of uncivilised people, so far from our own; whence all supplies of ammunition, money, &c., must be obtained. Let our Governors-General and Commanders-in-chief look to that; whilst I knit socks for my grand-children: but I have been a soldier's wife too long to sit down tamely, whilst our honour is tarnished in the sight and opinion of savages. Had our army been cut to pieces by an avowed enemy, whether in the field or the passes — let them have used what stratagems they pleased, — all had been fair. Akbar had shone as another William Tell; he had been the deliverer of his country from a hateful yoke imposed on them by Kaffirs: but here he stands, by his own avowal freely made, the assassin of the Envoy;— not by proxy, but by his own hand. I do believe, he only meant to make him prisoner; for the purpose of obtaining better terms and more money: but he is a man of ungovernable passions; and his temper when thwarted is ferocious. He afterwards professed to be our friend;—we treated with him;—great was the credulity of those who placed confidence in him: still they blindly did so;— even after the letter was received from Conolly, at Bhoodkhak, confirming the previous warnings of his intentions towards us. He followed us, with his blood-thirsty Ghilzyes. Mahommed Shah Khan, his principal adviser, I might almost say his master, is the most inveterate of our enemies. Akbar is a jovial smooth-tongued man; full of compliments and good fellowship; and has the knack of talking over both kaffirs and true believers.

To our cost, he did talk our chiefs over; and persuaded them of his friendship; but said that those sugs (dogs) of Ghilzyes were intent on murder and plunder; and totally unmanageable. In this way he hovered on our flanks and rear: and when our people were massacred and his bloodhounds in human shape were tolerably glutted with their blood, the scene was changed; although it was constantly reacted. In the distance, a group of horsemen invariably appeared: they were beckoned to; questioned as to what chief was present, — it was invariably Akbar, who always pretended good faith, said his 300 horsemen were too few to protect us from the Ghilzyes, &c., — and then, the following day witnessed a repetition of the slaughter, and pretended friendship; for that this friendship was a mere pretence, was acknowledged by him when he said, " I was the man who killed your Envoy with my own hand; I destroyed your army; I threw aside all ties of family, deserted every thing, for the faith of Islam; and now I am left to bear the opprobrium heaped on me by the Feringhees, whilst no one supports me: but were I in power, I would make the chiefs remember it!" and then he uttered maledictions on their heads. He has kept his word; has been a bitter enemy to all who have shown the slightest kindness to us; and grinds their money out of them by threats and torture.

A woman's vengeance is said to be fearful; but nothing can satisfy mine against Akbar, Sultan Jan, and Mahommed Shah Khan. Still I say that Akbar, having, for his own political purposes, done as he said he would do — that is, destroyed our army, — letting only one man escape to tell the tale, as Dr. Brydon did, — and having got the families into his possession; — I say, having done this, he has ever since we have been in his hands, treated us well : — that is, honour has been respected. It is true that we have not common comforts; but what we denominate such are unknown to Affghan females: they always sleep on the floor, sit on the floor, &c. — hardships to us. We have bought common charpoys at two rupees each; that is, a bed formed by four poles and ropes tied across and across them. Had we tables and chairs, we have not space for them; so many inhabit the same apartment. Individually I have no right to complain on this subject; as Lady Macnaghten, Mrs. Mainwaring, Mrs. Boyd, Mrs. Sturt, and I, occupy the same apartment. Capt. Boyd makes his bed on the landing-place of the stairs, or on the roof of the house; so that we have no *man*-kind amongst us, except the Boyds' two little boys, and Mrs. Mainwaring's baby. This little fellow was born just before the insurrection broke out in Cabul (in October): his father had gone with Sale's brigade; and we always call him Jung-i-Bahadur.

After so long enduring the misery of having gentlemen night and day associated with us, we have found this a great relief.

The Wuzeer gives us rations of meat, rice, ottah, ghee, and oil; and lately fruit. At first our food was dressed for us; but it was so greasy and disgusting, that we asked leave to cook for ourselves. That again was a matter of taste: one person likes what another does not. By us, a strong cup of coffee is considered a luxury; whilst an Affghan the other day, who had some given to him (he had never tasted any before), pronounced it bitter and detestable.

It is true, we have been taken about the country; exposed to heat, cold, rain, &c.; but so were their own women. It was, and is, very disagreeable: but still we are, *de facto*, prisoners; notwithstanding Akbar still persists in calling us—honoured guests: and, as captives, I say we are well treated. He has given us common coarse chintz, and coarse longcloth, too, wherewith to clothe ourselves;—I must not use the word dress: and making up these articles has given us occupation; increased by having to work with raw cotton, which we have to twist into thread for ourselves. We suffered more from uncleanliness than any thing else. It was above ten days after our departure from Cabul, before I had the opportunity to change my clothes, or even to take them off and put them on again, and wash myself: and fortunate were those who did not possess much live stock. It was not until after our arrival here (at Spéwakee, near Cabul) that we completely got rid of *lice,* which we denominated infantry: the fleas, for which Affghanistan is famed (and particularly Cabul), we call light cavalry.

The servants, of course, were worse off than ourselves; and, not having as good wardrobes as we had, communicated their pests, of the insect tribe, to the children they carried about; and thus the mothers obtained a double share. Bugs have lately made their appearance; but not in great numbers: the flies torment us; and the musquitoes drive us half mad. But these annoyances, great as they are, are the results of circumstances which cannot be controlled; and when I say this, I suppose I shall again be accused of prepossession in favour of the Wuzeer. We ought, however, to bear in mind, that the Affghans are not addicted to general ablution: they wash their hands before and after their meals, which is but *comme il faut*, as they eat with their fingers; and they constantly wear the same clothes a month. This is not economy. The Wuzeer will take his bath perhaps once a week; and change his clothes: and the women never think of doing so oftener; and only open their hair at such times; which is kept smooth for that period by the application of gum to its innumerable plaits. Here again is a difference between their tastes and ours, who so enjoy bathing twice a day.

The garden, or rather vineyard and orchard, I consider a great luxury: we walk in it every evening for an hour or two. A strong guard is placed there: but, except when it has been lately changed, the men do not annoy us. At such times they dodge about after us; but otherwise do not. Last evening, for instance, sixteen men, armed at all points, sat down in a row in the centre walk; and laughed and joked together: five or six were sitting eating grapes on the top of the summer-house; and a few were posted, seated on the walls; whilst we walked here and there where we pleased.

When we have marched since we left Buddeabad, Mahommed Shah's family, and some others, have accompanied us; and the best camels, largest kujavas, &c., have been selected for them; and when carriage runs short, they are served first. But this is only what we must expect. Mahommed Shah Khan, too, preferred Mrs. Sturt's riding-horse to his own; and took it. Mine was sent to Jellalabad. When Mackenzie went there, he rode, and lamed it; and it was left behind. There I was fortunate; as Sale has got it. Luckily I had a few rupees; and the only day I was not provided with a horse to ride, I hired one for two rupees six anas, a mere baggage pony; but it carried me safely.

Nothing can exceed the folly I have seen in the papers regarding my wonderful self; — how I headed the troops, &c. &c. It puts me in mind of Goldsmith's verses on Mrs. Blaze; in which he remarks, that " the king himself has followed her, when she has gone before : " and certainly I have thus headed the troops; for the chiefs told me to come on with them for safety sake : and thus I certainly did go far in advance of the column ; but it was no proof of valour, though one of prudence.

Troup and Pottinger have been told to be in readiness to go in to-morrow morning : so I now make up my packet, in case an opportunity should offer by which Troup can send it to Sale.

The only thing that has given me pleasure in the Indian papers, is a subscription set on foot by the civilians, to purchase a sword, to be presented to Sale ; because it shows that they appreciate his conduct ; and I know that he will value it most highly. I hear that after Futteh Jung was placed in confinement, his family had all their jewels, &c. taken away ; to the value of twenty lakhs. Some say this was done by Akbar and Sultan Jan ; others, by Mahommed Shah Khan. The latter had taken a lesson in such actions, when he despoiled Lady Macnaghten of her valuables.

22d August.—Our friends went back to the Wuzeer; and took my packets with them.

The Affghans still talk of some defeat they have experienced near Soorkhab: whence the celebrated miner has returned discomfited and wounded; and says he will not attempt to cope with our force. The Wuzeer has made the people of Cabul take their oath on the Koran to stand by him; and great excitement prevails in the city. Futteh Jung has arrived safely at Jellalabad; and has written from thence, that, if Akbar is his father's son, he will meet him in fair fight; for which purpose there is said to have been held a grand muster of troops on the Siah Sung plain; amounting to 25,000 infantry and 5,000 horse, who are to be headed by Akbar in person. I can scarcely believe that he will set his fortunes on the issue of a battle. A fair field and no favour is what we want: but he would be mad to meet our disciplined troops on the plain; when he knows that the fastnesses of his country give him every advantage over us, with any rabble he can collect. Besides, he is all but supreme now. He wishes to be king: but Zeman Khan has again got a strong party in his favour, and is endeavouring to regain the throne.

23*d.*—The prisoners from Ghuznee arrived quite unexpectedly:—Col. Palmer, Capt. Burnett (54th), Harris, Nicholson, Poett, Alston, Williams, Crawford, and Thompson.

Akbar says, he will send us away in three or four days, either to Bameean, Zoormut, or Soorkhab; twenty miles off, on the borders of the Loghur country.

24th.—Sultan Jan left Cabul with 300 men; to reinforce Shumshudeen, who has been signally defeated, we hear, at Carabagh; escaping with only twenty men. Some say Nott's force achieved this victory; but others that the Huzaras rose against him: so probably British gold has been weighed in the balance, and found more ponderous than the hatred of the Kaffirs.

Being greatly in want of medicine, Mr. Campbell went to the Sirdar to get some from Cabul; and he told him we were to move to-night or to-morrow. Mrs. Anderson, being too ill to travel, remains here.

25th.—A sudden order arrived for our removal; with a report, that Futteh Jung's and all the female royal family were to accompany us. Capt. Troup arrived in the evening to see us off, by Akbar's command. Mrs. Anderson, her husband and children, remained at the fort. Akbar has ordered every attention to be paid to her and the gentlemen; Mr. Campbell being left with the party to afford medical aid. Mrs. Trevor and eight children are also left here, in consequence of her being seriously ill with fever;

as also one of her children. A man of the 44th died of fever to-day; and was buried in the garden. Soon after the moon rose we left the fort; camels for kujavas and fifty ponies having been sent for our accommodation. All our ponies, &c., were taken from us; and on our removal, a certain number were sent. We fortunately purchased two ponies to carry our baggage. We were told we were to go to Killa Kazi, about seven miles from Cabul: but we made a long *détour* to avoid the city; and crossed the Loghur river: the road was very tolerable. After proceeding about five miles we came to several forts on our right; the first a large one; and were told it was called Killa Kazi. We passed a succession of forts on either side; but there was scarcely any one to be seen except a few men watching their grain heaps in the fields. On the right appeared much cultivation; judging from the dark shade: which, with an ill-defined line of irregular mountains, was all we could even speculate upon in the way of scenery. We had with us ten soldiers; so ill with fever as to require to be carried in kujavas: and Capt. Mackenzie and Lieut. Eyre were also suffering.

I was the only lady who rode; the others preferring the kujavas; on account of their children.

26th. — At daybreak we were still travelling;

and near sunrise found ourselves just opposite to Cabul; and about two miles distant, as the crow flies, from Baber's tomb. We saw the wall on the hill quite distinctly. We did not arrive at our ground till past seven: and took up our stations under some trees near the fort; which, I have been told, is called Kundah. Here there was no admittance; as Sultan Jan was in it, with his reinforcements for Ghuznee. This disproves a report of yesterday; to the effect that the people of Cabul had insisted on having Sultan Jan as a hostage for our safety. He had a number of good horses with him: and we recognised the Envoy's grey. His army consisted of about thirty men; but Inshallah! he is to be joined by lakhs. We are said to be guarded by 1000 men; but 300 were nearer the mark. During the morning we were joined by Dr. Berwick, Lieut. Evans, and the European soldiers who were left sick when we evacuated Cabul: they form a total of thirty-seven; but a few have been left for want of carriage, which is to be furnished; and they are to be sent after us; as also Lieut. Haughton. We this morning recognised the summer-house above Baber's tomb, Kerghah and the Pughman hills.

Judging from the time that we were travelling, about twelve hours; and taking the rate of the camels at about two miles per hour, deducting a fourth for halt; we estimate the distance we have gone at eighteen miles.

A letter has been received from Kandahar: Nott has marched in three columns with only 6000 men. He sent his camels out to graze the 3d March; and lost 2000. He left Kandahar on the 28th.

Shumshudeen has retired on Ghuznee: and, by the last accounts, Gen. Nott was within ten miles of that fortress. He is expected at Cabul on the 1st. Pollock's force is to move on the 20th. We are to march at moon-rising. We witnessed a parade of telling off the guards, &c.; and heard the retreat beat off at sunset. They use our drums and fifes; and have some bugles with which they sound for us to halt or advance. The sentries planted round our camp are a perfect farce. These men are the Pultans; who have no knives, and are mostly armed with our own muskets: I saw them place their pickets, in imitation of ours; and sentries walked backwards and forwards, with a ramrod in their hand; having stuck the butt end of the musket in the earth at their posts: so that, were it of any use, we might easily overpower them. We asked to be admitted into the fort: but though they said we might occupy one room when vacated by Sultan Jan; after his departure, they insulted the gentlemen who went to get it ready for us; and asked, how the Kaffirs dared to wear their shoes there.

We, therefore, spread loonghees to form a shade, as the heat was excessive; and at night it was very cold. At eleven the *réveillé* was beat by the drums, and performed by the pipes; a kind of repetition of one, two, three: and at midnight we were all ready to start.

27*th*.—We left camp soon after midnight. The Meer Akhor Ahmed Khan was very anxious that all the riders should follow the advance guard of half the infantry; the rest of which closed on our rear: then came the kujavas, followed up by the baggage; and their rear was closed by a strong guard of Affghan cavalry.

Another body of horsemen, about twenty in number, joined as riders; and kept near the Meer Akhor; who desired Lady Macnaghten's kujavas to be kept as the leading ones; and the camel had fine trappings, as if to mark it particularly in case of an attempt at escape.

We were between eight and nine hours on the march over a barren broken slip of land, bounded on either side by the hills for a considerable distance, until we passed a fort and chokey at Urghundee on our left; soon after which the road turns off to the left to Ghuznee. The ascent to Bala Maidan was long, but not difficult; and the view from the top of it, looking down on the plain above named, was very pretty; comprising a narrow valley, thickly studded with forts and diversified by cultivation; with lines of willows and poplars marking the water cuts; which here serve as hedgerows. We were taken to a fort; but not admitted into it: and after a time had tents pitched for us. Lady Macnaghten, Mrs. Boyd and three children, Mrs. Mainwaring and child, Mrs. Sturt and child, and I, occupied one division of a Sipahee's pall: there was another tent for the other ladies; two more for the gentlemen, and one for the sick soldiers.

We hear that Gen. Nott has arrived at Ghuznee, has blown up the new bourj in the city, and has put to death nearly every man, woman, and child found there. We cannot be surprised at the men taking signal vengeance; but we fear the news is too good to be true. We met on our road two horsemen; whom we supposed to be expresses. We met, also, several camels, bullocks, and donkeys, laden, for the most part, with assafœtida.

It seems a plan was proposed this morning, and negatived. I only heard of it by chance; so no thanks are due for courtesy to those, who, had the measure been carried, would have come to us for our share. The plan was, to get Ahmed Khan to make short marches, or halt; so as to allow Gen. Nott to hear where we are, and rescue us: and should it succeed, Ahmed was to receive two and a half lakhs. The scale before proposed was, I believe, again to be brought forward: Lady Macnaghten 10,000 rupees, Lady Sale 5000, Mrs. Sturt 5000, Capt. and Mrs. Boyd and family 5000, &c. This scale is said to be prepared according to rank and means; which I deny: the other captives are not wealthy any more than ourselves; and where the money was to come from, I know not. The Indian Government, it is said, offered to ransom us for that sum; and I believe would have given more: but this seems to have been a private and most *zubberrdust* arrangement.

There is a report, that all Cabul is in confusion, and the natives fighting against each other; and that our force has passed Gundamuk.

28th.—We left our encamping ground about two o'clock; and reached Tarkhana between eight and nine. Had I taken the ride for my own amusement on a good horse, instead of being driven about as a captive on a sorry baggage yaboo, I should have enjoyed it very much. The narrow vale we passed through was highly cultivated; the fields divided by willow and poplar trees, and the forts frequent. Near to Julraiz (the head of the spring) the scenery was particularly beautiful; the trees well clumped together; and the river, here clear as crystal, rapidly flowing to our left. The hills, also, assumed a novel aspect; having a foreground of lower hills of most uncommon form. Nearly opposite to the town was a triangular one, sharp as though it had been scarped purposely; next to it a semi-circular one, &c.; with the usual chain of mountains behind. Julraiz appears to be rather a large town, surrounded by forts. The scenery was varied; but the land always under cultivation until we reached our halting ground; where we bivouacked on the green sward, sheltered from the sun's rays by a double row of poplar trees; between which rippled a stream that empties itself into the Cabul river, which bounds our resting-place on one side. This river is at this place as famed for its clear limpid waters, as it is at Cabul for its dirty hue, being there quite red. We here got some small fish like gudgeons, some bad small apricots, sour grapes, and apples and pears, that had just arrived by a caravan. Here General Saleh Mahommed's troops looted five camels.

29th.—Marched at daybreak; and shortly afterwards saw a curious stone on the hill to the left. At about three miles passed Sir-i-chushm on the right; a fortified town, with a fort in front of it. Here are three preserves full of sacred fish. The name of this place signifies the "head of the spring." The road becomes daily more rugged.

On our right we passed a fine fort; called

Mustapha Khan Ke Killa. It was built by a person of that name. He is dead; but his son lives there; a very gentlemanlike man, wearing spectacles. As we passed he gave us *nan* (bread), and apricots prepared as a paste.

We halted at Killa Naziri; eight miles from our last resting-place. Here our troops again looted two camels.

30*th*. — Marched at two, A. M., sixteen miles to Gurdundewar, on the Helmund. At first we passed through a narrow defile with a stony road; after which the road was excellent, fit to drive carriages upon; except in a few places where there were rather awkward descents.

There were three steep ascents; one of which was very long. Very little cultivation; and but few forts seen on our route.

A man was met on the march, who said he was a cossid from Ghuznee: that that fort was in our possession; and that a force was to be sent to release us.

Shortly before we arrived at our destination, ten or twelve Huzaras were set upon by about 300 of our guard. They fired about fifty shots at them: killed one, wounded one, took two prisoners, and some loot.

There are two Yaghi forts here: the rest are subject to Akbar.

30*th.*—Left the Hah-i-Baba to our left: there was snow in the clefts; but none on the top, which is 18,000 feet above the level of the sea.

We marched about eight miles to the foot of the Hadje Gurk pass. The road led the whole way through a defile; at first very narrow and stony; with a tributary stream to the Helmund occupying nearly the whole of it.

There were several rocks which assumed the appearance of gigantic statues. One on the right representing a man seated on a bull couchant: another on the left, at first resembled a man clothed in the *toga*, standing on a pedestal. There were others, also, that it was difficult to suppose natural: they may have been ancient Buddhistic or Brahminic remains. After arriving at some forts and two tombs near a ruined fort, the valley became wider and fertile; being all planted with wheat, some perfectly ripe and some quite green.

On nearing our destination, the valley again closed up. We came to a fort dilapidated, but still inhabited. Every breach in the walls was filled with armed men. Our troops were drawn up in due form; our two drums and one fife struck up; the bugle sounded at intervals; and the men marched to this discord in the most appropriate manner; invariably missing both cadence and step, until we arrived at our tents.

Twice during the day's march there were shots fired in front ; and much talk of battle, which never took place ; though each time there were a number of Huzaras posted on the heights. These men have been for some time past besieging the forts here. The damaged one has been partially rebuilt; and the one opposite to it appears to be in perfect repair.

Our commandant is going with his army to fight : but I am not sure which side he takes. There was a skirmish this morning ; one party posted behind a sungah on the hill, which was forced, and the brave troops fled.

31*st.*—Marched to the forts of Kaloo. Found the road bad and stony ; with constant steep ascents and descents. Ascended the Hadje Gurk pass, which is 12,400 feet above the level of the sea; the hills barren ; grain was cultivated in the bed of the valley, where a silver serpentine stream meandered; and the hay, freshly thrown into cocks, reminded me of England. We crossed the river twice ; and with difficulty conquered a steep ascent to the fort, near which we encamped. A report that Akbar has been fighting with the chiefs at Cabul ; and that our force must be at Bhoodkhak to-day.

1*st September*.—Marched at daylight over the Kaloo pass. It is nearly four miles to the top of it. The road at first is narrow and precipitous; and for the most part little more than a steep path. From the top the view is very grand; resembling the waves of a very troubled sea, and composed of barren hills of every variety of shade and hue. We saw Bameean from thence: but though a magnificent scene was before us, it presented no pleasing object to those who expected to remain captives in that desolate region. The only plant here is the Koole-Huzara, or Huzara Cass, a kind of furze that is very prickly, and grows in bunches: it is used for fuel. As we neared our destination (Killa Topchee), we entered a very narrow but highly cultivated valley: the grain short in the stalk, but particularly fine in the ear. This day's march was seven miles.

3*d*.—Marched at daylight seven miles to Bameean. The road wild and uneven, with narrow paths and many ascents and descents. This valley is nowhere more than a mile broad; but it is very fertile, and produces particularly fine grain. Plenty of beans and pease are cultivated here; the former very small, the latter small and hard. The tamarisk and barberry were abundant, and a shrub with yellow berries. We halted for a short time opposite a fort, near which were many cows.

Here we got some mast (curds), which we found very refreshing. Looking back from hence, we saw Zohak behind us, on a high point. At Bameean they refused to take us into the fort; and we pitched our tents just under the ancient fortress and city which were destroyed by Jhenzhis Khan; when upwards of 300,000 persons perished. The caves, ruins, and towers, extend for miles. There are two large images which have been described by former travellers: opposite to the largest was our encampment.

We had scarcely settled ourselves in the tents ere the General beat, in consequence of the people of the fort and the regiment disagreeing: so we went on about a mile, to such a wretched fort, that we asked leave to remain in tents; which was with difficulty obtained: but the Khan said he would endeavour to get a better fort for us tomorrow.

4*th*. — Saleh Mahommed Khan's lady came to visit Lady Macnaghten. She is young and fair, with a fat round face; and comes from Loodianah; where, it is said, she was a dancing girl. Her information is, that Futteh Jung is a prisoner, or has been put to death: his family, she says, are expected here in a day or two.

From the 5th to the 9th we made excursions

to see the caves, &c. At first some difficulty was made: but the General sent about thirty men to guard us and our pencils; for several went intent on sketching. I only copied the frescoes that were on the walls and ceiling near the large image; but Mr. Eyre made some very pretty and correct sketches of Ghoolghoola (the ancient city), &c.

9th. — I have daily been begging hard for permission to go and see the ancient city; but am at last put off by a direct refusal: the soldiers, it seems, are over-worked in keeping watch over us in camp; and to relieve them we are to be taken into one of these horrid forts.

We went to the fort formerly occupied by Dr. Lord.

Long ago, to prevent a recurrence of disputes which had formerly arisen amongst us regarding distribution of accommodation, &c., we elected, by vote, a committee of three gentlemen, whose fiat was indisputable — Major Pottinger, and Capts. Webb and Lawrence: the latter also undertook to be our purveyor; portioning out our rations generally with his own hands (servants being scarce), as well as the food for the soldiers.

On our going into the fort, the committee, having examined the miserable sheds built round the square of high walls with corner towers and a gateway, at first decided that the five best rooms, or rather most convenient ones as regarded privacy, &c., should be destined for the ladies; and we were to draw lots for them, or arrange amongst ourselves. Finally, it was requested that the choice might go by seniority. Lady Macnaghten of course had the first choice. I had the second; and took a dark cow-house; the only light admitted being from a door down a long narrow passage and a hole in the roof. This was for Mrs. Sturt, myself, the ayah, and *the dog;* and was decidedly the best apartment there, to my taste. We soon *set to:* and by dint of hard working with sticks and stones, in which I bore my part, assisted by Mr. Melville until both of us got blistered hands, we knocked two small windows out of the wall; and thus obtained darkness visible.

10*th.*—We were fortunate in our selection; although our nightly visitant, in the shape of the largest bug I ever saw, was sufficiently disgusting: but Lady Macnaghten, Captain and Mrs. Boyd, and Mrs. Mainwaring, with the children, had no rest in the three rooms they had taken; which all communicated with each other. They had capital *shikar* all night: and in the morning got leave to pitch a tent at the gate, and reside there.

11*th.*—When we were at Tai Khana on our way to this place, a Sipahee came to us and said that there were about fifty Hindostanees, amongst our guard, who were willing to join us; and that Saleh Mahommed Khan was a man who would do any thing for money. This was told to Capts. Johnson and Lawrence; and they agreed to sound him on the subject; which they did: but he laughed at their offer; and pretended to imagine they were only joking.

This morning early, Capt. Lawrence came to ask if we would allow a conference to take place in our room, as being the most private place. We assented. Saleh Mahommed Khan, the Syud Morteza Khan, Major Pottinger, Capts. Lawrence, Johnson, Mackenzie, and Webb, assembled; and our bed, spread on the floor, formed the divan. Here in the course of an hour all was settled. The gentlemen present signed their names to the paper; in which we promised to give Saleh Mahommed Khan 20,000 rupees, and to insure him 1000 rupees a month for life; and that if the government did not extricate us from this difficulty, we would be answerable for the money. Thus they held the promise of five British officers as sacred. In heading the paper, they insisted that we should do so in the name of Christ; as rendering it perfectly binding. Saleh Mahommed declared to us, that he had received orders to remove us farther (to Khooloom), and to set out that night: also, that he had another letter from Akbar, ordering all who were not able to march to be put to death. He seems anxious that we shall not receive any news from others; and had his two drummers severely flogged, for telling us that the Kuzzilbashes with Khan Shireen Khan had risen against Akbar, and that the latter had fled to the Kohistan.

12th. — Saleh Mahommed Khan hoisted the standard of defiance on the walls, — white, with a crimson edge and green fringe.

Two Huzara chiefs have tendered their allegiance to Major Pottinger; as also Zulficar Khan, the Naïb of the province, who, we heard, had fled. Another man has been appointed in his room; and has paid 1000 rupees to Saleh Mahommed for his appointment: which money was laid out in purchasing khelluts (for the chiefs who came in to us) from a Kaffila fortunately passing by.

A report that the Andersons, Trevors, and Bygrave have got safe to our troops: but as this is coupled with Troup's having gone to Ghuznee, we fear it is not true; more especially as we are told that our force is still on the other side of the Khoord Cabul pass; and the last accounts from Ghuznee are, that Gen. Nott was one march on the other side of it.

13th. — A large party travelling by, supposed to be the Meer Hadje and his family. Saleh. Mahommed Khan determined to seize them. They pulled the Moollah off his horse; who only proved to be a Sheikh somebody, a relation of the Hadje's; so they were all *bien quittés pour la peur*, and proceeded on their way in double quick. There is a talk of arming our men, if we can get muskets. Our valley is now almost hermetically sealed at both ends. Akbar is at Bégram in the Kohistan; the Meer Hadje and Zeman Shah Khan quiet at Cabul.

The Meer Akhor went off at night with his Juzailchees; taking with him sundry ashurpees which he had received from myself and others to change for us. This is particularly inconvenient; as we are about to purchase all the ottah procurable, in order to lay in a little commissariat of our own; and, if Akbar sends troops against us, hold out till our own people come to relieve us. We have appointed Capt. Johnson our commissariat officer.

Kurrim Beg came over to us, and Meer Hassun; and with much form and ceremony swore on the Koran to be faithful to us. The latter is the person whose fort Dr. Lord burnt; and on which subject there was much angry discussion, *pro* and *con.*, in the Indian papers. He offered his fort to us: it has a name, which the wits pronounce as *fool-hardy*; and say it is synonymous with our attempt. The only persons who are against the measure are Gen. Shelton and Col. Palmer. As the latter has already been tortured at Ghuznee, he possibly fears a repetition of barbarity, should we not succeed. The former says, we are precipitating matters with Akbar; whom he considers as our friend. I believe both have at length signed the paper. They could scarcely do less; as our signatures were to exonerate the five officers whose names were superscribed as answerable for the whole account, which we were of course to pay our shares of.

I wrote to Sale to-day; informing him of our resolution to hold out till we received assistance, even should we be reduced to eating the rats and mice; of which we have a grand stock.

14*th*. — Zulficar Khan, Salamid Khan, and other chiefs, joined us.

It would be great injustice to Major Pottinger not to mention the active part he took in affairs. From his perfect knowledge of the Persian language, and his acquaintance with the manners and customs of the people, he well knew how to manage them, and take advantage of the slightest opening on their part in our favour. His coolness and decision were only equalled by the promptness with which he met the wishes of the chiefs; giving them *barats* on the neighbouring lands, empowering them to receive the government rents, &c.; all which documents, though he executed them with an air of great condescension and with the gravity of a judge, he well knew were mere pieces of waste paper: yet they had a magic charm for the time; which was all we required. I had again an opportunity of writing to Sale; as another messenger is sent, in case the first should no reach his destination.

At night we were roused by the sounding of the cracked trumpet, and the drums beating to arms; which, in our *yaghi* (rebellious) position, was a little astounding. It seems that a body of horsemen were hovering about the ruins near the images; and were suspected to be some of Akbar's troops. Saleh Mahommed sent out his men in skirmishing order, or rather disorder: however, it answered our purpose; for, whoever they were, they *made themselves scarce.*

15*th.*—A letter was received from some one, whose signature in cypher was not to be made out; stating that all Cabul had risen against the Wuzeer; that Nott's force was at Maidan last Wednesday, and Pollock's at Bhoodkhak; that Akbar had fled to the Toba mountains towards Kandahar to the Ghilzyes, and Shumshudeen Khan to the Kohistan.

Another letter came from Mohun Lull, corroborating the account of the insurrection in Cabul. He himself had fled to the Kuzzilbash quarter with his family: Zeman Khan had fled to either the Kohistan or Kuzzilbash quarter; and the Kuzzilbashes have taken a decided part in the business. A light force is said to have been sent to our aid: it is therefore decided that we are to march to-morrow; taking with us two kurwahs of ottah, which is all (out of four) that we can carry; being very short of cattle. This ottah was purchased by the subscription I before mentioned.

16*th*.—We marched to Killa Topchee on a fine sunshiny morning; which we hailed as a presage of the future. We were not, however, without considerable anxiety; for our present state was replete with danger. We had every reason to believe that the Meer Akhor, on leaving us, had gone to Akbar, and revealed our plans; and consequently every man we saw was suspected to be the *avant courier* of troops sent to reclaim us: and the cheering hope of an escape was considerably clouded before we had been an hour on the road. Those who travelled in kujavas, of course, could not keep pace with those who rode: our equestrian party, of which I formed one, had halted; and, to screen themselves from the sun, had taken shelter under some huge masses of rock. Here Saleh Mahommed Khan came up to us; and speaking in Persian to Capt. Lawrence, told him that he had succeeded in getting a few muskets; which, together with ammunition, he had brought with him on a camel: and requested that he would ask the men, which of them would take them; it being his wish to form a small advance guard of Europeans, as a *show*. Capt. Lawrence then said, " Now, my lads, here's Saleh Mahommed Khan has brought arms and ammunition for some of you: who volunteers to take muskets?"

I blush to record, that a dead silence ensued. Thinking the men might be shamed into doing their duty, I said to Lawrence, " You had better give *me* one, and I will lead the party;" but there was still no offer: and he told our General, that it was useless; and he had better take them on. It is sad to think the men were so lost to all right feeling.

We encamped near the small forts. Here a letter was received; stating, that on Tuesday Pollock's force fought from mid-day to midnight; and eventually forced the Khoord Cabul pass, charging the enemy as far as the hills north of Cabul to the Jurra Tunghee, leading to Tagow; that on Wednesday morning Nott attacked and pursued the enemy as far as Siah Sung; that meanwhile the Kuzzilbashes seized the city, and partially looted it.

Mahommed Akbar Khan and Mahommed Shah Khan are said to be — *nowhere!*

Sultan Jan and Shumshudeen Khan had been

previously defeated at Maidan ; as also Sultan Ahmed Khan.

Reports have just arrived that 2000 horse from Khoolloom are following us up to take us thither.

17*th.*— At two in the morning we were roused by the arrival of a horseman with a letter from Sir Richmond Shakespear ; who is coming with 600 Kuzzilbash horsemen to our aid.

We marched eleven miles to the forts at the foot of the Kaloo pass ; again admiring the silvery serpentine stream and the haycocks near it. We arrived at our ground at mid-day, and were sitting under the walls of one of the forts, sheltering ourselves from the sun until the arrival of our tents; when, at three o'clock, Sir Richmond arrived; and was received, with *one* exception, with heartfelt pleasure. That one, Gen. Shelton, could not forget the honour due to his rank as the senior military man; and was much offended at Sir R. not having called on him first, and reported his arrival in due form. Even were this a military duty, Sir Richmond was perfectly exonerated in its omission; for the greater part of us ladies and some gentlemen had seated ourselves where he must pass, anxious to offer our acknowledgments to him for his prompt assistance.

He told us, that Gen. Nott had gained two victories on the 28th and 30th, at Ghuznee and

Maidan; and that Gen. Pollock had beaten Akbar at Jugdaluk and Tézeen. He also, most considerately, informed me of Sale having been struck by a spent ball without injury; and congratulated me on our gracious Queen's bestowal of the highest order of the Bath upon my gallant husband; — a distinction, I believe, unparalleled in his present rank; and therefore the more dearly prized.

We now have accounts we can depend upon of the position of our armies. Pollock is encamped at Siah Sung; and Nott expected to march on to Cabul to-morrow. Akbar is supposed to have taken refuge in the Ahmedzye country.

18*th*. — We marched to Gundundewar over a very stony road, having a serpentine river on our left. Crossed the Hadje Gurk pass; which is at an elevation of 12,400 feet above the level of the sea; but lower than Kaloo, which is 14,000. At the end of the pass, the river appears to gush through immense portals of solid rock.

During this march, many curiously formed rocks were seen at a distance; one bearing a strong resemblance to a giant climbing up the precipice; another, so perfect when near, as to render one doubtful whether the bull couchant was not the remains of ancient Hindu sculpture. We did not fail to drink of the mineral spring as we passed it; and whilst so employed, attracted the attention of a party of Affghans; to whom Major Pottinger recommended a hearty draught of this sparkling liquid; which, however pleasing to the eye, is far from being so to the palate; being very like ink. The grave Affghans drank a full cup of it; exclaiming, "Shookr!" and "Joor Ustie;" — praise be to God! and they would grow strong upon it. They then stroked down their beards; and wended their way with great satisfaction. The latter part of our road lay among a narrow path, on either side of a tributary stream, bounded by a high and precipitous range of slatestone rocks. We soon came to the Helmund; which we crossed, and encamped on its bank. Nearly opposite to us, a part of the rocks presented the form of a seated figure of Boodh.

19*th.* — We marched two hours before daylight, and crossed the Onai Kotul; a succession of ascents and descents, and some of them very steep, ending in a defile: after which the road was very stony. The grain was still green in many parts; but some of it was not only cut but carried away. We passed Killa Onai, Killa Suffard, and Killa Mustapha Khan: at the latter, breakfast was prepared; — *nan* (native sweet cakes) and tea for all who chose to partake of it *en passant.* The proprietor of this fort is a friend of Saleh Mahommed Khan's; and had given us bread and preserved fruit as we passed before. From hence we went on to Sir-i-Chushm; and diverged from the road to see the preserve of fish there. I asked the name of the fish; but all they knew was that they were fish; that they were held sacred, and fed; and that any one who caught, or even touched, one would die shortly afterwards. The streams were very clear, and the fish innumerable. Four miles from this place we took up our old ground under the poplar trees at Tarkhana. We were not yet considered as safe even here, and Sir Richmond Shakespear felt much anxiety at not receiving any accounts of troops coming to our aid; as he had written to Gen. Pollock to send a brigade to meet us. As Sultan Jan was believed to be hovering near, there were some thoughts of our going into a fort: however it was decided that we should remain in our tents.

We had proceeded but a short way on our journey, when a horseman arrived with a note informing us, that Sale was close at hand with a brigade. I had had fever hanging about me for some days; and, being scarce able to sit on my horse, had taken my place in a kujava; the horrid motion of which had made me feel ten times worse than before I entered it. But this news renovated my strength. I shook off fever and all ills; and anxiously awaited his arrival, of which a cloud of dust was the forerunner. Gen. Nott was near Urghundee, and consequently close to us; and Gen. Pollock requested he would send a brigade to our assistance. This he refused, much to the disgust of his officers, alleging that his troops were fatigued. On this, Gen. Pollock sent Sale with a brigade, at a few hours' notice. He left Siah Sung two miles east of Cabul; and made a forced march on the 19th (his sixtieth birthday) to Urghundee: he halted there that night; and on the following morning left his camp standing, and marched to meet us. At the pass near Kote Ashruffee he left his infantry to hold the position, and proceeded at the head of the 3rd dragoons. A party of Sultan Jan's men were in this neighbourhood; and some Kokhes in the immediate vicinity were driven off by the Juzailchees. Had we not received assistance, our recapture was certain: but as it was, they dared not attack the force they saw. It is impossible to express our feelings on Sale's approach. To my daughter and myself happiness so long delayed, as to be almost unexpected, was actually painful, and accompanied by a choking sensation, which could not obtain the relief of tears. When we arrived where the infantry were posted, they cheered all the captives as they passed them; and the men of the 13th pressed forward to welcome us individually. Most of the men had a little word of hearty congratulation to offer, each in his own style, on the restoration of his colonel's wife and daughter: and then my highly-wrought feelings found the desired relief; and I could scarcely speak to thank the soldiers for their sympathy, whilst the long withheld tears now found their course. On arriving at the camp, Capt. Backhouse fired a royal salute from his mountain train guns: and not only our old friends, but all the officers in the party, came to offer congratulations, and welcome our return from captivity.

21st.—We marched to Killa Kazee; and great was the contrast of our present happiness and comfort, compared with what our state had been, when we last bivouacked under the trees at this place. The obnoxious fort was deserted; but the troops obtained forage there; and the place was destroyed by fire: as also a fort of Sultan Jan's. But guards were sent to the Kuzzilbash forts near us, to protect the property of our friends. A reward has been offered for Capt. Bygrave, and it is supposed he will be brought in to us shortly. At three o'clock we resumed our march to Cabul; and passed through the great bazaar; where the shops were shut, and all looked very desolate, and unlike the busy city it was when we were here last year, and the inhabitants found their trade prosper under our rule. We were greeted, on our arrival at the camp at Siah Sung, with a salute of twenty-one guns.

And now my Notes may end. Any further journals of mine can only be interesting to those nearly connected to me.

ADDENDA.

On the 20th of October, the Envoy wrote to Sir Alexander Burnes, in consequence of information he had received from Capt. Trevor, which indicated an unquiet state of feeling among the people of Cabul. But Sir A. Burnes, on whom the intelligence department devolved, assured him that Trevor must be mistaken; as *he* knew nothing of any meditated rising of the people: and that all was as it ought to be. Notwithstanding this, Trevor assured the Envoy that a number of Ghilzye chiefs had left Cabul for hostile purposes.

On the 1st of November, Sir A. Burnes congratulated Sir William on the prospect of soon leaving Cabul in a perfect state of tranquillity. We might attribute his anxiety to calm the Envoy's mind, by assurances of the peaceful feelings of the people of the country, to anxiety on his part to succeed to the situation to be vacated by Sir William: but it appeared questionable whether he would permanently have done so; as Col. Sutherland had, it was said, been nominated for the appointment.

There can be no doubt, from what we have since heard from the Affghans, that Sir A. Burnes wrote to Sir William Macnaghten for a regiment: and that no aid was given, either to him or Trevor, Anquetil or Mackenzie, is well known. Where the blame rests, it is not for *me* to determine.

Not only did Taj Mahommed Khan, but also the Naïb Shureef, warn Sir Alexander. The latter was very intimate with him; and they were both well known to most of those officers who at all associated with the Affghan gentlemen.

Mention is made of the Naïb in one of the Bombay papers; in which he is represented as a very respectable person, — a Naïb in Capt. Johnson's office. Khan Shireen Khan is the head of the Kuzzilbashes; and Mahommed Shureef was his Naïb, or the governor under him;— a man of large estates; who, from his adherence to our cause, has had to fly his country, with what little he could save; but leaving landed property, worth above two lakhs of rupees, to the mercy of his enemies, the Barukzyes. Naïb Shureef paid a large sum for the interment of the bodies of Burnes and his brother. It was asserted that he was deceived, but his intention was equally good. After the return of the British force to Cabul, the bodies were reinterred.

Taj Mahommed Khan and Naïb Shureef have both paid every attention in their power to the hostages, left in Cabul: and, as far as regards Mrs. Sturt and myself, they sent us, whenever they could obtain a secret conveyance, various little comforts. Tea, sugar, stockings, gloves, and money we received: and much, which they sent, never reached us.

Taj Mahommed Khan is the son of Gholam Mahommed Khan; who formerly assisted Shah Shoojah in his fruitless attempt to gain the throne. His family were long the hereditary Wuzeers of the country. That family are so influential, that they can hold their ground with all parties. We leave him in the Wuzeerat. Jan Fishan Khan is now, as he says, only the poor Syud Mahommed. Two of his brothers have fallen in battle: one son was burnt alive, when a child: another has had his throat cut; though he begged hard for life, stating that he was a little child, and never could have harmed any one. The wretched father, with the remnant of his family, accompanies us to India. He never was rich. He possessed lands in the Pughman valley; a fertile vale, with magnificent vineyards and orchards. Despoiled of them, he is all but a beggar; but looks for the favourable consideration of the Government of India.

A trifling subscription was raised by Sale and some officers, to enable him to purchase camels, &c., that he and his family might travel with us.

In the absence of actual returns, I believe that the force, which left Cabul, was nearly as follows:—

4 Horse Artillery guns.	4th Local Horse - - 70
3 Mountain Train do.	Envoy's Escort - - 70
Bengal Sappers & Miners 20	2nd Shah's Cavalry - 500
Shah Shoojah's do. - - 250	Half Mountain Train - 30
Queen's 44th - - 600	5th N. I. - - - 700
1 Troop H. A. - 80	37th Do. - - - 600
5th Cavalry - - 260	54th Do. - - - 650
1st Local Horse - - 70	6th Shah's - - - 600

At the last stand, on the hill at Gundamuk, there remained —

20 Officers.	4 or 5 Sipahees.
50 men of the 54th.	300 Camp followers.
6 of the Horse Artillery.	

Amongst them all about twenty muskets.

In reading over these Notes, I believe I have not done justice to some of the men who were our fellow-captives. The day after that on which Saleh Mahommed Khan offered them the arms, a few men of the artillery, and perhaps, in all, half a dozen others, asked for and obtained them. Swords were difficult to procure for the officers:

Lieut. Eyre, not being able to get one, took a musket; which was very troublesome and heavy; as, from the wound he received at Cabul, he has lost the use of one hand.

It is now said, that though we all at the time believed Saleh Mahommed's assertion, that Akbar ordered the death of those who could not march, it is probable that this was a fiction. No one actually *read* the letter, that I can discover: and he probably wished to enhance the value of his releasing us. The order for our being sent to Khoolloom was read by several of the officers.

Here follow copies of a few notes that have been recovered. The first is not dated; but, if I mistake not, I have made allusion to the order for cutting away the weeds that grew on the ramparts; lest they should facilitate the enemy's entrance into the cantonments. The Affghans had first to cross the ditch, twenty feet wide.

No. I.

TO LIEUT. STURT.

Has the breast-work on the Musjid been improved? This Lieut. Sturt was to have done yesterday. It must be, and as effectually as circumstances will admit, done to-day.

The bridge at the rear gate does not seem to be understood. The planks must be always kept ready to lay down. The breach of the captured fort ought to be strengthened. (The officer must be told, on the appearance of any people near it, to warn them off, and immediately let a party fall in near it); this latter does not apply to Lieut. Sturt.

Can any thing be done to the magazine or other forts during this quiet day?

Weeds on ramparts to be cut.

My dear Sturt,

    I send you the above for your attention and consideration, to do what you can.

                          Your's,

          (Signed)   W. K. E.

No. II.

LIEUT. STURT. *Immediate.*

My dear Sturt,   *3d Dec.*

    On my return from the Envoy's I heard you had taken out a gun at the Bazar fort. I hope there is no risk, although I feel rather uneasy about its having been done before the work for its protection was completed; but as it has been done, you must look to the work, and carry it on without the least delay. See that this is carried on.

                      Your's,

          (Signed)   W. K. E.

I was not aware you intended to take it out, and I hear the Brigadier was opposed to it. I hope, however, for to-night the gun is safe: to lose it would be disastrous.

No. III.

My dear Sturt,

It is deemed too bad that we should suffer ourselves to be bullied in the way we have been to-day outside the Siah Sung gate, to say nothing of people being fired at every night coming to us with supplies; therefore it is determined that you throw up some sort of flêche, or other work, to hold a dozen men or so, which would keep these fellows at a more respectable distance, protect our animals and camp followers, save our bridge, and do away with the necessity of a cavalry piquet. If we have a quiet night, the General wishes you would plan out such a work on paper, and have it marked out on the ground, ready for the 200 Sappers and Miners to commence on the first thing in the morning, and as many other workpeople as can be got. The Brigadier has spoken to you about a trench across the road from our ditch to the Captured fort. [No. 1.] The enemy set us a good example last night. You must have thought it necessary when you went to it and returned this evening.

Your's truly,

4th Dec. 8 P.M.   WM. THAIN.

Another line for the last-named trench is mentioned, which would be shorter than from our ditch, viz., from a barricadoed door in the old bazar near the S.W. angle.

W. T.

No. IV.

My dear Sturt,

In rear of the old commissariat godown the rebels have prepared a platform to-day, about twelve feet by four. Hay says they were looking at them all day from the Bala Hissar; that they began it at about one P. M., and seemed to have finished it before dark, and left it then; and that they seemed to be trying it, by walking on it, before they went away; it seemed to be a contrivance for crossing our ditch. The enemy appeared more numerous to-day than for some days past.

Your's truly,
(Signed)   WM. THAIN.

10*th Dec.* 8½ P. M.

No. V.

My dear Sturt,

Have we the means, by taking the beams of some building, of making a bridge over the canal? and how long would it take?

The guns, I fear, cannot cross otherwise, or the carriages for the bridge over the river.

The scarping the bank of the canal would render it practicable for the cavalry and baggage, and save some time. How long will it take to complete the opening for the egress of the troops? Pray attend to all this. I have told Pottinger to ask for a guard to protect our party; but the bridge might be prepared directly, ready to lay down the morning we go. Send for the Sappers, and see what you can do as to this. How many bullocks will be required to draw the carriages to the river? This we must get assistance to do just before we march.

Your's,
(Signed)   W. K. E.

[No date, but, from the context, a few days previous

to our leaving the cantonments, and Sturt making the bridge of gun-carriages, which was effected the day we started (the 6th of January).]

No. VI.

My dear Sturt,

The General wishes to know what you have done about cutting a passage through the rampart for our exit; if the Sappers are unable to do the job, you might have an European working party, if you will let me know the number you require; and the work should be done to-night, if possible.

Your's sincerely,
(Signed)   W. GRANT.

30th Dec.

No. VII.

My dear Grant,

A party of forty Europeans with the regular Sappers will do the job in about three hours: all inside is cleared away.

I cannot help giving the warning before doing this to-night. If we do not march to-morrow, we shall want a gun and a very strong guard, to prevent the Ghazeeas entering.

Perhaps the General is not aware that about 500 men were on the point of forcing the gate to-day, and, being prevented, tore up the remaining portion of the canal bridge, which now no longer exists. While giving this warning, I have ordered the work to be begun now; therefore, if it is desired to be stopped, send to me; if not, send the Europeans. I am not answerable if accident happens, as I now wish you to tell the General that, in my opinion, no other than concealed measures should be used for moving out, until a few hours before that event takes place. If we march to-morrow, it should be done or commenced now; if not, it is my deliberate advice — do not execute it, or you endanger cantonments.

Yours ever,

(Signed)   J. L. D. STURT.

Thursday, 30th Dec. 1841.

The dhooley bearers just returned are specimens of what can be, is, and will again, be done by these men, if we place even the smallest unguarded confidence in them.

When Istalif was taken, the book of Gen. Elphinstone's Orders was found there.

To show how inaccurately it was kept, I am told, by those who saw it, that the orders of the 11th and 12th were inserted before those of the 10th of December. The book was made over to General Pollock; and does not agree with General Elphinstone's last memoranda regarding Brigadier Shelton; as he is there thanked for the assistance always given by him to General Elphinstone.

APPENDIX.

TREATY.

ARTICLES of the Treaty entered into between Sir William Macnaghten, Envoy and Minister, on the part of the British Government, at Cabul, and the Sirdar Mahommed Akbar Khan, Mahommed Osman Khan, Sultan Mahommed (half-brother of Mahommed Akbar), Mahommed Shureef, Kuzzilbash, Mahommed Shah Khan and Khoda Buksh Khan, Ghilzye Sirdars, and the principal Chiefs of the Tribes:—

1. Immediate supplies to be furnished to the troops, to any extent required, as also carriage cattle.
2. The British troops to evacuate Affghanistan.
3. An offensive and defensive alliance to be formed.
4. The Ameer Dost Mahommed Khan and all his family to be released.
5. His Majesty Shah Shoojah Ool Moolk to have the option of remaining in the country as a private individual, to be treated with all honour and respect, and have a guaranteed stipend of a lakh of rupees annually, or, if he so wishes it, to be allowed to accompany the British troops to Hindoostan, taking all his property and family with him, only giving up such effects as had formerly belonged to the Ameer Dost Mahommed.

In the event of carriage not being procurable for his family, they are to remain in the Bala Hissar, and be treated with all honour and respect; and on the arrival of the Ameer and all other Affghans imprisoned in India at Peshawer, the former are to be transported with safety to India.

6. All the sick and wounded to be left under the care of the Sirdars at Cabul and to be treated as guests.

7. All the ammunition, guns, and small arms, if the means of transport are not procurable, to be made over to the Sirdars.

8. All surplus property of officers, for which carriage might not at present be procurable, to be left in charge of Zuman Khan, and be forwarded to India the first opportunity.

9. No man to be molested on either side for his actions during the war. Such chiefs as had stood stanch to the King to be allowed either to accompany his Majesty, taking with them all property, or remaining in Affghanistan, to be treated with every respect.

10. Any British subject wishing to remain in Affghanistan, for the purposes of trade, to be in no way molested.

11. The troops at Jellalabad to evacuate that fort, ere the Cabul force commences its march.

The forces at Ghuznee and Kandahar to quit those places as soon as the season would admit of their marching.

12. The Sirdars, Mahommed Akbar Khan and Osman Khan, or any other chiefs wishing to do so, to accompany the troops on their march to Peshawer.

13. Four hostages to be given by us for the full

performance of the above articles, to remain until Dost Mahommed Khan arrives at Peshawer.

[Capt. Trevor accompanied the Sirdars back as one of them.]

11*th December*, 1841.

On the 12th, Major Pottinger was informed by the Envoy that he was to be a hostage.

THE END.